Meeting the

Meeting the "Other"

Living in the Present:
Gender and Sustainability in Bhutan

Rieki Crins

Eburon Delft

2008

I would like to acknowledge the generous sponsorship of Brooklyn Bridge/TBLI.Group, without whose help this book would not have been possible.

ISBN: 978-90-5972-261-3

Uitgeverij Eburon
Postbus 2867
2601 CW Delft
tel.: 015-2131484 / fax: 015-2146888
info@eburon.nl / www.eburon.nl

Graphic design: Textcetera, The Hague
Cover design: Studio Geert Hermkens, Amsterdam
Cover photo: © Oksana Perkins/Shutterstock: *Dancers in Punakha Dzong, Bhutan*
All other photographs in this book are by the author.

Contents

Research prologue, Bhutanese contexts introduced

In this chapter, I will delineate my first encounter with the country that inspired me to write this book. This book is my narrative of 17 years experience with meeting the "Other" and with the "Other" I mean the people and the culture of Bhutan.

After my stay in a Bhutanese village in 1990 (my first episode), I went back in 1999 (second episode), just to visit the country. After that, I went back almost every year to visit and to do research in the country. The last research I did was in 2004 (third episode): I had conversations with Bhutanese people to gather data for this book. I also visited the country in 2005 and as late as 2007.

The first chapter of this book is a result of the first experiences I had with Bhutan in 1990, and the following chapters are constructed around the research in 2004.

How it began

In the autumn of 1989, I received a letter from a professor who taught anthropology at the Free University in Amsterdam, where I was studying anthropology. The letter stated that the Free University at Amsterdam and the Wageningen Agriculture University were looking for students who were willing to conduct research in a country called Bhutan. I remember that I was in the last year of my master's studies, and I was required to undertake fieldwork in order to complete my course. I had always dreamed of conducting anthropological fieldwork in a place that still was "untouched" by westernisation. Up to now, however, there are not many places in the world that allow a student to conduct research in such romantic settings, where people still lead lives unspoilt by globalisation, westernisation, TV, Coca Cola, and MacDonald's.

But Bhutan? I never had heard of it before! I referred to the Encyclopaedia Britannica (in those days, I did not have access to the Internet) and found only a very brief description of Bhutan. Not much was written about the country. The encyclopaedia stated only that Bhutan is an absolute Buddhist monarchy situated in the Eastern Himalayas. I also learnt that the people there carry swords and that it is inhabited by bears.

This certainly did not tell me much about the place. This is the ideal place, I thought, realising that I would like to go to Bhutan to conduct fieldwork. I wrote to my professor, telling him that I would love to visit Bhutan. Shortly afterward, he informed me that I had been chosen as one of the members of the team that would be visiting Bhutan. The team comprised three students of anthropology and three students of irrigation technology. We were invited to join a programme organised by the Department of Agriculture of the Royal Government of Bhutan. The Bhutanese government needed information on how Bhutanese farmers grow crops, particularly rice, in order to facilitate the implementation of improvements in and for the agricultural sector and to seek possible ways to increase crop yield. The aim was to achieve self-sufficiency in rice production and to reduce the import of rice from India and other foreign countries.

A British irrigation engineer hired by the Bhutanese government drafted a policy. Three student teams – each consisting of an anthropologist and a student of irrigation technology – were sent to three villages situated in three different regions of the country. I was sent to a village in the northwestern part of the country. The university organised an orientation session for all six of us, since we had no idea of what to expect from our stay in the country. We assumed that we were being sent to a country that would resemble Tibet, because Tibet was very close to Bhutan and the Buddhism followed in Bhutan is related to Tibetan Buddhism. Each of us had to choose a partner; I chose one of the three irrigation engineers, Marleen. We got along very well.

There was not much to prepare, because we did not know what to expect. As suggested, we assumed that Bhutan would look like Tibet, with towering mountains and snow-laden land. Although we had prepared ourselves to face all kinds of weather, we did not know what to expect with regard to food or accommodation. We only had heard that the meals and lodging provided would be very basic.

After a long journey by plane via New Delhi (India) and Kathmandu (Nepal), we arrived in Paro, Bhutan, in February 1990. Our small plane landed on a short landing strip between lofty mountains. Paro International Airport was a small building, not much larger than a barn. The air was crisp and fresh, and I felt as though I had landed in a fairy tale country.

The houses looked like Swiss chalets with Asian features. We saw impressive buildings amid rice terraces. The city of Paro comprised one line of old wooden buildings along a road, at the end of which was a gigantic fortress. It looked very oriental and familiar. It reflected the mental image I had of Switzerland in the Middle Ages. The Bhutanese people had Mongolian features, and both men and women wore colourful clothes. The women wore long dresses called *kira* that they draped around themselves, with a belt around the waist and two silver buckles, one on each shoulder. The men's attire included a kind of rope, which, as we learnt, was called *gho*.

A woman from the Dutch development organisation picked us up from the airport and took us to the capital, Thimphu; it was a two-hour drive on a small road through winding mountains. Thimphu looked like a small village – no traffic lights or commercial billboards. It resembled an exotic mountain hamlet with an Asian feel. The Bhutanese government had rented for us a modern apartment made of concrete in the new part of the town. We were to live in this apartment for the first week of our stay in Bhutan; during this week, we also would be briefed about what to expect.

We noticed that Thimphu lies at an altitude of 2,400 metres above sea level. We discovered several aspects of life here; for example, walking was slightly difficult and water took a considerably longer time to boil than it did back home. In February, winter set in at Thimphu; we had a *bukari* (a wood stove) in the living room, which helped us stay warm and comfortable.

After a week in the capital, Marleen and I were sent to a village named Tsachaphu. Ours was the most difficult post because the village was a day's walk from the town of Punakha. The village had no access road and could be reached only by foot and/or on horseback.

A French Tibetologist living in Bhutan and a Dutch linguist studying the Bhutanese languages conducted a three-day training session for us regarding the dos and don'ts during our stay and fieldwork. I must confess now that this training later proved to be very important. Despite this training, however, we were still unsure about what to expect.

Finally, the day arrived on which we had to leave for our post. We drove four hours to the middle of nowhere in a huge Toyota High Lux provided by the Department of Agriculture. During the final leg of our journey, we passed through rice terraces and a dry riverbed. The car stopped at a wooden shack that served as a store. Some men already were waiting for us there. They helped us carry our luggage (bedding, food, kerosene, candles, and backpacks) up the mountain. We had to take gifts for the villagers, such as dried chillies, tea, and betel nuts. We followed the Po Chu, or the Father River, up the mountain. The landscape was spectacularly beautiful; it seemed as though I was travelling through three climatic zones and three seasons at the same time. If I looked skywards, I could see snow-capped mountains. I was walking along a path lined with trees that had autumnal-coloured leaves. After a few hundred metres, I found myself in a tropical microclimate with big, beautiful, blue butterflies and orchids, and where the sun shone bright and warm. So we reached Punakha. This town is located at a low altitude and is much warmer than Thimphu. From Punakha to Tsachaphu, we had to climb about 1,000 metres. While the biodiversity that surrounded us was stunning, the climb was arduous and, at times, I doubted my ability to complete the trek. The porters, in contrast, were physically fit for the climb; they ran up the mountain slopes, while we barely could keep pace with them.

At one point, I felt like giving up, thinking, "I cannot go further. I feel dead." At that very moment, one of the porters pointed out the village in the distance. Although it looked very close, it still was an hour's walk away. I did not know what lay in store for me.

Researcher's Context

For a social scientist, it is very difficult to get access to Bhutan to do research. The Bhutanese government does not give research visas to Westerners easily. I have been told the reason for this is that the Bhutanese government is afraid that these Western researchers do not understand the Bhutanese cultures and therefore write untrue stories. Secondly, they disturb the people in their daily life and have not been respectful toward the Bhutanese religion and customs in the past. Respected scholars who have been living in Bhutan have been "blacklisted" because of writing about the Bhutanese culture and history that have insulted the Bhutanese very much. Later in this book, I will give an example.

The Bhutanese government wants Bhutanese to fill the research jobs as much as possible. Anyhow, I have been lucky that I received a research visa in 1990, and then again to do my last research in 2004.

I understand very well this reluctance of the Bhutanese government toward researchers and especially anthropologists. I always feel like an intruder when I am doing research and interview people. I personally feel that I want something from them and they offer it generously, and I receive the information but do not have to offer much in return.

As a Western researcher, I feel that I have a responsibility to respect the culture where I am, and that I have to be aware of my own bias as a Western researcher looking at "the other."

I also am aware of the responsibility I have of my ontological and epistemological assumptions. I have been granted access to a unique culture and I want to tell my story with respect and with self-reflection. I have the feeling that that is what I owe the Bhutanese people in return for their many hours of talking with and to me about their way of living.

So, what can you expect in this first chapter? First, I will give a brief introduction into Bhutan as background of this book. Then, I will go back into the village where I stayed in 1990. This description of the village is an example of how most Bhutanese live and have lived. It is a description of traditional village life, a style of life most Bhutanese lived about 20 years ago.

Kingdom of Bhutan: The context

Bhutan, the small Himalayan kingdom, is sandwiched between India in the south and China in the north. Bhutan has a population of about 650.000 and is the size of Switzerland. It remains the only Mahayana Buddhist country in its Tantric[1] form in the world. Because of the country's geographical isolation and its self-imposed political and cultural isolation, the classical culture of Bhutan was able to evolve undisturbed for more than twelve hundred years. Bhutan

---

1 The Tantras were a series of "revelations" that took place from perhaps the fourth century onward mainly in India (Samuel, 1993). According to Samuel, "Tantric Buddhism as practiced in Tibet (and Bhutan) may be described as shamanic" (Samuel,1993:8). In chapter 4, I will go deeper into Buddhism in Bhutan.

never has been ruled by a colonial power and could preserve its own identity over the years. Most other Himalayan states – for example Ladakh, Sikkim, and Mustang – have been absorbed by foreign powers.

Bhutan's economy is one of the worlds smallest and least developed, and is based on agriculture and forestry that provide the main livelihood for more than 80 percent of the population. Rugged mountains dominate the terrain and make the building of roads and other infrastructure difficult and expensive. The economy is aligned closely with India's through strong trade and monetary links and dependence on India's financial assistance. Most development projects, such as road construction, rely on Indian migrant labour. Bhutan's hydropower potential and its attraction for tourists are key resources. Model education, social, and environment programs are underway with support from multilateral development organisations. Each economic program takes into account the government's desire to protect the country's environment and cultural traditions. For example, the government, in its cautious expansion of the tourist sector, encourages visits by upscale, environmentally conscientious tourists.[2]

Until 1907, Bhutan was a theocracy and was ruled by the Shabdrung, a theocrat, similar to the Dalai Lama in Tibet. In 1907, Bhutan became a monarchy. In the 1960s, the third king started to open up the country to development in a slow and careful way, to preserve its own culture.

Fifty years ago, except for a very small proportion of the elite, the social structure, value system, and lifestyle of the Bhutanese did not differ very much from that of their ancestors of around 1500. In those days, the vast majority of the population spent their time as subsistence farmers, almost totally dependent on the yield of a few acres of agricultural land and adjoining forest. If there was a small surplus, it was bartered, since money was not used and to a lot of people unknown. All goods had to be transported on mules or horses, or on the back of people themselves. In 1960, health care was almost absent, except for two trained doctors and a few dispensaries. Average life expectancy in 1984 was 48 years, whereas now it is 66 years (Ministry of Planning 1997).

In five decades, much has changed. Learning from the mistakes made in neighbouring countries, Bhutan chose its own way of modernisation, to fit in with its culture and respecting the ancient values and traditions. In this context, one can speak of a particular Bhutanese development approach. The way Bhutan handles and plans its development is influenced partly by India, on which the

2   https://www.cia.gov/library/publications/the-world-factbook/geos/bt.html

country is very dependent. But partly it is typically Bhutanese and embedded in the culture and traditions of the country where religions such as Buddhism and indigenous religion play a major role. Bhutan, as a Mahayana Buddhist country, is opening up to the outside world slowly. This small Himalayan kingdom is known only to a relative small number of outsiders and scholars. Since 1990, Bhutan has slowly developed a tourist sector and a limited number of tourists can visit the country every year.

Life in the present: Village life in Bhutan

I read back notes in my journals of the first trip, called "the first episode of my research":

In 1990, after a long walk I arrived very tired and covered in sweat in the village where I had to stay for six months. When I saw the house where I had to live, I could cry! No electricity, no plumbing, no chairs, and tables. In short: no comforts from the twentieth century. I needed a shower and a cold drink after the long walk. My landlady, Am Zam, offered me butter tea instead. This is Tibetan style black tea with salt, a pinch of soda, and butter. It tastes more like soup than tea. I had to get used to it.

All the people in the village came to look at Marleen and me, and we stared at them. To me, they all looked the same: same face and same clothes. Everybody was wearing very dirty clothes and my landlady was very dirty, except her face.

No house in the village had indoor plumbing and the water had to be carried to the house. Water was used mainly for cooking and making tea. Washing was not a big issue; people eat with their hands and everybody uses his/her own plate and cup; this is cleaned by licking it clean after using.

Later, I found out that in the middle of Neptenka, the hamlet where I stayed, UNICEF had provided a water installation, a tap where one could fetch water much more easily than to go to a mountain stream in the forests. UNICEF placed the tap in the village without consulting the astrologer or the *ngejums* or *pawo's*.[3] The result was, according to some Bhutanese, that three people in the village became ill with meningitis. This was, they said, because the water deity Lu was disturbed. She became angry because her habitat was violated without asking her permission. She made the villagers ill. Later, a villager who became ill – because of the deity Lu, who was offended and made him sick – destroyed the tap. Five months later he reconstructed it, after having done the right rituals for Lu, asking her for permission to rebuild the tap.

---

3   *Ngejum*, female shaman; *pawo*, male shaman.

I found out that everything in the village was embedded in rituals. Deities stipulated the whole life of Bhutanese village people. Before we came to the village in Timphu, we had had a brief training about the complex life in the village.

We had learned some basic things to say, as *kuzuzangpo la* as "a greeting" and *lob she geh la* to say "goodbye." I realised that nobody was greeting us. My landlady did not greet us, either, but after a while – we were sitting in her house and we did not know what to do – she offered us butter tea and *dzip* and *dzou* (puffed rice and a kind of popcorn) as a snack. After the tea, she showed me my room, which was actually her storage room. Here, I had to stay for six months. Marleen was living with a family a ten-minute walk from my house. My quarter was not big enough for two.

The first weeks in the village were very tough. Every day was the same. I realised how I as a Westerner was conditioned by time. In the village, there were no clocks. You got up in the morning at the crack of dawn; Am Zam was doing all kind of rituals to chase away the evil spirits of the night. She was burning incense and saying mantras and making the fire to prepare breakfast (rice, curry, and butter tea); after breakfast everybody did what they had to do for the day. There was no weekend and, although the days are named after planets, to me every day was the same. I realised that I was upset with it and for a reason I do not know, my watch became very important to me. I was already confused being in a totally alien world. I became very afraid of losing time and, with that, losing control. The watch was my connection to my Western world. It gave me a kind of comfort. But, here in Bhutan, I missed that comfort! I realised that it was impossible to ask people when something would happen. For example, I heard that the basic health workers would come to the village to give some basic treatment to the sick people and pregnant women. The standard answer to my question was *nabah natse,* which means "any time after tomorrow." This answer I got for all my questions in regard to time. When the moment was there, people called me that today the health workers are coming.

Then, there were a lot of rules about "good" days and "bad" days to do something. For example, only on Fridays were you allowed to sweep the floor and throw the dust out. Other days, you could sweep the floor but the dirt had to stay in the house. Monday was a good day to travel, and so there were auspicious days and inauspicious days.

The first four months, we did not have a good translator and to talk to the people was almost impossible. The children, though, were very helpful and creative in communicating with us. They pointed to things and told us what the name was in Dzongkha. Later, this was a blessing, although at that moment, it was very frustrating. I wanted to do research and to be able to talk to the people. There was a lot going on and I did not understand what it was. I could not ask anybody. I tried to observe as much as possible and just write down what I saw. I did not always understand what I saw. Later, when I had a good translator, I checked all my observations and asked the people about the meaning of it. Much later, I realised how important and valuable it was just to observe. This way, the villagers got used to us and we did not bother them with annoying questions. But this we realised much later.

In February, not much activity was carried out on the land; people were mending houses and fences. One household started to build a new house. Some people helped them with pounding the mud to make the walls of the house. During the pounding, men and women were singing beautiful songs; some were mantras (kind of prayers to attract the good spirits and some were kind of naughty songs to tease the opposite sex). Much time was spent on rituals.

Marleen and I both spent most of the time visiting all the households in the village. This was a time consuming task because the hamlets are far removed form each other and one had to climb on steep terraces. To walk from one hamlet to another one could take more than two hours. But we did this most of the time. Later, the villagers told us that they appreciated that very much. In the beginning, the villagers kept a bit of a distance from us because they did not know what we were doing in the village. The villagers thought we came to spy on them for whatever reason. But later, the people got used to us and did not see us as a threat anymore.

We tried to help with all kind of errands; some were way too heavy for us. The women were so strong; they could carry heave loads and dung to the fields, and I could not even lift the basket that women carry on their back.

After one month, I got used to the life in the village and I started to like the food very much. Although... It was almost the same every day. The vision of chocolate, crème, and sweets disappeared. Also, the people were not the same anymore. I got used to the Mongolian features of the people.

I realised that it was convenient not to wash all the time, and going to the bathroom: you go in a bush where you are. I also realised that I was the only one who was polluting the area with toilet paper and hygienic towels. Later, I saved them up and burned them in the forest.

Once I made a big mistake to throw waste in my landlady's stove while she was cooking. She became very angry with me because I had offended the fire deity. Now she had to burn incense and perform a ritual to restore the harmony.

I realised that by being in the village and having time to be there, although life was very much the same every day, I learned so much. I noticed almost every day that something very unusual to me happened. First of all, I enjoyed the quietness of the place. There is a deep quietness, nowadays rare to be found in the world. Then, there was the living with animals. I walked close to the Po Chu River and I saw water otters playing. I could go so close to them, and they did not even look at me. They were not afraid at all. Sometimes in the morning, when I had breakfast in the house of a neighbour, birds flew into the house (there are no glass windows) and sat down on the edge of my plate to eat some rice with me. One day, as was sitting at the fireplace of Am Zam, a big bug walked up to me. As a reflection, I killed the bug with my hand with a loud clap. My landlady was very upset because of this. She screamed at me that I should not have killed the bug; this was very bad for my karma. I noticed that all the villagers were very aware of not killing other sentient beings. This could be a reason why the birds and other wild animals did not feel threatened by humans. On the other hand, the villagers liked to eat meat and most households had pigs. The way to slaughter a pig was to tie the poor animal up to a tree in a way that the pig kills itself. In this way, no negative karma will be inflicted on the one who is going to eat the pig. Only this way, the pig suffers a slow and painful death. The poor animal was screaming for help.

I noticed how gentle men and women cared for their children. Children were very free to do what they wanted till the age of 12. Most children in the village did not go to school. Only the children from a few households were sent to school in the cities, and had to live there with relatives. When a boy or a girl becomes twelve year, he or she has to help with the work on the farm or in the house.

After some time, I regarded the village as my home. The smells of the wood fires and the incense, the sounds of the drums and prayers in the houses at a far distance and close by, and the beautiful lights, became so familiar to me. I got very attached to the friendly and calm people in the village. After some time, one family adopted me as their daughter, according to Okhum, Nakhum, and Nam (three sisters who were the heads of the household). It is better to become a family member than to be a friend! My relationship with Am Zam was not as easy as with the other villagers. I noticed that people in the village felt sorry for me that I had to live in the house of Am Zam. People gossiped about her and she never attended at big rituals in neighbour's house, although everybody else from the village was there. The first month I did not know why this was. Am Zam was a very religious woman and she was a *ngejum* (shaman). My being in her house was very disturbing to her because I made so many mistakes. I offended the deities every day by doing things that were not good: like killing bugs, throwing paper in the fire, cleaning the room on a inauspicious day, walking to Punakha on an inauspicious day, whistling in the house, stepping over a pan with rice, and so on. One day, I became ill and my legs were so painful I could not walk anymore. The neighbours said I was ill because of the evil eye that was sent for Am Zam; because she was a *ngejum,* she could protect herself from evil and she sent it to me. The village monk came to my room to do a *puja* (ritual) to send away the evil spirits that made me ill. Later, a translator found out that Am Zam belonged to the Zap caste, a former slave caste. She used to be the servant of a high lama. After the abolishment, the government gave her land and a house in Tsachaphu. It seemed that she still was stigmatised.

With this story of my experiences in the village as a fieldworker, I want to point out that being there in the village influences life in the village. We were just as 'interesting' to the villagers as the villagers were to us. Without interaction, fieldwork would not have been possible.[4]

Inquiring the village

Tsachaphu is situated in a fertile valley. Not all of Bhutan is that fertile, and in some parts of the country, it is harder for the people to grow their food. This village, Tsachaphu, is situated a day's walk from the "all weather road." The path toward the village is a small path through rice fields, forests, and rivers, sometimes a bit steep. In the rainy season, many small streams have to be passed. Only humans and horses (animals) can walk this path.

The village is situated at the end of a beautiful valley. The altitude is about 1600 meters high and the climate is subtropical. Winter is cold but there is no snow or ice, and summer has a monsoon with heavy rain in the months of July and August.

About a one-and-a-half hour walk from the village are hot springs due to tectonic activities. These springs are regarded as holy and beneficial for one's health. In wintertime, they attract a lot of people who stay from three days up to one month. These hot springs create the possibility for the villagers to sell some of their produce in order to get some cash; the villagers need to buy dried chillies, tea, kerosene, and betel nuts. Because the path between Punakha and the hot springs is narrow, and in the rainy season muddy, it is not easy for the villagers to bring their produce to the market in Punakha on a regular base.

The village consists of nine hamlets; each hamlet consists of one to nine households. In total, there are 19 households and around 118 inhabitants.

---

4 Source: Crins & de Graaff, 1990.

History of the village

Most of the people of the village did like to talk about the past. Whenever I asked a question about the past, people responded that talk about the past attracts evil spirits. The facts we learned came from the government and one or two old people who used to be village Gup (headmen).

It is not known exactly how long people have been living in the village. But some people think that people were living there about 150 years ago. Until the 1950s, only barter existed between neighbours and friends and reciprocity in work. The society was based on a feudal system in which there were landowners and landless people. Also, the monastery owned and still owns land in the village area. The landless worked for the owners of land. In 1956, the feudal system was abolished and, due to land reform, landless people received land from the government.

In this period, landless people from other areas settled in. All land was said to be measured and recorded. The government changed the tax to be paid in kind into money. The barter system decreased and a monetary system slowly appeared (yet, barter still is more important in daily life than the use of money). Another form of tax that the people have to pay is *chapdaula* and *gandaula*,; two times a year every household has to send one member for compulsory labour for the community or government. People have to help build a school or to maintain a *dzong* (fortress). The tax payments to the monastery were at the time of the research (1990) reduced to a fixed amount of rice for those who sharecrop the land – 40 percent for the sharecropper and 60 percent for the owner.

Although the feudal system was abandoned, it still left its traces in the village. The landowners of the olden days possess the biggest houses and own the most land, while the servant families live in smaller houses. The servants, who used to be called *zap*, still form a separate group and have their social life within their own group. *Zap* refers to the slave caste. These are people whose ancestors have been abducted from the Indian *Duars*. My landlady was from the *zap* caste and she used to be the servant of a high lama. She also was a *ngejum* (oracle/shaman). She received the land and the house she lived in from the government. She has three sons from different partners. Her sons help her with the farm and she earns some extra payments, mostly in kind, by telling the future by reading rice or doing rituals (going into a trance) to help sick people to become better.

Religious context in the village

All the villagers are Drukpa and Drukpa Kagyupa, but there is a lot of influence of the pre-Buddhist belief. Buddhism and pre-Buddhism are mingled completely. Many different deities and spirits play important roles in daily life. Every household has its personal deity, and this deity is the protector of the house and family. There is Lu, the protector of the land on which the house is built. Every village has its deity; the deity of the village is Fola, a male god. The deity of the valley is Katshap; he is a warrior deity and the lord of the whole valley up to Punakha. Next to these deities, there are deities in rocks, water, air, forests, and caves. People are very respectful toward these deities and behave according to their rules in order not to disturb or offend them.

The *ngejums* and *pawo's* in Tsachaphu are the mediators between all the deities and gods. They can predict the future by reading rice. Farmers will consult them when a cow gets lost in the forest; she gives them directions where to find the animal. These *ngejums* hold important functions in the village community; they function as doctor, psychiatrist, and priest, and are able to attract good and avert evil. *Ngejums* and monks/lamas practise the rituals side by side and they are not competitors; the even perform some of the rituals together.

In Tsachaphu, there is no lama but there is a *Getre* (a retired monk). He earns some money and food by performing *chokus* (rituals) and he has some astrological knowledge. He also can read and write Dzongkha. If people borrow rice from another household, he writes it down in a book with names, date, and amount. Reciprocity is a common way for the households to help each other. Only relatives help each other "for free." Other people are very strict in paying back labour time or doing chores for each other.

Almost all the people in Tsachaphu depend upon the natural environment they live in. Nature also is recognised as inspiration. There is an entire hierarchy of gods and spirits/demons who live in the rocks, in the water, in the earth, and the fire. The god Mahakala is Bhutan's protective deity and each valley has a god warrior who reigns over the entire valley (Katshap in my valley). All of these gods are to be kept as friends and the demons to be avoided. The practice of many rituals is necessary; lamas, as well as *ngejums* and even the common people, are occupied on a daily basis with performing the rituals.

In Tschaphu, early in the morning when everyone is awake, incense is burned in the house to purify the air and remove negative energies. Before harvesting, beautiful *tormas* (small sculptures made of rice or wheat) decorated with colourful little pieces of thread are put in the fields to attract evil spirits and entrap them in the thread.

In the village where the research was conducted, the warrior god of the valley is honoured with offers of eggs, *arra* (rice wine) and rice; this takes place yearly near a source in the forest. Until recently, animals were sacrificed. This was called a *Bön* or pre-Buddhist ritual. Currently, animals no longer are killed for ritual purposes.

Yearly, each household takes part in a great *choku*. This is a ritual that can last for three days, depending upon the wealth of the family. Monks and lamas hold a three-day period of prayer to thank the family's God for a good harvest as well as serving as a request for fertility and health for the farm and the entire household. Usually, people from the entire valley are invited to partake of the copious meal and abundant drink.

Everywhere in Bhutan, and particularly in the villages, there are *stupas* and small rectangular stone piles called *chorten*. *Stupas* are part of official Buddhism and the *chorten* contain something valuable inside, such as money or a gem as a sign of thanks to the deity who made the person better.

Bhutanese birth, marriage, divorce, and death

Presently, Bhutan has a good health care system; throughout the country, there are hospitals and basic health units. Since recently, every Bhutanese has free access to this health care. From where many people live, they have to walk for days to reach the paved road that connects the country; it is difficult for the people in remote villages to consult a doctor in case of an acute illness. Villagers in Tsachaphu used to get a visit once a month from the basic health worker, who performed a medical examination, consulted pregnant women, and helped people in need. These health workers come with horses and set up a big tent in which they examine the sick women and children.

In these remote villages, death was a frequent visitor. Many babies died in an early stage, and adults were attacked by wild animals or died of snakebites. Most women in the village had many children, but many died very young, due to bad hygiene and unclean drinking water.

In Bhutan, death is not the end of a lifetime but a next stage to a new life, and therefore something positive. Everything in Buddhism is focused around the concept of reincarnation and karma; it determines where and how a human will be reincarnated. Only the soul is important, and based on deeds and thoughts, it eventually will be shown in nirvana. The human body is only a vessel and represents nothing more.

After death, the soul starts a search for a new existence on earth. This journey takes seven weeks. During this time, the soul encounters friendly as well as deterrent divine figures that will try to lead it from the right path. The *Bardo Thö-dol* (or Tibetan death-book) serves as a good preparation. The lamas read from the *Bardo Thödol* while they keep track of the soul on its way to a new incarnation. By means of a death-horoscope, they will choose the right moment to cremate the body. In Bhutan, most corpses are cremated; until recently, dead babies were entrusted to the river and children up to 12 years of age received a "heaven-funeral." These ways of burying the bodies is a symbol of giving the bodies back to the elements such as air, fire, and water. Burying into the earth is less suitable because of the earth spirits (de Vries, 1997: 118). Some of the high lamas who possess large amounts of spiritual knowledge and powers are able to mummify themselves or dissolve themselves so that only their nails and hair remain. This is called a "rainbow-funeral." For the common people, cremation is the only option.

During our research in the village, two old men died. The whole village is involved with the death ritual. The dead person has to be taken to Punakha to be cremated. People from the village have to carry the body all the way to the Dzong in Punakha, where the cremation ground is. Everything is determined by an astrologer. For example, only a person who is born in a stronger star sign can carry the dead body, or can put the body in a fetal position after he or she has died. Someone born in the year of the snake can handle someone born in the year of the rat, but not vice versa, and so on. Also, the day that a dead body can go out of the house, and when it is carried to the cremation ground, is determined by astrology.

In the village, one dead body had to wait for three day outside the house before it could be carried to Punakha. If there is nobody born in a stronger star sign, the person who will carry the body will have the face painted black so the *dhip* (negative energy, force) that is with the death body will not recognise the person who will be protected by the black paint.

A cremation is accompanied by many dinners, and many people in the village help cook the food. At the time of the research, most households had death insurance; people paid the *Gup* (village headman) a small amount, and if a person died, the family got the money to be able to do a full ritual. It was the only insurance people had at that time.

The birth of a child is a joyful event. In Bhutan, girls and boys are welcome equally. Nevertheless, it is very convenient for a family if there are more daughters than sons. Daughters can inherit the house and land. Sons go to monasteries or just leave, or go to live with the family of the wife. In Tsachaphu, women who gave birth were assisted by their husband and sometimes by the husband's brother. For three days after birth, the mother and child are not al-

15

lowed to receive visitors because there is too much *dhip* in the house that could make people sick.

Marriage can be arranged by mutual agreement. In most cases, the man moves in with his wife. He is regarded as a valuable labour force since there is a shortage of labour in the village. There is no marriage ceremony, sometimes a lama is asked to give a blessing but in other places in Bhutan, there can be very elaborate marriages rituals and procedures (Lham Dorji, 2003).

Divorce can be arranged by mutual agreement, but if there are conflicts, these can be solved with the help of the *chiepen* (messenger) or the *Gup* (village headman). If the problems cannot be solved within the village, the couple can go to the Dzong-court. Sometimes, compensation has to be paid for children by the father if he leaves his wife.

In Tsachaphu, family members or members of the same extended family help each other without expecting anything in return. But for families that are not members of the same family line, reciprocity is important and strict rules apply to the way people interact.

Lands are looked after by cousins/relatives and sharecropping is practised at the end of the harvest. In most cases, at the end of the year (mostly winter months) people from urban areas contribute to the annual *chuko* (a ritual that lasts for three days depending upon the financial situation of a household) in terms of providing money and edibles such as meat, oil, sugar, etc. The people in the urban areas also provide financial support to their rural cousins/ families.

While the men and women are engaged in the field and domestic work, children help their parents by looking after the cattle, and collecting firewood and manure. The grandparents or the elderly help by looking after the younger children. In times of illness, death, or even during the *chuko*, relatives/cousins from other households help the family. In Tsachaphu, only the children from three households went to school; they were in boarding school in Thimphu or in India. In the other households, when the children reach the age of 12 years, they have to help with all the work in and around the house. They are a very important additional workforce for the household.

In the urban communities, it would be very unusual if there were no relatives/cousins from the rural areas living in with a family. In most cases, children of cousins/relatives go to study in the cities, as they believe that education there is better. Parents/grandparents also live with their families in the urban areas, although it sometimes is a large strain on the financial situation. But they in turn help their children by looking after their grandchildren when they go to work.

Making a living

The closest market in the area is too far away to bring the produce there. It takes about a 12-hour walk with horses. All the people in Tsachaphu are self-sufficient farmers, and all economic activities are based on barter. Cash money is of minor importance. Rice is the most important good and it is used as currency. *Kira's, gho's*, chillies, and labour can be paid in rice. If cash is needed, people sell rice. One family told me that they divide the crop in three every year. One part is for their own consumption, one part is a donation for religious purposes, and one part is to sell or barter. Some families have orange trees and can sell the oranges. Others are selling betel nut leaves, cheese, and butter. There was no electricity in the village and refrigerators are too heavy to carry to the village, so butter and cheese have to be sold in a short period of time.

Some households have horses, which they rent out as beasts of burden, and this brings in cash, too. Once, I made the mistake of thinking of one household as very poor. This family lived in a very simple shack, made of just pieces of wood put together, and it was very cold inside. The wind blew through the walls. It looked very poor. Later, I noticed that this family actually was very rich; it had many horses and lots of land. They were living in a temporary "hut" because they were planning to built a new house; they just were waiting for the right time to start building the house.

All households have pieces of land in the valley. Every household grows irrigated rice in summertime, and in wintertime, people grow wheat, buckwheat, and mustard. In the home garden, people grow chillies, potatoes, onions, and garlic. To complete the diet, the forest provides all kind of important products like mushrooms, green leaves like spinach, herbs, and spices (cinnamon and pepper). All households own livestock like cows, pigs, and chicken. Bulls are needed for ploughing and cats to eat the mice and rats.

The activities to grow rice starts after all the winter crops are harvested. The cattle eat the leftovers from the land. People consult an astrologer when to start ploughing. The astrologer also is consulted about the right time to start with the transplanting of the seedlings in the paddy fields. Several different kinds of local varieties of rice are grown in Tsachaphu. There are two kinds of red rice and four kinds of white rice. Rice is treated with great respect before eating it. The government of Bhutan tried to convince to villagers to grow the "high yield variety" rice to have more crops per year. Some villagers grew one *langdo* (a measurement that means the amount of land that one person can work in one day). This rice was not popular with the people. The people complained it did not taste good and it gives "heart-pain"; the seeds need chemical fertilisers and had to be threshed with a machine that needs kerosene. The traditional rice could be threshed with the feed and did not need chemical fertilisers. Later, the villagers just refused to grow the miracle seeds from the green revolution. It was a first sign of modernisation that came to the village when the government tried to convince the farmers to grow the high-yielding variety rice seeds instead of the traditional seeds.

My stay in the village was an incredible experience; I started to love the people there. All the time I am in Bhutan, I like the people from the villages so much; they have such a good sense of humour and an internal peace, and their faces are relaxed and happy.

Reflections on this first episode

The first month of my stay in the village was very tough for me. I suffered from what I believe was culture shock. To be in a total different environment, where there is nothing from the Western world, had a deep impact on me. To me, the village was a cosmology on its own, with its own rules and regulation, imposed by nature and guided by gods and deities. People were adjusted to this cosmology for survival and many rituals helped them to cope with hardships, fortune and misfortune. It took some time, but after a while, I adjusted myself.

With the story of my experiences in the village as a fieldworker, I would like to point out that being there influenced life in the village. We did not change the life of the people but we stirred up some things.

In one incident, Marleen's landlady was jealous of her, because her husband was our translator for a short while and we spent the first weeks together. His English was so limited, though, that we had to stop using him. Simultaneously, his wife put a lot of pressure on him; she did not like it that he was with us all the time. His wife was not very nice to Marleen, and one day she gave Marleen old rice offerings from the altar for dinner. This was the moment that Marleen had to move to another house in the village. Only one house had space for her, the house of Phuba, the man who had destroyed the water tap because he became ill with meningitis, and because of the disease, he became deaf. Phuba was the black sheep of the village and people gossiped about him. We liked him a lot; he was a kind and funny man. Marleen was allowed to move into the attic of his house, and she had her own ladder from outside to reach the attic.

One evening, it was already dark and I went to Marleen to visit her. While walking up the ladder, I caught with my flashlight a pornographic image. On the ladder was a wooden tablet with an image of a naked woman that perfectly carved out every detail of her private parts. The private parts were painted red. I called Marleen and asked her what this was? Marleen saw it and did not know what it was or what it meant. At that time, we had a translator and we asked him what it was. He said that it was a *dorji*. Phuba had made it as protection against gossip. We would think that an image like that at our door in the Netherlands would increase gossip. Another protection against evil and gossip in Bhutan is the phallus. Big phalluses are painted on houses and doorknobs; handles of spoons have the shape of a phallus. Many houses have a wooden phallus on every corner of the roof.

This symbol of protection goes back to the "divine madman" in the fifteenth century who could ward off evil forces with his private part.

I do believe that we were just as "interesting" for the villagers and the villagers for us.

We got to know each other and we got to like each other in those years. Today, I still meet people from the village. Many children are grown up now. My Am Zam has passed away and her sons have children now.[5]

Reflections on the stay in the village and the report

I give this description of village life to describe how I experienced life in a traditional village in Bhutan. The description is based on the report I had to write for the Department of Agriculture. The report describes how this rural community uses traditional irrigation technologies.

After our stay in the village, we presented our report to the Department of Agriculture in Thimphu, the capital of Bhutan. Our finding was that the people in the village knew best how to use the resources they have to grow rice of high quality in an organic way. Also, the yield was enough to feed the community. The policy we used as a framework for our research was drafted by an English engineer, and it turned out not to be suitable at all for the small traditional community. It was drafted for a far more modern, highly-developed irrigation scheme.

The village headman was asked by the Department of Agriculture to encourage the farmers in the village to try the "miracle seeds," but the farmers were reluctant. At first, they were a bit suspicious toward us being in the village. They thought we might be there to spy upon them. But this was just in the first week. The bottom line was that the villagers did not like to use the so-called "improved seed" to have more crops a year, because this rice did not taste good. All the farmers in the village were asked by the village headman to try to grow this rice on a small plot as a test. They did not like to do this but

---

5   Source: Crins' diary and research (in: Crins & de Graaff, 1990)

they wanted to help the village headman because he had been approached by the government to do this.

This so-called "miracle" rice needed chemical fertilizers that the people had to buy. It had to be threshed by a machine, and the machine needed fuel, which had to be bought with money and carried to the village. The local rice did not need all this; it was grown organically. So our advice was not to develop a cash crop rice area; other places in Bhutan closer to the road would be more suitable.

I realized that the research method was very Western and the world that I encountered was deeply religious. Religion in the village structured life and work: How and when to grow the crops, on which plot it had to grow, when to sow; it was all in the hands of the gods. This was a totally different method than the policy on which we had to base our report. In the beginning, being in this religious community was very confusing to me, and I felt very alienated. It was completely different than "my" world.

In the beginning, I felt very guilty being there in the village, wanting to know everything the people did. I felt like a busybody interfering in the daily life of the people. But being limited to observations in the first months turned out to be helpful. I realized that the concepts with which I had to work were strange and did not fit into the cosmology of the village. At first, it was very frustrating not to be able to talk to the people.

Observation turned out to very valuable. I translated my observations into themes of my world, and later I checked my interpretations with an accomplished translator who was trained in an English school in India. Still, it was a Western world meeting an Eastern world; I realized that I had to find a bridge to enter so I could try to understand this other world. The themes about which my Western mind was most interested and curious about were religion, gender, and sustainability as I encountered them in the village.

Chapters to come

In Chapter one, I will describe how this book came into being, I will go into the research and methodology as it was done in 2004. I will close this chapter with self-reflection and the central research questions. Finally, I will give a summary of the argumentation I follow in this book. In chapter two, ten conversations are related, and in chapter three, I explore theories as a framework for this research. Chapter four consist of a description of the history and the religion of Bhutan. In chapter five, I will explore gender relations in Bhutan, and in chapter six, I will describe what sustainability means in the Bhutanese context. Chapter seven is the conclusion, with self-reflection on my stay and doing research in Bhutan.

How this book came into being

"Beauty through my senses stole; I yielded myself to the perfect whole."

Ralph Waldo Emerson

As you have seen in the previous chapter: I have had a experience that is Bhutan, where the logic of the animist / Buddhist religion determines: that life is entirely experienced in the present, that human gender is conceived of as part and parcel of the cosmos, and where spirituality is everywhere and immediate. In Bhutan this experience is identified (explicitly) with 'sustainability'. Experiencing Bhutan has revealed to me that 'sustainability' is not a partial quality of politics, economics or of society as we see it in the West; sustainability is either a total ontology (as in Bhutan) or it is self-contradictory. In a fragmented lifeworld as in Western (post-) modernism, the holism characteristic of traditional Bhutan culture is just what is lacking (and what will go lacking in Bhutan as it modernizes). In this book I wish to show you my experience of 'sustainability' especially in terms of gender and sustainability, and indicate what such an experience (reflexivity) signifies to me as researcher." I explored literature on self-reflection and reflect on my own activities and interactions in the process of doing research and writing this book.

In this book I try to make you (the reader) think differently about what sustainability is and what its relation to gender is by showing how my experience of Bhutan changed my thinking about sustainability and gender.

As we have seen in the previous chapter, this first stay in the village has led to this book. I could never have completed this work without the knowledge I gathered during that time. I lived in a house with a Bhutanese woman and her three sons and became close to most of the other villagers. They shared their lives with me and it was a very valuable gift that these people and the Bhutanese government allowed me to conduct this kind of fieldwork that most researchers can only dream of. In 1990, Bhutan was still closed to the outside world. There were hardly any telephones, only a very basic hospital in the capital and no television.

In the first weeks of my stay in the village I discovered that the people did not say hello or goodbye. To me this was very strange and sometimes upsetting because the only Dzonkha – the Bhutanese language – I knew was *kuzuzangpo la* and *Lopchegeh* which means "hello and goodbye". When I visited a household nobody said anything to me. I would sit on the floor and think: 'oh my God, I am not welcome here', but suddenly, tea and snacks would appear and people came to sit with me. We spoke with our hands. My interpreter spoke only a few words of English.

Later, I realized that it was impossible to ask people about their past. They refused to talk about it. They would say that talking about the past attracts evil. It was just as impossible to talk about the future. I asked my landlady when the big *choku* (ritual) would be held in her house. She always replied *nabah natse*, which means "the time after tomorrow". But then suddenly she would call me and say "today the *choku* will be".

I asked the people in the village if they would tell me when a village meeting was scheduled, so I could attend. They called in the middle of the night: "Rieki! Meeting!" The time to do things was entirely set by the astrologer, and some of the times he pointed out as auspicious were a bit strange to a westerner such as myself.

After a few weeks of my stay in the village I had a new interpreter who spoke better English. I asked him if he wanted a cigarette. He replied that he did not smoke. Ten minutes later he asked me for a cigarette, I said: 'you do not smoke, don't you?' He said, 'the moment you asked me I did not smoke, but now I smoke'. The same happened when I asked him who was cooking our meal. 'Do you put cheese in the curry?' I asked. He said: 'no'. Later I saw him putting cheese in the curry. I said to him; 'I thought you do not put cheese in the curry and now you do it'. Again he said, 'the moment you asked me I did not put cheese because it was not the right time. Later, it was time to do it'. That was when all of the pieces of the puzzle fell into place: that is why people do not greet or say goodbye. It does not matter: In the moment you are either there or you are not .

Could this way of living in the present , reflect on the gender relations (no marriage ritual, no stigma on separation) and sustainability as a way of life? I shall elaborate on in the coming chapters. What I experienced in the village was that religion is celebrated as a mix of Buddhism and animism; the animistic believe in deities in the soil, air and rocks and astrology is used to determine the time at which actions have to be done or undertaken. I would like to know if this is an overall way of life in Bhutan? I will explore these themes in the chapters four, five and six.

The book

My intercultural exploration is informed by my training as a Western anthropologist but in this book I confront myself as a Western researcher in interaction with Bhutanese whose view of Bhutanese culture is biased by my Western intellectual engagement. In this sense the themes of this book are explored and written in a post-modern humanistic tradition.

I will not go into Buddhist theology, which is beyond the scope of this book. I will describe Buddhism and pre-Buddhism as it is celebrated in Bhutan and how I witnessed it. Buddhism and Pre-Buddhism are strongly connected to the history of the country and in order to understand contemporary Bhutan, a basic knowledge of Bhutanese history and worldview are necessary.

By "post-modern humanistic tradition" I mean that this book recognizes an ethical code in human conduct[1]. My own ethical code in writing about the "other", to identify the inner logic. (Gardner & Lewis, 1996) With this inner logic I refer to the Bhutanese religion and value system with its different realities. I try to avoid 'a-historical generalizations, based upon the observations of the "objective" researcher.' (Gardner & Lewis, 1996:23)

In this book, my aim is to show and explain religion, gender, and sustainability as a single *gestalt*, and I reflect on the experience and what it reveals to me as an researcher.

---

1   www.uq.net.au/slsoc/manussa/humbud.htm

I was impressed by what I saw as a high level of gender equality and the respect people had for the natural environment. I want to know if the political and economic changes of the past 17 years have endangered the traditional "relaxed" gender relations and the respect for the environment.

I explored the themes in an interdisciplinary way and encouraged the Bhutanese people to speak. Although this book is not an anthropological book, by writing about "the Southern other" I am aware of my responsibilities as a western researcher. I am very aware of the colonial heritage of anthropological methodology and its contribution to imperialist discourses about the Southern "other". 'We have to keep in mind that anthropological representations are not neutral, but embedded in power relations between North and South, it is about the notion that one has no right to "speak" for other groups, and the ascribing of legitimacy only to "authentic" voices.' (Gardner & Lewis 1996:24)

This book is my story of my experience in Bhutan. I listened to the stories of the Bhutanese people. I tried to highlight the richness and diversity of human existence as expressed through different languages, beliefs and other aspects of culture as Gardner and Lewis (1996) pointed out.

Reflection on doing research in Bhutan

It was not easy to obtain a research visa for Bhutan. I understand the reluctance of the Bhutanese to admit Western researchers to come to their country to study the Bhutanese culture and write about it in a way to present it as the "truth" or to speak about "the other", as Gardner and Lewis stated. During the 1980s, cultural anthropology paid scant attention to self-reflection in the field and in ethnographic writing. More attention was paid to the hardships an anthropologist has to endure during fieldwork in a non-western setting and in the remote corners of the world. Limited attention was paid to interaction with "the other". The anthropologist had to stay objective and find an answer to the research question. To me this approach was mechanical as not right, in the interaction with the "other". Many realities are happening and my presence there had a significant meaning for the interaction with the people and the research.

During my own fieldwork I realized the impact of my presence in the village. In the first two weeks people asked us what we were doing there and if we were working for the government. We also noticed that the people complained to us about the hardships of daily life. Later when they became used to us, this attitude changed dramatically. I learned to observe and to listen; it was very important that I interact with the people, help them if needed and to be compassionate.

The villagers started to trust us and they came many times to ask for help when they were sick or injured and needed medical care. One village monk gave us Bhutanese names and a family adopted us as their daughters. Being accepted in this community gave us access to very interesting happenings. In the course of my many other visits to Bhutan I encountered openness, trust and friendship. I saw this non-Western culture with my Western eyes. I realized that the meaning of observations are not always are what it seems to be. There were multiple realities and layers to be discovered. Being an objective researcher was a challenge and with the interaction of other humans a strange and mechanic concept that is not appropriate in the interaction with humans and cultural analysis.

My first stay in Bhutan was a profound experience. At first everything was alien to me. Coming from a highly developed country to a village in a remote part of the world was disorienting, to say the least. I spent the first month in culture shock, but I subsequently adapted to the Bhutanese environment. My second trip to Bhutan was like a homecoming. I was thrilled to be smelling the familiar scents, and hearing the beautiful Bhutanese language again. Bhutan had become very familiar to me, almost like a second home. I felt the same way in all of my other later visits.

At the same time, although I feel comfortable in the Bhutanese culture, it is not the culture I grew up in. Some aspects of the Bhutanese culture are very different from my own. Sometimes I encountered the "Asian" or "Bhutanese" way in my interactions and did not understand it at all. I realized that there are layers of values, hierarchy, and customs that are profoundly different than those in my world and are thus difficult to grasp.

Reflecting literature on researcher's behaviour in another context

My research is based on anthropological methodology, so it is important to reflect on the history of anthropological methodology.

Marcus and Fischer (1986) give an overview of the history on anthropology and ethnography methodology . It points out my own "problem" as a Western researcher studying "the southern other".

In the view of Marcus and Fisher, twentieth-century anthropology is different from what it had been in the mid- and late nineteenth century:

'Then, as a burgeoning field of Western scholarship in an era imbued with pervasive ideology of social progress, it was dominated by hopes for general science of Man, for discovering social laws in the long evolution of humans toward ever higher standard of rationality. For contemporary socio-cultural anthropologists, the most prominently remembered intellectual ancestors of that era are Edward Tylor and James Morgan in England, Emile Durkheim in France and Lewis Henry Morgan in the United States. Anthropologists characteristically, pursued ambitious intellectual projects that sought the origins of modern institutions, rituals, customs, and habits of thought through the contrasts of evolutionary stages in the development of human society. Material on contemporaneous "savage," or "primitive," peoples served them as living cultural analogies with the past. Theirs was an era of "armchair" ethnology. Although travelling occasionally, they depended on sources as traveller's accounts, colonial records, and missionary scholarship for firsthand data. These major writers, among others, set the agenda for the style, scope, and subject matter of anthropological debates into the twentieth century.' (Marcus & Fischer 1986:17)

'The critical transition in the nature of British and American anthropological scholarship came during the beginning of the twentieth century. There was a professionalization of the social sciences and the humanities into specialized disciplines of the university.' (...) 'Divisions of academic labour, specializations by discipline, the taking of distinctive methods, analytical language, and standards, all became the order of the day. Finding an institutional place in the university as one of the social sciences, anthropology has been the most disorderly and interdisciplinary of disciplines to both the delight and despair of the academic establishment'. (Marcus&Fischer1986:17)

'An important shift has made a distinctive kind of method the centre of social and cultural anthropology in its new disciplinary placement as a social science and this distinctive method was ethnography. Its main innovation was bringing together into an integrated professional practice the previous separate processes of collecting data among non-Western peoples, done primarily by amateur scholars or others on the scene, and the armchair theorizing and analysis, done by academic anthropologist. Anthropology is a "research process" in which the anthropologist closely observes, records, and engages in the daily life of another culture-an experience labelled as the fieldwork method-and then writes accounts of this culture, emphasizing descriptive detail. These accounts are the primary form in which fieldwork procedures, the other culture, and the ethnographer's personal and theoretical reflections are accessible to professionals and other readerships.' (Marcus & Fischer 1986:18) Marcus and Fischer point out that if the locus of order and the source of modern anthropology's major intellectual contribution to scholarship were to be identified, it would be the ethnographic research process itself, bracketed by its two justifications. One is the capturing of cultural diversity, mainly among tribal and non-Western peoples, in the now uncertain tradition of anthropology's nineteenth-century project. (...)

'As an ethnographer, the anthropologist focuses his or her efforts on a different sort of holism: not to make universally valid statements, but to represent a particular way of life as fully as possible. The nature of this holism-what it means to provide a full picture of a closely observed way of life-is one of the cornerstones of twentieth-century ethnography that is currently undergoing serious critique and revision as we have seen in the writing above'. (Marcus & Fisher 1986:-23)

Clifford summarises some important questions for an anthropologist: 'Who has the authority to speak for a group's identity or authenticity? What are the essential elements and boundaries of a culture? How do self and other clash and converse in the encounters of ethnography, travel, modern interethnic relations? What narratives of development, loss, and innovation can account for the present range of local oppositional movements.' (Clifford, 1988:8)

He puts the emphasis on Western visions and practices in ethnography. Modern ethnography appears in traditional and innovative forms. According to Clifford, ethnography is a hybrid activity; it appears as writing a collection of modern collage and a way of understanding a diverse world.

He points out that this century has seen a drastic expansion of mobility, including tourism, migrant labour, immigration and urban sprawl. More and more people travel the world. In cities on six continents immigrants have come to stay. The "exotic" is uncannily close. Conversely, there seem to be no places left on the planet where the presence of "modern" products, media, and power cannot be felt. One no longer leaves home confident of finding something radically new, another time or space. Difference is encountered in the neighbourhood; the familiar turns up at the ends of the earth. Cultural differences are no longer a stable, exotic otherness; self-other relations are matters of power and rhetoric rather than of essence. A whole structure of expectations about authenticity in culture and in art is thrown in doubt. One can conclude from Clifford that beautiful exotic places do not exist anymore, that cultural authenticity has been lost in the modernist age.

As Soules (2007) points out: 'Traditionally, change has been interpreted as disorder, a chaos, as loss of authenticity. But in the global intermixture of cultures that we have witnessed in this century, the authenticity of former cultures may not be lost in quite the ways we imagine them to be: "local authenticities meet and merge in transient urban and suburban setting," according to Clifford (1988). This complex process of acculturation, of meeting and merging, poses a predicament for the contemporary student of culture: the student of culture must consider both "local attachments" – regional dialects and traditions and general possibilities.' (Soules, 2007:1)

Marcus and Fisher (1986) noted that the contemporary debate is about how an emergent post-modern world is to be represented as an object for social thought in its various contemporary manifestations. According to Marcus and Fischer: "discussions of current intellectual trends can be weightless and unconvincing if they do not concern themselves with the situations of particular disciplines. For us, developments in contemporary anthropology reflect the central problem of representing social reality in a rapidly changing world. Within anthropology, ethnographic fieldwork and writing has become the liveliest current arena of theoretical discussion and innovation. Ethnography's concern is with description, and present efforts to make ethnographic writing more sensitive to its broader political, historical, and philosophical implications places anthropology at the vortex of the debate about the problem of representing society in contemporary discourses." (1986:vii)

Marcus and Fischer believe that their examination of social and cultural anthropology's "experimental moment," reveals much about this general intellectual trend. 'Anthropology is not the mindless collection of the exotic, but the use of cultural richness for self-reflection and self-growth', as Marcus and Fisher (1986: ix) state.

'Accomplishing this in the modern world of increased interdependence among societies and mutual awareness among cultures requires new styles of sensibility and of writing. Such exploration in anthropology resides in the move from a simple interest in the description of cultural others to a more balanced purpose of cultural critique that plays off other cultural realities against our own in order to gain a more adequate knowledge of them all.' (...)

According to Marcus and Fisher, 'twentieth-century social and cultural anthropology has promised its Western readership enlightenment on two fronts. The one has been the salvaging of distinct cultural forms of life from a process of apparent global Westernization. With both its romantic appeal and its scientific intentions, anthropology has stood for the refusal to accept this conventional perception of homogenization towards a dominant Western model. The other promise of anthropology has been to serve as a form of cultural critique for us. In using portraits of other cultural patterns to reflect self-critically on our own ways, anthropology disrupts common sense and makes us re-examine our taken-for-granted assumptions. The current predicaments in sustaining these purposes of modern anthropology are well illustrated by a pair of recent controversies. Both make their strongest points about distortions in the ways non-Western peoples have been portrayed in scholarship, which has depended on descriptive, semi literary forms for its expression' (1986:1)

Marcus and Fisher and Lewis and Gardner but also ecofeminists like Merchant (1980) and Radford Reuther (1996) inspired me to do the research and writing this book in a compassionate way as much as possible towards the society that I encountered and that had let me in. Being in Bhutan made me aware of my own assumptions and my own background that was very different than those of the people I was researching. My "objectivity" is biased by my own background and self-reflection could clarify my place in analysing the "other" culture. This method was against my training in the 1990s when I was studying cultural anthropology. My advisers instructed me to do research in an "inter-subjective" and positivist way. I always had problems with this method because of what I had gleaned from the works of Marcus and Fisher and Lewis and Gardner. But in this book, I do not want to enter this debate on anthropology further because it is not the theme of this book. I want to write this book about my visit to Bhutan in a style that is fluctuating in a sense, that I am changing and the topic is changing. I want a style that contains this change but does not lock it up in a cage. I approach my meeting the people of Bhutan from both a Western and a Bhutanese perspective, as I experienced it.

Reflecting literature on Self-reflection

In regard to self-reflection I find the work of Crapanzano (2004) very enlightening; he speaks to my own struggles in analysing the "other culture". According to McGee and Warms: 'The underlying concept of Crapanzano's work is that anthropologists construct meanings by writing ethnography. Although ethnographic data themselves are mute, the act of writing is a literary construction of the author. As previous analysis shows, Crapanzano takes apart and examines rhetorical devices in ethnographic writings. The method for this critical analysis is called deconstruction, which reveals interpretations and hidden biases that authors have for justifying their authority. Deconstruction does not resolve inconsistencies, but rather reveals underlying hierarchies involved in conveying information. With this knowledge, we can look at texts with a different, more critical perspective. Deconstruction forced anthropologists to become sensitive to their unconscious assumptions and authorities'. (McGee & Warms, 2004 see footnote 1)

According to Mc Gee and Warms: 'Crapanzano is one of the post-modern anthropologists who claim that objectivity does not exist in cultural analysis. Crapanzano demonstrates this principle by analyzing ethnographic writing of others. One of Crapanzano's analyses is on *Deep Play: Notes on a Balinese Cock-*

fight by the symbolic anthropologist Clifford Geertz. The cockfight is a traditional gambling for prestige in Bali. Geertz depicted symbolic meanings in the
cockfight and explained how these meanings influenced the Balinese lives.
Crapanzano states that Geertz' writing is far from objective descriptions of
Bali culture because Geertz controlled the texts by using various rhetorical devices. Crapanzano first points out the non-existence of the author in the texts,
or a lack of reflection. Geertz described Bali society as if his presence did not
affect the people in the society. Since Geertz was not a member of Bali society,
he must have influenced the Balinese behaviours and thoughts just by being
there. Crapanzano argues that Geertz did not consider this impact. For example, Geertz stated that the Balinese did not pay attention to him, and therefore,
they acted 'as if he simply did not exist'. (McGee & Warms, 2004)[2]

Crapanzano argues that Geertz's view is not necessarily accurate. As Marcus and Fisher (1986) point out, just because Geertz felt like a non-person does
not mean the Balinese viewed him as one. Recent decades have witnessed a
profound challenge to the purpose and styles of theory that have guided the
social sciences since their late nineteenth-century emergence as academic disciplines. 'Crapanzano argues that ethnographers tend to mix what they believe
natives think with how natives actually feel. This mistake stems from authors'
attempts to establish their authority regarding the accuracy of their texts.
When an author does not distinguish between his own view and native's views,
readers tend to forget that the author's voice is the only one they hear in the
writing. Therefore, readers feel as if the text is transmitting an objective reality without any bias or interpretation of the author. Another point Crapanzano
makes is that anthropologists generalize the whole population of a particular
society. For example, based on his experience with a group of informants in his
research, Geertz described Balinese character as follows: 'the Balinese never
do anything in a simple way when they can contrive to do it in a complicated
way,' [...], and 'the Balinese are shy to the point of obsessiveness of open conflict'. (McGee & Warms, 2004:603 see footnote 1)

'Crapanzano argues that this kind of generalization reveals a conventional
attitude of anthropologists in front of their research subjects. Anthropologists
tend to separate themselves from a population they are studying and reject
to see the people as equal individuals. Crapanzano claims that Geertz, as an
anthropologist, separated the "anthropologist" and "his Balinese".' (McGee &
Warms, 2004:603 see footnote 1)

2   See also: http://www.mnsu.edu/emuseum/cultural/anthropology/Crapanzano.html

Reflecting on ethnography in Bhutanese context

According to Ramos (1992): 'In the world of ethnography certain images are created of entire peoples which remain undisturbed in the readers memory. The lovely and companionable Pygmies, the proud and intractable Nuer, or the headhunting Jivaro are evocations that come easily to mind'.(Ramos, 1992:48) Bhutan is therefore seen as Shangri-la, the country with a policy to increase "Gross National Happiness" instead of its Gross National Product. However, Westerners tell another story. Wikan (1996) has a different story about Bhutan than Crins. (1990, 1993, 2003). Both anthropologists conducted research in Bhutan in 1990. Each one of them has a different account of Bhutanese culture. According to Ramos, each ethnographer produces a unique portrait of the people studied is neither news nor it is surprising, since field experiences are forged as much by the ethnographer as by the people. This becomes evident when two or more anthropologists study the same people. When several ethnographers are working simultaneously in the same general area, it is easier to appreciate the twists and turns of personal preferences in describing a culture. (Ramos, 1992) I will reflect on my own experience in Bhutan in regard to the writing, when describing my observations of gender relations.

I will also examine Wikan's view of gender relations as she depicts it in a life story of an old nun. Wikan's *The nun's story. Reflections of an age-old, post-modern dilemma* (1996) tells the story of a Bhutanese woman of 76 years old who had become a nun at 19.

'My Candidate for a post-modern life is the following: a woman, now 76, who was a nun till she was 19. Then she got raped by a monk and had to leave the nunnery because she got pregnant. The child died at birth. After a while she got raped again a second time by a nobleman. The child lived, and later the mother got married- to a man who was a runaway monk. He has been in a monastery since he was seven, but now on an age of 30, had to flee – because he had a fornicated with the wife of the district governor. Now he and the former nun teamed up. Together they had two sons – so there were three, with the son she had of the nobleman. The middle son was sent off to become a monk, but ran away and married. His wife had two daughters by each of his two brothers. But when he kept womanizing, she decided it was too much, and took off, leaving her children with grandma. Thus fate again made a mockery of the ex-nun's desire to devote herself to spiritual matters. At 60, she redone a nun's habit and told Grandpa she was finished with sex. She kept on running the household but withdrew more and more to meditate. Then the government decided to take her house and land to make a volleyball court. If anything has unhinged Grandma, this is it. For a while it is good to give birth even to a child conceived in rape, nothing but sorrow ensues from being evicted from your home and losing your family's sustenance. You want to know more? A typical life this is. Though the specifics are unique, the changing fates and circumstances are common enough. Where? In the most traditional of societies, Bhutan, which has been "post- modern" since the dawn of time'. (Wikan, 1996: 279)

According to Wikan, the old nun's life is a prototype of post-modern life; she presents an extreme example of a typical condition of things falling apart as normal in Bhutan. Interestingly by writing and publishing this article about a pre-modern society also for Wikan things fell apart. She was blacklisted and could not visit the country for a long time. She writes as a Western scholar about the life of an uneducated poor woman in a traditional pre-modern country. Her article focuses on the woman's hardships, and she delineates the callous and cruel society in which this woman lives .

Wikan analyses the position of an old woman who had been the victim of a cruel, male-dominated society. Is Bhutan a cruel male dominated society? What about the monks? Had they not taken a vow of celibacy? These questions should be answered before supporting an analysis like Wikan's.

According to Crapanzano (2004), anthropology is a moral science, a science that explores ways in which people regulate and evaluate their associations with each other, on the communal and intimate level. Anthropologists are immediately implicated in the world in which they do their research. This has been noted time and time again and is, in fact, the concern of most ethics committees. However, preoccupation with the anthropologist's conduct in the field and with the consequences of his or her research for those studied, however important it is, should not blind us to our own moral communities. Crapanzano refers to the way in which our descriptions of the lives and cultures of those we study determine our attitudes towards them and toward ourselves. We assume enormous moral and political responsibility in our construction and representations of our subjects. In this line lies my problem with Wikan's story. My question is, can she make this kind of deduction from a one woman case?

I believe the Bhutanese who were very upset with Wikan's story would agree with Crapanzano :

'If in the name of one science or another, we dismiss most everything the people we study hold important – their religion, their values, their expressive culture, their culinary habits, their sexual practices – as epiphenomena, ultimately reducible to some ecological adaptation, evolutionary responses, cognitive predispositions, or genetic make-up, we devalue those people, sully their under-standing of themselves and their own world, and promote our parochialism'. (Crapanzano, 2004:4)

Anthropologists have to be aware of "ethnocentrism"; they have a responsibility to listen to the voices of the people that they study, and not only what they have to say about themselves but also what they say about the researchers and about themselves. (Crapanzano, 2004)

According to Crapanzano (2004), today's anthropologists are less concerned with imaginative processes than with the product of the imagination, despite their frequent references to the imagination. Nor have they really shown the concern for individual imagination that Joseph-Marie de Gerando advocated in the methodological treatise he wrote in 1800 for the *Societé des Observateurs de L'Homme* one of the founding documents in French anthropology. The in-dividual has always been something of an embarrassment in anthropology. Crapanzano's concern is with imagination and, as he calls it, "the hinterland, the Beyond". He is concerned with openness and closure, with the way in which we construct, wittingly or unwittingly, horizons that determine what we expe-rience and how we interpret what we experience. Crapanzano's point is that when a horizon and whatever lies beyond it are given articulate form, they freeze our view of the reality that immediately confronts us. 'Was it not for the fact that once that "beyond" is articulated, a new horizon emerges and with it a new "beyond". The dialectic between openness and closure is, according to Crapanzano, an important dimension of human experience and imagination and worthy of anthropological considerations' (Crapanzano 2004:2).

Now, I'd like to address the question: Where do I stand in regard to eth-nography? My view is much in line with Crapanzano but I want to be careful not to fall into the trap of cultural relativism. Cultures are different, and this enriches the world, but I do not think we can accept that all views in the world have equal value. There are ethics that are universal applicable, for example on human rights (although this is a Western concept).

To me, being in another culture and writing about this culture comes with a responsibility. A researcher has to be aware about his/her own position and opinions: "How do I view this culture?" "what does this view mean?" "Where does it come from?" "Am I aware of my (e. g.) Western eyes?" I agree that self-re-flection can be a helpful tool in becoming aware of one's own ethnocentricity.

Towards a research question

In this book, I explore themes that in my Western mind are: gender and sustainability.

I'd like to address this book as placed somewhere between me and my meeting with the people of Bhutan, on the bridge of my construction of that relationship, which is like three bridges next to each other: religion, sustainability, and gender. And they are not objective themes out there; they are my experimental constructions.

I shall take a society that is living in the present, or in the now (as the Buddhists say), as a point of departure (see also Marx, 1961). The connection of the gender relationships, the sustainable awareness in the country, and change, are the focus of this book and very relevant themes in the contemporary Bhutanese debate on sustainability and gender. It is important to acknowledge these subjects now, before modernization and development take their toll on the traditional life of the Bhutanese and the uniqueness of the country.

In this book I focus on the Buddhist majority. In the South of Bhutan there is a Hindu population from Nepal but this group will not be included in this book.

My aim is to structure this book along the line of the concepts of social ethics, gender, and civil society, but in a wider context.

In addition to gender and sustainability themes, I will address values and religion. I want to know how the Bhutanese value the themes that I find important in my meeting with Bhutan.

Combinations of facts such as living in the present, a high level of gender equality, a pristine environment, and respect for the environment together with a spiritual form of life are brought in relationship to each other in this book. This combination brings me to the following research questions.

My research questions are:
How and what kind of insight is produced when I, a Western researcher, meet the other?
How can one find the otherness in oneself and become the "other?"

How can I contribute, through the development of reflexive arguments, to an understanding of gender and sustainability in the Bhutanese setting? In my reflections, studying the "other" is crucial; by studying the "other", I may start to understand my own feelings, interpretations, and prejudices.

As we have seen in the previous chapter, my meeting with Bhutan was a meeting with a totally different world. The village was a complete alien cosmology for me. This, to me, was meeting the "other" – a meeting with a strange, very religious world in which everything was different than in my world. Because this world was so alien to me, and I had to survive for six months in that alien village, I had to adjust to that environment.

Slowly, by being there, and later in my many visits in Bhutan, I found that otherness in myself by learning more about the culture.

The Bhutanese development discourse is dominated by preserving the traditional values and culture. According to Marx, however the moment a society tries to keep its traditions they are gone. With the emergence of a market economy and the introduction of money the society is changing. Money undermines the ability of the past labour to obtain the present value is given to past labour for future gains. (Marx, in: Elster 1987)

Because of my 17 years of experience I will address the impact of a market economy on the traditional life in Bhutan. What kind of influence does a market economy have on a traditional society that is living in the present?

Methodology

I wrote this book in order to answer my own questions about everyday Bhutanese life. Knowing Bhutan as one of the last undisturbed Mahayana Buddhist countries with a strong pre-Buddhist heritage.

I wanted to ask the respondents "obvious" questions about my Western categories, such as gender relations, their sense of nature, environmental sustainability, and religion.

To gain insight into the themes of religion gender and sustainability in my meeting with Bhutan, I have studied the literature on these themes. It is impossible to gain an understanding of values in Bhutan without having some familiarity with its religion. Mahayana Buddhism in its Tantric form is the state religion. This form of Buddhism incorporates many aspects of indigenous religion and an esoteric system of deities and practices. Since English literature on Bhutanese Buddhism is scarce, I studied the literature on values in Tibetan Buddhism that made reference to Bhutan.

The second category in this book is gender: gender relationships in Bhutan are different from those of the surrounding countries and in Asia as a whole. To put these gender relationships into theoretical perspective, I explored the gender debate. There are few empirical studies of gender in Bhutan society and I had to find a framework in which to place Bhutanese gender relations.

The third category in this book is sustainability, which I try to approach from the Bhutanese perspective although I conceive it from my Western view. In addition, I raise the question how has changed these concepts. I explored Marx's philosophical anthropology and especially his theory of alienation as a model for change in Bhutan. I chose Marx because the people in Marx's ideal society live in the present and are not alienated from the means of production.

I carried out my empirical research along the line of qualitative inquiry (Hosking 2006). It means that qualitative inquiry holds space for relational processes in which social constructions are socially produced between human beings. As a consequence, I am part of my own inquiry. Simultaneously, I recognise multiple local-contextual knowledge fields and practices. Bhutanese ones, as well my own knowledge fields or practices which are just one of many communities of practice. I also understand my inquiry as an intervention method (Hosking 2006)[3]. Subject-object are not independent; self and other are co-constructed self realities, relational realities and self is part of other – not a part of and based on hidden assumptions. (...) As a Western researcher it means being reflective while observing Bhutanese culture, the relation between subject and object, and the power games. In order to understand the values in Bhutan or what the Bhutanese people find important, the research methodologies employed were open conversations, semi-structured interviews, informal discussions, narratives, and literature.

The leading questions for the conversations were partly inspired by Schwartz and Bilsky (1990). Their theory of the study of values is suitable for cross-cultural settings, and is universally applicable. I used this theory because it helped me to make a checklist of questions about daily Bhutanese life. The other questions were grouped by theme: religion, gender and sustainability.

My translator and I travelled to different places in order to speak with informants of different ages, education and life experience.

The research was carried out in February and March 2004, the second episode of my quest. I interviewed 30 men and 26 women, from farmers to ministers, in rural and urban areas. To interview the respondents who could not speak English, the Centre for Bhutan Studies provided me with a translator who arranged for all the road permits and papers. I discussed my list of questions with her so that she could translate them into Dzongkha. The questions are available for inspection.

---

3   www.geocities.com/dian_marie_hosking/qi.html

More than 20 languages are spoken in Bhutan. (Chakravarty, 1996:62) Almost every valley has its own language, and many of these languages are not related to any other. The younger generation and all the people with English medium education speak English. I was able to interview 35 western-educated Bhutanese informants who spoke English. I identified the respondents according to age, sex, profession and education.

Of the 26 women, 13 were living in Thimphu, the capital of Bhutan. Ten of the 26 had no English medium education. The education of the other 16 women ranged from sixth grade through a masters degree. Three of the women had a masters degree and three a bachelor's degree. Four of the women were farmers, three were shopkeepers, two were nuns, one was a minister, one was a hotel manager, one was a policewoman, one was a housewife, four were senior civil servants, one was a hotel manager, three were students, three were hotel receptionists, one was a librarian, and one was a waitress.

Among the 30 men, 12 were living in Thimphu and they all are educated. Nine of the men had no English medium education, six were farmers, one was a workman and three were monks. Among the men who spoke English, four were students, one was a filmmaker, four were teachers, one was an engineer, one was a businessman and seven were senior civil servants. The other 21 were educated from level class 6 to class 14, seven respondents have a masters degree and one has the doctorate.

The youngest respondent was a girl of 16 and the oldest was a man who guessed that he was around 70. Ten of the men were single, 11 of the women were single and two were divorced.

In order to visit more parts of Bhutan I hired a car and a driver. Our first trip was to Punakha, where the annual *Punakha Dromchue*, the three-day New Year's festival, is held. This means that many people from the villages went to the *Dzong*. Next to the religious festival in the *Dzong* a carnival and market had been set up to cater for and entertain the people. At the festival we interviewed farmers from the countryside. After two days we drove up to Trongsa and Bumthang in central Bhutan. Bumthang is a religious site where many saints lived. Guru Rinpoche visited Bumthang several times. After Bumthang we drove to Trongsa Wangdi, Paro and Haa (West-Bhutan).

We spent our last two weeks in Thimphu where we wanted to interview people with a higher education and senior government workers. Having the conversations was easy as I visited most of the respondents at their workplace and they all had time for me. Each conversation took about two hours. In Thimphu I had to schedule interviews with high government officials. All the other respondent were visited; we just asked them to talk with us for a while. All of the respondents agreed to interviews. In chapter two I will explore these conversations.

Bhutan was unlike any other Asian country that I had visited. It was a kind of a Shangri-La. There was no noise pollution, no air pollution and no billboard pollution. There was hardly any crime. As a woman I could go freely into a bar and have a beer; Bhutanese women were comfortable doing the same. This would be unheard-of in India, Bhutan's neighbour. Men and women have a re-laxed way of interaction; they work and live together as equals. I love the Bhuta-nese sense of humour and the liveliness of its elderly men and women.

1999, the second episode of my journey

In 1999 I returned to Bhutan and at first sight little seemed to have changed in the nine years since my last visit. On closer inspection, however, tremendous changes had taken place. For example, there were hospitals, schools, an infrastructure, and the capital had grown, with all the positive and negative consequences.

I was very impressed by the country's economic development, but I learned that many Bhutanese in the higher ranks of the civil servants were frightened by it. Those who had studied in western countries and who were living a more western life-style in Bhutan are afraid of losing their Bhutanese values and tra-ditions. I noticed that the maintenance of traditional values and customs is a concern for the higher educated people. This concern is reflected in govern-ment policy. Within the official documentation of Bhutan, fundamental im-portance is given to the maintenance of traditional values and customs despite modernisation. Buddhist beliefs and institutions are constantly cited and em-phasized in commentary. As Pema and Pain (2000) out it:

> 'The establishment of the Special Commission for Cultural Affairs in 1985 is
> seen as a reflection of the great importance placed upon the preservation of the
> country's unique and distinct language, dress, arts and crafts which collective-
> ly define Bhutan's national identity.' (Ministry of Planning, 1996:193, in: Pema
> and Pain 2000:219)

The publication of *Driglam Namzha* (Bhutanese Etiquette) by the National Library of Bhutan hoped to 'serve as a significant foundation in the process of cultural preservation and cultural synthesis'. (Pain & Pema (2000:219)

Much of the recent writing on Bhutan has focused on the more formal and materially evident aspects of tradition and culture, religious institutions and their ceremonies, the monarchy, architecture and textiles. Not so much atten-tion has been given yet to social interaction. Bhutan's traditions are unique and worth studying, because Bhutan is the only surviving Buddhist Himalaya kingdom that has preserved its traditional culture. Continuing to preserve the country's cultural and traditional heritage is vital for the Bhutanese to know their culture and its social relations. It is the people who make the arts and crafts and the cultural and religious institutions. One example of this are the gender relationships. The Bhutanese tend to take these relationships for granted, but these are worth studying.

In 2003 the UNDP and the Department of Planning conducted a gender pilot study. The Bhutanese society is marked by high level of gender equality unique in Asia. Located in a geographical region where prejudice against women is common. Bhutan accords the same legal rights to both men and women, and gender discrimination is claimed not to be a significant problem. Both men and women have equal status and opportunities. There are no sharply defined male/female domains and in most cases women own and inherit land and assets. (Kunzang Choden, 1999; Brauen, 1994; Crins, 1997) This is what I observed during my stay in the village, where all the land and houses were owned by the mother and preference for inheritance was given to daughters. Couples lived together without the marriage ritual. Divorce was easy and not stigmatized.

Bhutan was blessed with relaxed gender relations, matrilineality and matrilocality. It would be interesting to incorporate the Bhutanese view of gender. I wanted to know how the Bhutanese comprehend gender in relation to their religion and values. Is there a defined role about how women or men should be, according to Buddhism? Ahough there is no God in Buddhism as I know it from my Christian background I was curious if people have an image of God and what gender God has, according to the Buddhist Bhutanese?

Another aspect of Bhutanese culture and world-view is their respect for nature and animals. The environment is respected and a profound sense of stewardship for the natural environment prevails. This respect for nature pervades the country and is a pillar of the state's economic development policy. Is this consciousness a central Buddhist value?

And is it derived from ancient values? As this is manifested in government policy. Since 1988, the government has measured its "Gross National Happiness" and strives for economic growth that serves the country while respecting its culture, history, philosophy and environment and in line with this is good governance.

Scientific research on social, cultural and political changes in the Bhutanese society is still in its nascent stage. Bhutan is a country in transition and the social structure of the country can still be described as traditional. Now, however, the country is changing as it is slowly opening up to the outside world.

'The historical evolution of Bhutan provides a manifestation of considerable

39

and complex transition through which contemporary Bhutanese policy came into being. Its religious, political and ethnic institutions had been uniquely secured through the historical process, which has shaped the typical Bhutanese personality in which a clear separation between spiritual and temporal realms is not recognized.' (Ramakant, 1996:12)

This background is the cornerstone of this book. To understand religion in its Asian context, because religion plays a very important role in all spheres of Bhutanese life, and to understand the changes is Bhutanese values, Bhutanese Buddhism and the local pre-Buddhist religion will be discussed in this book. This book adopts three perspectives: one is based on literature; the second is from conversations as illustration of the Bhutanese reality, or the opinion of the Bhutanese on the subject and the third is my perspective on my findings and reflections.

In chapter two I start my inquiry with conversations with ten Bhutanese. On request, the transcripts of the 56 interviews are available for inspection.

Chapters to come

In chapter three I will describe the theoretical framework of this research. Chapter four describes the history and the religion of Bhutan. In Chapter five I will explore gender relations in Bhutan and in chapter six I will explain sustainability means in the Bhutanese context. Chapter seven offers some conclusions based on my self-reflections and on reflections in and on interactions with Bhutanese during my stay and doing research in Bhutan.

In next chapter two ten Bhutanese conversations are worked out.

Bhutanese conversations

In this chapter I present some of the conversations I had with the respondents in 2004. I selected these ten conversations (of 56 total) due to their richness as well as the differences in age, education level, profession, and place of living of the conversation partners in order to gather as many different views and opinions as possible.

The structure of the conversations

In 2004, I conducted conversations with 56 Bhutanese inhabitants, with each conversation lasting one to three hours. I wanted to enter these conversations on a level of reflection. I have been to Bhutan, as you have seen in the prologue. In chapter one I presented my questions. I have reflected on my first and second episode in Bhutan, and now I seek to give voices to the ones I have been reflecting on.

In conducting interviews with respondents who did not speak English, I utilised the services of a female interpreter. Most respondents in the urban areas (more than 30) were western educated; consequently, I could interview them in English. It would be too much to present them all here in their complete form; therefore, I chose 10 conversations that offer insight into the Bhutanese way of living.

As stated in chapter 1, respondents were identified according to age, sex, profession, and education. The interviewees ranged in profession from farmers up to ministers in rural and urban areas and included lamas, monks, and a nun as well as shopkeepers, workers, farmers, and business people. We travelled to different places in order to include different ages, education levels, and amount of life experience. In other words, I sought to elicit responses from all levels of the population of Bhutan.

Prior to the interviews, I structured the questions into three groups focusing first on gender relations, then religion, and finally sustainability. Before ending the interviews, I asked several questions that combined the three subjects of focus. Then, I ended the interviews by asking whether the interviewees wanted to add anything to the discussion.

The space of knowledge that I am meeting here is about what people value in regard to religion, gender, and sustainability. I wanted to know how Bhutanese perceived the world; the main aim of these questions was to explore how religion, gender, and sustainability were valued, as well as to determine if a change had occurred on these themes due to modernization. I wanted to explore my perception vis-a-vis their perceptions.

The last leading questions on how my conversation partners conceive the world and what they value are based on a theory of Schwarz and Bilsky (1990), who proposed the theory of a universal psychological structure of human values that identifies the facets necessary to define human values and specifies the types of value contents that people from all cultures are likely to distinguish. The theory derives these types from a set of universal human requirements. Schwartz and Bilsky make three distinctions in value content – namely, because values are goals, they must represent the interests of some person or group, although some values may serve both individualistic and collectivist interests.

Bilsky and Schwartz collected different motivational domains of values derived from the literature on needs, social motives, institutional demands, and functional requirements of social groups. These domains are:

1) Enjoyment domain (pleasure, a comfortable life, happiness, and cheer)
2) Security domain (security values, family security)
3) Achievement domain (capability, ambition, and social recognition)

4) Self-direction domain (daring, decision-making, creative, independent, intellectual)
5) Restrictive-Conformity domain (obedient, polite, clean, and self-controlled)
6) Pro-social Domain (helpful, forgiving, loving, and equal)
7) Social power domain (leadership and authority, social recognition)
8) Maturity domain (broadmindedness, wisdom, mature love, a world of beauty, standing up for one's beliefs)

Although Bilsky and Schwartz claim that the structure of these domains of identifying values is universal, I realize that the values are Western. Because I perceive the Bhutanese in their social context from my Western view, the tools available for me to work with are Western. I used this method as a start to explore certain values people have, and to try to determine if those values are different than my Western values in regard to the themes.

By giving voice to the researched, I can learn if these domains have any values for the Bhutanese world.

I have to address another question that I cannot answer now, but I hope to be able to answer in the last chapter: How will this meeting between the domains, values, and my three themes influence the 56 conversations? Do Bhutanese people recognize these domains and values, or are there other Bhutanese domains and values?

To start with: I focused first on the gender relations. I was interested in incorporating participants' views on gender as they could shed light on gender relations seen and experienced by all levels of society, from farmers in rural areas through highly educated senior government officials. I wanted to know how people see genders in relation to religion. Do men and women have a defined role according to Buddhism? What gender does God have according to the Buddhist Bhutanese?

For answers to my research question, I included a list of several questions about religion. I asked the respondents about the role religion plays in their lives and what religion means to them. Of all the respondents, one man is Hindu and one woman is Christian; the remaining are all Buddhist. The majority of the respondents belong to the Drukpa Kargyupa Buddhist School. The nuns and two lamas interviewed belong to the Nyingmapa Buddhist School. These different schools are not strictly separated; In both schools, the same saints are worshiped and religious practitioners are free to marry if they have not taken the vow of celibacy.

While I give the conversation partners voices, I try to become wiser myself and this result is in chapters four, five and six. But the main aims of the conversations are to give Bhutanese their voice. In order to hear what they say, I have to reflect on my prejudice on the voices: How do I recognize a value and how do I find a relation between a theme and a value?

Questioning in the actual conversations

I started the interviews by asking background questions about the level of education, profession, and where people came from (what part of Bhutan). I asked participants if they were married, if they lived in an extended family, how many children they had, and if those children were going to school. Then I asked several questions about labour division within the household and on the farm (if living on a farm). I wanted to know if work activities were carried out by both genders or if certain work was not done either by the women or the men. A majority of Bhutanese people are farmers and involved in agriculture. As in most rural communities, all of the household members are involved in the production and generation of food and income. I also asked both men and women if they perform religious rituals (*pujas*) to determine if differences exist in performing rituals between the genders. I then asked if people were happy with their lives and if they wanted to change something; if they indicated yes, I asked what they would like to change.

I asked 24 general questions about gender-related ideas, worldviews, and dominions based on my previous experiences in Bhutan. These questions dealt with daily life, wishes for the future, what is important to people, freedom of movement and choice, but also what status means to the respondents and power. My own experience is that in Bhutan people with status are persons who are very popular; these people are highly regarded because of the good deeds they have done. Status is ascribed to a certain person because of his or her good deed for society; sometimes such deeds are rewarded by the king, who makes that person *"Dasho"* (comparable with "sir" in England). Similarly, I sought to determine what power means to people in Bhutan.

In addition, I asked 14 questions about religion – what it means to people, how people think or imagine where they come from, and whether a creation myth exists (Buddhism does not believe in a creator). Bhutan has many *ngejums* and *pawos* (shamans); therefore, I wanted to know if people consult them.

I was also interested in what "a good" person is to the people to whom I talked – namely, what qualities a good person has. In its definition of "Gross National Happiness", the Bhutanese government states that the accumulation of knowledge is more important than the accumulation of material things. In interviewing participants, I wanted to know what knowledge meant to them.

Furthermore, I asked six questions about sustainability, including if participants had heard of the word *sustainability* and what it meant to them. Because Buddhism has no creator as in the Christian tradition, I was curious about how the Bhutanese perceive the creation of nature – put simply: What do you think makes nature grow? In addition, because of the ecofeminist theories, I wanted to know if women have the same relation with nature according to the respondents. Moreover, due to the shortage of human resources in the villages and the unpopularity of farmers as a profession, I asked all the respondents if they wanted to be a farmer or an educated farmer (an "educated farmer" is the Bhutanese way of describing a farmer who works with modern tools and produces for market).

I made a checklist with 35 short questions based on Bilsky and Schwartz's (1990) value content theory, including the eight domains addressed earlier. The goals of these questions are to identify gender values and sustainable values. I asked about (1) joy in life, (2) security in life, (3) ambition and recognition, (4) freedom and independence, (5) self-control/politeness, (6) love, equality, and helpfulness, (7) authority and power, and (8) wisdom and knowledge. The answers to these questions were listed in an Excel file and made available for inspection. I talked to 19 persons with no education, 9 women and 10 men. Another 11 had education through form 12 (7 women and 4 men), and 26 persons had achieved some post-graduate education, up to and including a Ph.D. (9 women and 18 men). In addition, 19 respondents live in Thimphu; the remaining 37 live in villages and small towns.

In the subsequent sections, I first briefly introduce *the context of the interview and some characteristics of the conversation partner (in italics)* and then present some highlights in the conversation concerning the subject.

Tandin

Tandin is a 25–year-old male who lives in Simtokha, Thimphu. He studies at the Simtokha Cultural Institution (a boarding school) in form 14. He studies Sanskrit, Tibetan, Dzongkha, and English. I met Tandin at the Centre for Bhutan Studies, where he was working as a translator during his school holiday. This centre is an autonomous research institute dedicated in promoting research and scholarship on Bhutan.
Tandin is a very friendly open young man, he tells me that he loves to talk to foreigners and he likes it to talk to me. Tandin calls me Madam La , "la" is a polite form of addressing someone who is senior to you.

We sat outside the building in the sun so we could talk.

'I am single and I come from Tashiyangste in East Bhutan. I lived alone with my mother. My mother sent me to school, but I also had to work on the farm because I was the only one who could do it. I helped my mother [with] all the work that had to be done, except for weaving. I also carried dung. I liked helping my mother but the neighbours told me I was working too hard. Also my mother was worried about me, because of my hard work, she was afraid that I would become ill and catch TBC.

Next to school and work at the farm, I had to earn my own money and I did every year *whoolla* (compulsory work for the government).

I am a *gomchen*,[1] I can read the holy books. My dream for the future is to study abroad for a master's degree; but I do not have the money for it.

As said before I did all the work at my mother's farm.'

I asked him why women do not plough: 'It is too hard work for women; the bull could attack a woman, bulls are scared of men. I did carry dung but a saying is "if men carry dung, his knowledge will go down and he will become stupid. Students are not allowed to carry dung because their brain is very sensitive".

'My mother is the head of the household, she managed the farm. But government stimulates the father, but the father was more engaged with non-farm activities, father passed away a few years ago.'

'Women have to cook, women get a stigma if they do not cook. My mother managed everything and she guided my father when he was still alive. Men are careless, women are better.'

'The village *gomchen* advised my family to send me to school. My father and mother send me to school. I like what I am doing, I like studying and my ambition is to become a high-school teacher. I like to teach Dzongkha. As a teacher I can reach a higher incarnation in my next life.'

I asked him who would inherit the property in the village.

'When my mother dies, the house and land will go the person who will take care of it "depends of convenience, who is there". I will have a job, I will not go back to be a farmer. To be a farmer is not good for your karma, because as a farmer you kill many insects and that is not good. To be a teacher is much better for your karma.'

Do you have a hobby?

'As a hobby I like to watch the news and I like to talk to foreign tourist, just as I like it to talk to madam la here. I do not like to go dancing. "I hate it", but I like to be with my friends.

'I am independent and I can do and go wherever I want, but I respect society.'

---

1   Gomchen: a male lay religious practitioner, sometimes married.

What would you buy if you had a lot of money?
'If I had a lot of money, I do not know what to buy, I would share it with my family, especially my mother. I would like to buy religious items and books.'
What does status and power mean to you?
'Status to me means a person who has much devotion. The persons with lots of status are the King, Je Kempo, and minister Jigme Thinley. I like to have status – that is one reason for me to become a teacher, teachers have a lot [of] status. Because they help other people and they are an example. Power is when people can comment [on] other people, like a boss and rich people. Money is power. A person with power is the king. His majesty has "transcendental power".'
I asked Tandin if he had to choose something nice for himself or something nice for his family, what would he choose.
'I would choose for myself and share it with my mother.'
Are men and women equal?
'Men and women are equal but "men are more intended towards evil".'
Are you religious and what does religion mean to you?
'I am a Buddhist and religion means to me helping other people.'
Where do people come from?
'I always think about my creator. Before I did not believe in reincarnation and to me the creation myth from the monkey god is just a story. I think also about where people come from, "everything is created by everything, we are in a dream".'
Did you ever want to become a monk?
'I would like to be a monk but I cannot become one because I have to help my mother.'
Do you consult an astrologer *or* ngejum *or* pawo*?*
'Sometimes I go to see a *tsipa* (astrologer) before I go on a journey, I will ask the *tsipa* about a good day to start travelling. I am not going to a *pawo* or an *ngejum* because they belong to the Bon religion, I do not believe in Bon. Religion (Buddhism) is very important to me because "it guides us, it shapes society because it lets people [be] reborn as lamas and *rinpoches* who help the people to a better incarnation".'
Why are there so many monks and only a few nunneries?
'Before all the household had to [send] one son to the monastery to become a monk, they were forced to go. Women are not as good as men in controlling their mind. That is why there are only a few nuns and so many monks. Girls have to take care of the farm and the parents.'
Can men and women reach the same level of enlightenment?

'Yes, women can reach the same enlightenment as men, they do not have to incarnate 9 times, it is only an old folk's belief. "A good person is a person who respects others and helps others".'

What does knowledge mean to you?

'Knowledge is deeper than reading, people who are dealing with society and know what to do that is good for the people in society, that is knowledge.'

Sustainability?

'Sustainability is "something that last[s]". People try to be sustainable in a religious way, to sustain the way of life.'

What makes things grow?

'Emptiness, everything is a dream, nothing really last[s].'

Can people help nature?

'Due to greed, nature is changing; we have to recycle and to be aware of the pollution.'

Do men and women have the same relation with nature?

'Men are more inclined to harm the environment, women stay in the house. As a farmer you hurt the environment, by ploughing you kill many bugs, etc. Mother earth feeds us and mother earth provides us with food just like our own mother.'

Do you enjoy nature?

'I enjoy nature a lot, I like the sun. Nature means to me "it is not made by humans". Although I do not trust nature in providing my family with food: "sometimes you have too [many] crop[s] and sometimes not enough crop[s]. A salary is better, you can trust money". My mother's fields are not fertile enough, she has to put dung and there is a lot of animal damage.'

Are you happy to be a man?

'I am proud to be a man and I would like to be man again in my next incarnation. To me being a man it means, "to be more free, a woman has to give birth, this is difficult and painful". A woman is therefore more vulnerable and has more worries. Due to the physicality men are freer'.

What is an ideal man to you?

'An ideal man is to be like the king or the minister Jigme Thinley.'

Are you happy?

'I am happy with my life "due to previous incarnation were I worked so hard, I can study now".'

Do you feel secure as a man?

'I feel very secure as a man, "when travelling, women can be attacked". Although in the jungle I am scared of wild animals and I am scared to die. I am also afraid in India.'

Do you have a wish for the future?

'My wishes for the future are to become a teacher and to help people.'

Do you have a hero?

'My hero is the King of Bhutan, because he went to the south of Bhutan to fight the Bodo guerrillas from India. I would like to be a hero one day.'

Have you ever taken a risk and would you take a risk in the future?

'I took a risk once to fight my boss, I fought for the rights of people, but my boss did not like that, my boss wanted to dominate everybody. I helped the people although there was a chance of losing my job. I have no money and I am not interested in business. I also do not want more land because there are no human resources in my village.'

Are good relations with neighbours and other people important to you?

'To me [...] good relation[s] with neighbours [are] very important, "you have to respect society. You have to respect women and men the same way".'

Do you show it when you are angry?

'When I am angry I try to hide it, but with friends I will show it, but the best is to control it. To me it is very important that people are polite, although *driglam namzha* are sometimes outdated and people [in] high position[s] take advantage of poor people [at] lower levels of society. Many rules should be more contemporary and equal for everybody.'

And how about nature?

'One has to respect nature [in] the same way, because nature is vulnerable'.

Are humans and animals equal?

'Men and women are equal, but animals have less mental power. But as a life force, animals are equal, but animals are greedy.'

Compassion is an important value in Buddhism. What does it mean to you? What does love mean to you?

'Compassion means "not to be greedy and to be equal with everybody". Love means: taking care of everybody.'

Would you like to marry?

'I [would] like to stay a bachelor; I do not [want] to marry in the future, too many worries. "Men have more physical power and women have more mental power, men have to listen to women".'

What does God mean to you?

'God means to me: "Universe is God, we ourselves are God, I am God we only need a teacher to find it".'

And wisdom?

'Wisdom to me means, "People who respect society and with wisdom one can earn money". In general women are wiser than men. Nature is very wise, because without a summer there will be no cultivation of the land [...] Nobody knows if God is wise, it is like a dream. To me God is a woman".'

Pema

Perna is a 20-year-old single female living in Thimphu. A graduate from class 8, she is policewoman. I saw Pema in Thimphu while she was doing her job guarding the entrance of a government building. I asked Dorji, my translater if it would be possible to interview that young police women? We asked her if she would be interested in talking to us, while she was on duty. She had time to talk to us. We were sitting on the steps of the entrance of the building.

Pema is from Pemagyatsel East Bhutan: 'My parents still live in the East, and they have a farm. I helped with all the work except sewing, shopping, and financial shores. I am a very good weaver and I like to knit and to clean my house in my free time. Here in Thimphu I share my house with roommates – they and my family in the East appreciated a lot the work I did and do, because I like cleaning. I help to perform all the rituals and I call in the monks to do the *puja* in the house. At home in the East I help my smaller sisters and brothers with schoolwork.

'Here in Thimphu I am on duty every day for four hours as policewoman. I do not like my job, but I have to do it for 5 years and then I will be free. Because the government paid for my education I have to do this work for 5 years. Every day after my duty I like to go home and do the knitting, cleaning, and washing.

'On the farm in the East I did all the work; I carried dung and [my] brothers did this too. I did not plough the fields; I do not know why this is.

'My father and me are the most responsible people of the household, but my oldest sister is the head of the house. She does all the weaving. Although my father is not educated, it was he who sent me to school. I chose to be a policewoman because this job was available. But I do not like this work. In general I am not very happy with my life and I [would] not like to marry in the future. Marriage and children mean a lot of responsibilities and I do not know if I like this. Most important in life to me is my family. I am independent and can do what I like. I live on my own. I used to sing in a bar and I was very popular. People always ask me to come [and] sing but I cannot do it, I have a duty as a police.'

What would you buy if you had a lot of money?

'If I had money I would like to buy a car. I can buy what I want; I do not need permission from anybody to spend the money.'

What does status and power mean to you?

'Status to me means "I know my status as a woman and I find it not fair. Men have a better life. Men are free to gossip about women and they can do whatever they want". "To me status have the lady officers on senior level within the police force".'

Are you happy? Would you like to change your life? If yes, how?

'If I could change my life I would like to become a business woman [...] I would love to have my own business like a store.'

Are men and women equal?

'Men and women are not equal; women are lower than men, because women are less religious.

About religion'?

'I am Buddhist and religion means, "helping others is religion".'

How do you imagine a creator, your creator?

'I imagine my creator as something very powerful. The creation monkey god from Tibet is the explanation where people come from.'

Would you like to be a nun?

'Once I was interested in becoming a nun, but I had to earn money so I became a policewoman'

Are you going to a pawo/ngejum?

'When in need [to,] I visit a *pawo*; for example, when I am sick. Religion is very important to me although women are less religious than men due to their physicalities, but I perform *pujas* on a regular base.' 'And I think men and women can reach the same enlightenment".'

What is a good person to you?

'A good person is a religious person.'

Have you heard about sustainability?

'Sustainability is important for the future generations. Nature makes that things grow, and people can help nature by taking care.'

Can people help the deities?

'People cannot help the deities and gods because they are powerful.'

Do you enjoy nature?

'I enjoy nature a lot. I like to be in the forest and in the mountains; "they are so beautiful". I trust nature as a provider for food; in my village, my family lacks human resources to work the land. I think nature is much stronger than humans.'

Are you happy to be a woman?

'I am not happy with my life because being a woman means: "a woman can take better care of others". An ideal woman is "a woman who is single and independent".'

Do you feel secure being a woman?

'I feel insecure with other people, sometimes I am even afraid of other people. But in nature, in the forest or in the mountains, I feel very secure and happy. In general I feel threatened [by] gossip. People gossip [a] lot and I do not like it at all.'

Do you have a wish for the future?
'My wish for the future is to become a businesswoman.'
Are men and women the same?
'Women are cleverer than men.'
Are good relationships with others/neighbours important?
'It is important to have good relationship[s] with the neighbours, otherwise you will fighting all the time. It is very important that people are polite "otherwise there will be too much pressure in society".'
Are men and women equal? How about animals?
'Men and women are equal, and the only difference between humans and animals is that animals cannot speak and think. I have more respect for women than for men. Women are cleverer and are more caring than men.'
What does compassion mean to you? And love?
'Compassion means helping old and sick people with all kind of chores. "Love is when a person loves all humans and all living beings".'
What does God mean to you?
'God is "a force who helps all sentient beings". I think God is male.'
What about wisdom?
'If a person can help all other people, than he/she is wise and wisdom is more important than money: "money comes and goes, wisdom stays". [...] "Women are wiser than men".'

Tupto

Tupto is a 46-year-old married female. She lives in Jakar Bumthang. We met Tupto in the restaurant of her daughter were she helped her. We had lunch, and after lunch we talked.
'I am a housewife and I am helping my daughter who owns this hotel and restaurant in Jakar. I have two daughters and two sons who are all adults and married. All my children went to school.
'I own a farm but I gave it to tenants. I got the farm from the government – it belonged to Nepalese migrants who left Bhutan in the beginning of 1990. My husband is a retired army man. I weave and my husband does all the household work in my house.
'In the evening I like to watch movies and shows on TV. When my children were small they all helped in the house and the boys and girls did all the same work.
'Sometimes I like the work I have to do and sometimes I do not like to do the housework. My husband likes to help me, he does not mind doing the house-

hold chores. I help my daughter by taking care of the grandchildren and I help with the hotel and restaurant.

'I do all the *pujas* that need to be done. If I could change my life, I would like to have my own business. I am the head of the household and the most responsible person. I make all the important decisions.'

Do you have a wish for the future?

'My wish for the future is to go to a *Gompa*[2] to read the holy scripture and to meditate. This way I can prepare myself for a better incarnation after I die.'

What is important to you?

'[What is] very important for me is education for my children so they will have a good future. It would be nice if they could work for the government.'

Who inherited the property?

'I inherited everything – [the] farm and house–from my parents; I got most of the property.'

Do you like to go out?

'I do not go to parties – do not like it very much. I would like to have just one good friend. I am free to do what I want and I can go where I want to. I am not afraid, I am known as a very brave woman.'

Are men and women equal?

'To me men and women are equal.'

What would you buy if you had all the money in the world?

'If I had a lot of money I would like to buy a nice house.'

What about family, is this important to you?

'To me my family is very important; if I had a lot of money, I would share it with [my] family and poor people.'

Religion?

'I am a Buddhist and religion means to me is the base for life, death, and afterlife. I imagine my creator as *kon chog sum* (the triple gem, Buddha, *sangha,* and the scriptures).'

Where do people come from?

'People come from karma and incarnation. You do not have to become a nun to be religious; you can train your mind to be religious also as a laywoman.'

Are you consulting an astrologer or a pawo/ngejum?

'I only consult an *ngejum* or *pawo* when I am desperate (with sickness or bad fortune) and if there is no lama to go to.'

Why are there more nuns than monks?

---

2   Buddhist monastery

'I think that there are more monks than nuns because men are more successful in religion. Men and women can reach the same enlightenment – there is no difference. There are female and male gods, for example Khandro.'

What is a good person?

'A good person is a person that helps others.'

What does knowledge mean to you?

'Knowledge means [the] desire of the heart; let your heart speak, what you feel in your heart.'

Sustainability?

'I [have] heard of sustainability, it means being good to nature. Without nature, there will be no life. Nature grows because of fertility and an invisible force. People have to take care of nature and people can help the gods who live in nature by praying and doing *pujas.* Nature means life. I respect nature very much. Nature is powerful and stronger than humans.'

Are you happy to be a woman?

'I am happy to be a woman, but in my next life I would like to be a man. [For a man] it is [...] easier to be religious. I do not know an ideal woman, never thought of it. I am happy with my life.'

Do you feel secure as a woman?

'I feel very secure as a woman, although I am afraid of becoming ill. In nature I am afraid of wild animals.'

What would you buy if you had a lot of money?

'If I had the money I would like to invest in a business [of] my own. I would like to take that risk; I never before took a big risk in my life. I would not invest in a farm, too [much] hard work.'

Are men and women the same?

'Men and women are the same, only physically they are different.'

When you are angry, do you show it?

'I hide my anger, it is very important that people are polite, Driglam Namzha is important because it teaches you how to behave and it saves the traditions.'

Are humans and animals equal?

'Humans and animals are equal; animals suffer like humans – pain and hunger.'

What does compassion and love mean to you?

'Compassion means to help others and love means to take care of others.'

What does God mean?

'God means that he/she is there when I need God. God is male and female.'

And wisdom ?

'Wisdom means that you have many friends to help you if you are wise. Wisdom is more important than money [which] comes and goes. Nature is wise because it lets everything grow.'

Pema

Pema is a 53–year-old male who is a hotel owner and retired teacher. He lives in Jakar, Bumthang. I met Pema through his son, who was once my Bhutanese guide when I was in Bhutan with a group tourist. We met in Jakar and Pema (his son's name is also Pema) invited me over to his house to have dinner with his father. I was able to interview his father before dinner.

'I studied history, geography, and anthropology in Bhutan, India, and New Brunswick, Canada. I have a master's degree. I am married and I have 4 children. My wife is not educated. I have a farm, but my sister-in-law takes care of it in Tang. I also own an orchard; I have workers to take care of it. I am a wealthy man for Bhutanese standards.

'When I was young, I had to do the same work as my sisters on the farm. I also had to carry dung. But men are ploughing because you have to be strong to handle the ox. In Tang, where my wife and I come from, men and women do the same work except [for] ploughing. There is no taboo on carrying dung. I love the work on the farm.

'I also helped with all the *pujas* for good fortune for our house and land. Life is changing a lot; for example, before the annual *choku*, the most important one was an event for the whole village. Sometimes this *choku* took 3 days and all villagers were invited to eat and drink. Nowadays it is only a family event; neighbours and villagers are not invited anymore. So the village *puja* is disappearing. Because of modernization I am afraid that we will lose more of our traditions.'

What do you like doing when you are not working?

'I like to read and listening to the BBC world service in my free time. My mother and my wife [weave] and my wife takes care of the financial chores.'

Who is the head of the household?

'In my house, all the important decisions are discussed and taken jointly by my children, wife, and me. I have the last word though because I am highly educated. I made all the decisions in regard to [the] education of my children, and my parents sent me to school. Later I could freely choose my profession.'

Are you happy with your life?

'I like very much my life at the moment; my wishes for the future are to have more hotels. I like the hotel business [and] meeting all kind of people. Sometimes we had guests, very strange westerners who demanded so much, we had to laugh a lot about their behaviour. More and more tourists are coming to Bhutan; having a hotel is good business.'

What do you find very important in life?

'Education is the most important thing for me in life. All my kids are educated.'

Who will inherit your assets?

'In Bumthang, it is the custom that women inherit the property, but this is changing. There is a law that dictates [giving] each child an equal share, but this does not happen very much.'

What do you like doing?

'I like to play archery a lot and I like to meet friends. If I had a lot of money I would like to buy more hotels as I said before.'

What does status and power mean to you?

'Status means: "status you get from your rank; you cannot buy it". Some people just have it. The *Dasho Dzongdha* (district governor) is a person with high rank and status, people are frightened of him, and he has a big personality. I do not like to have status; I like [being] a simple man.'

What about power?

'President Bush has power.'

Would you like to change something in your life?

'I would like to change the Bhutanese society, like "Tsa Wa Tsum and Driglam Namzha"–these traditions are from 1616 and very outdated; it has to change and the bowing has to stop. Everybody should be treated equal. We have to preserve our traditions, but they have to be more contemporary.'

Are men and women equal?

'My wife is [a] housewife; she is not educated. In Bhutanese tradition a woman is 150 times less than a man. But everybody, men and women, are alike. Women are powerful and not less than men.'

What about religion?

'I am a Buddhist and religion means "a belief". I do not know how to imagine the creator. People come from history; insects came on earth and everything incarnated until humans. And there is the creation myth from Tibet.'

Did you ever want to become a monk?

'I never wanted to be a monk. [I] did not like it. But I do *pujas*. I visited several times a *pawo* and an *ngejum* in Tang (central Bhutan) when I was sick. Religion means "root of culture".'

Why are there so few nuns and so many monks?

'Nowadays there are many nunneries where nuns can study the higher teachings of Buddhism. Before, this was not possible. Women and men can reach the same enlightenment and they're female and male gods. A good person must be helpful and kind to others. "Knowledge is useful to you in daily life".'

Have you heard about sustainability?

'Sustainability means to preserve what you have for future generations, everything what we have: culture, tradition, and nature. This means that there will be life all the time.'

What do you think makes things grow?

'Everything is interconnected this is how nature works, collective *karma*. [...] People can help nature by taking care, planting tare trees, and protecting [them].'

Are you happy to be a man? Do you feel secure being a man?

'I am happy as a man, being a man means: "in society man can do everything, make important decisions, sometimes men can make better decisions than women". "An ideal man is a man that helps, is gentle and compromising". I am happy with my life and I like nature that is what is around.

'I do not feel very secure being a man because I have a lot of responsibilities – that scares me sometimes. I do not feel secure with or in nature I am afraid of climate change, the environment is changing'. "Until now nature provides my family with food, I do not know if this will be in the future due to climate change and the destruction of the environment". 'My fields are not fertile anymore I have to use fertilizer.'

How about men and women – are they equal – and how about animals?

'Men and woman are the same. [From a] religious point of view, animals are the same as men.'

What does compassion mean to you? And love?

'Compassion means to be compromising and gentle. Love means happiness. I did not have a marriage ritual.'

What does wisdom mean?

'Wisdom means useful knowledge and wisdom is more important than money.'

Sonam

Sonam, a 53-year-old Nyingmapa male monk, lives in Bumthang. He is single (Nyingmapa monks can marry). We met Sonam in a store in Bumthang and asked him if we could talk to him; he liked the idea. In the store, we sat down and talked. The owner of the store did not mind, and she liked listening to us. Sonam is a caretaker of a small monastery. Most of the time he is alone in the monastery. He is a very funny man and talks a lot. I was disappointed that I could not talk to him in his native language. He has many stories. Dorji my translater said: 'he talks

too much and his stories are very strange, I do not know if I can translate them all, but I will try'
The text that follows is the translation from my interpreter, from Dzongkha to English.

He tells me that, as a Nyingmapa monk, if you are highly educated as a monk on religious teachings and have developed you awareness on a high level, you will dream about your consort (wife, female companion); if this happens, you will meet her soon and then you can marry her.

He was a student of Dilgo Khyentse Rinpoche. He became a monk when he was 15 years old, when his mother put him in the monastery, where he became a student of Rinpoche. In the monastery, he does all the work – cleaning, cooking, and working in the fields. He makes offerings to the spirits around and meditates two to three hours a day.

He likes to pray, and meditation gives him a lot of pleasure. He does not like to work in the fields, but he has to grow his food and clean the monastery; he would like to spend all his time on meditation.

Before he was monk, he helped his mother and did the ploughing and carried the dung.

Are men and women equal?

According to Sonam, women are equally good as men. There are high female incarnations like Khandro, who has holy sight and can help you reach enlightenment. However, for example, a bad woman can marry a good man, who can prevent her from going to hell, although he will lose some of his position. Yet if a bad man marries a good woman, she cannot help him.

Who was the head of your household?

When he was still living with his parents, it was his grandmother who was the head of the household. She made all the important decisions.

What are your wishes for the future?

Sonam has one brother who is also a *gelong*. Sonams wishes for the future are that someone will take care of him when he is old. Most important in his life is religion. Sonam can and likes to go to places alone, but only in Bhutan or in other Buddhist places in India. He can walk to Thimphu (200 km), but he does not like to go to faraway places. If he had a lot of money, he would spend it on religious purposes.

I asked Sonam about status and power and what these mean to him.

Sonam does not know about status, but he knows about power. To him *Kundun* (high incarnation of a lama, like the Dalai Lama) has power because he takes care of all the *gelongs*, who are disciplined. To Sonam, *Kundun* and the police monk have power; the police monk beats you up if you are not disciplined in the monastery. He was once a police monk; he did not like it because he had to beat up small children. The only change he would like to make in his life is that he would like to meditate more. According to Sonam, men and women are equal.

About religion?

Sonam is Buddhist, and religion to him means that religion can help one reach nirvana.

How do you imagine your creator?

He sees his creator as the system of incarnation. Sonam has a strange story about the creation of people: We come from very small men who only lived 10 years (*tselu chupa*). These small humans were very bad people. They were incarnations of very evil creatures. The worse they became, the smaller they became. Then there was a God, Gesar Jambha, who thought these people were good so they started to become taller and became normal people.

Sonam also mentioned the Tibetan creation myth of the monkey, who is a previous incarnation of Chen Rezig. Chen Rezig was Pakpa, so the monkey came to him for religious teachings in India. At this time, Tibet was a dark place, full of demons. One big demon came and changed into a beautiful lady. The monkey did not want to make love to her and asked Pakpa if he could stay with her; Pakpa said he could stay with her, and after a while they had children. The children went to Tibet and they will pray to me.

Do you consult a pawo or ngejum?

Although Sonam is a lama himself, he consults *ngejums* and *pawos*.

Why are these so many monks and only a few nuns?

According to Sonam, in the Nyingmapa sect nuns also receive high teachings from masters. However, they are a little bit lower than monks. If they want to marry, it depends on previous incarnations. Women can reach the same incarnation as men. There are female and male deities; Sonam makes offerings to all of them.

What is a good person to you?

To be a good person depends on your previous life. If you were good in a previous life, you will be good now.

What does knowledge mean to you?

Knowledge depends on the society in which you live. If you live in a village, you need knowledge to be able to make a living in the village. For example you need to know how to do the *pujas* for the deities in that village and you need to know how to work the land.

What make things grow?

In a previous life, some trees grow on land; if a tree does bad things, it will reincarnate on a cliff where it is difficult to get nurturing for the roots. It is difficult to live on a cliff as you can fall of it too – or a river. If a river is bad, it becomes a waterfall.

Can people help the deities?
People can help nature by taking care of it, and one can help the deities by cleaning the *lhakang* and special places that belong to the deities.

Are you happy to be a man?
Sonam is very happy to be a man, and he can work to become a better life. However, he finds it difficult to be born as a man; he would like to be with his teacher, but he has to stay in the small monastery. If you can be with your teacher, you have been a very good man in your previous life because then you are wealthy. An ideal man is a man who is wealthy and able to study.

What does nature – your surroundings – mean to you?
Sonam loves nature, and nature means to him karma of previous life.

I asked him if nature provides him with food.
He said only as you work for it. I trust nature in doing so because nature will always be there. We have to be kind to nature because nature is kind to you.

Do you have a wish for the future?
His wish for the future is to reach nirvana.

Do you have a hero?
His hero is the King of Bhutan because he fought the Bodos from Assam. Becoming a hero depends on previous lives.

Sonam is a monk and he is mainly interested in reaching enlightenment. To him it is important that people are polite to follow the writings of Driglam Namzha and the Shabdrung. People have to respect these rules and etiquette.

Do you show it when you are angry?
When he is angry, he hides under blankets.

Are men and women equal?
To Sonam, men and women are equal and men and women can do the same things. God takes care of you – that is the meaning of God to Sonam. God has both genders.

What is wisdom to you?
Wisdom means kindness, and again it depends on previous lives if you have wisdom.

Neten

Neten is a female who lives as a nun (Nyingmapa) in Tang in Bumthang. She is 25 years old. We visited a nunnery in the mountains in Tang. We asked the head nun if we could talk to one of the nuns, and Neten agreed to talk to us. She spoke no English, so this is the translation of our conversation.
Neten is from Mongar. Her parents are farmers. Her brother is a *gelong*. There is no one at home, only her old parents, who do not work much.

Nowadays Nyingmapa nuns can study the same scriptures as the monks. The Gangden Tulku (incarnated lama from Gangden) established this nunnery and arranged for nuns to study the same as monks. Before, this was not possible. Neten likes to study and pray. Every day she gets up at 5 o clock and prays until 6. At 7 there is breakfast. At 8 she studies till 12:30, then eats lunch. In the afternoon, she studies and does chores, like cleaning and cooking. She does not meditate yet; only after completing standard 9 will she start to meditate.

Would you like to change your life?

She never thought about her life and if she could change it, but now she thinks about it. She would like to be a monk.

Who is the head of your household?

At home, her father and mother were both the heads of the household. Together they made all the decisions. Neten made the decision to become a nun by herself. She came to the nunnery on her own. She likes the life in the nunnery. Her wish for the future is to receive teachings from high lamas.

Can you do what you want or do you need permission from anyone?

Neten is free in what she wants to do, but being a nun, she needs permission from the head nun if she wants to go somewhere. There are strict rules in the monastery. If she had money, she would offer it to the lhakang. She does not need permission if she wants to buy something.

What does status mean to you? And power?

For Neten, her teacher has a lot of status, as does her *kempo* (studied lama). Neten does not know a female *kempo*, but now women can also become *kempo* and the Gangden Tulku expect from this nunnery the first female *kempo* from Bhutan. According to Neten, at home her parents have power; in the nunnery, it is the *kempo* who has power. She does not like to have power – it is too much responsibility.

If you could choose something nice for you or for your family, for whom would you choose?

To Neten, her nunnery is her family now; if she had to choose something nice for her or her nunnery, she would choose for the nunnery.

Religion?

Neten is a Buddhist nun (*Nyingmapa*). Religion to her is the only thing you can take with you after you die.

How do you imagine your creator?

Creation is a matter of incarnation to Neten. She must have been good in previous lives, which is why she could become nun in this life.

Where do people come from?

People come from the monkey god.

Why did you become a nun?

Neten became nun because is afraid of dying. The teachings she receives as nun help her to overcome this fear. Neten never visits *ngejums* or *pawos* because they belong to the Bon religion. Bon is for this life and Buddhism is for the afterlife – the afterlife is more important. Religion is important to get a better incarnation. There are more monks than nuns because nuns are not allowed in the *dzongs* at night. They do not need nuns in the *dzongs*.

Are there male and female gods?

There are male and female gods; they are equal, and men and women are equal too.

What is a good person – what qualities must a good person have?

To Neten, a good person is a person who is religious. It is a person who prays a lot and who is good to all sentient beings.

What does knowledge mean to you?

Knowledge to her means the same as gold.

When you look outside, you see all nature. Where do you think nature comes from?

To Neten, a combination of all elements of nature let things grow. People can help nature by taking care of it and not destroying it. When Neten is in nature, the autumn season reminds her of the impermanence of life.

Are you happy to be a woman?

Neten is not happy being a women. She does not like her period and she feels that women are weaker than men. She does not like to be a woman because of her physical body. An ideal woman is a religious woman.

Neten feels very confident as a woman. In general she feels safe, but sometimes she is afraid of bears. She is also afraid of being raped while she is travelling. Her wish for the future is to get an initiation to be able to meditate.

Do you have a hero/heroine?

Her hero is *kenpo* lama. She would like to be a heroine too.

Are animals and humans equal?

Animals and humans are equal, only animals cannot talk.

What does compassion mean to you? And love?

Compassion means to Neten, if you can solve others' pain and sorrow, then you have a lot of compassion. Love to her means a sound relation with other sentient beings.

What do you think about power?

Humans are more powerful than nature; we can control nature. Power is negative.

What does God mean to you?

God has no form and does not tell you what to do – you have to decide in life what to do. Although God does not have a form, you can visualise God with your mind. Jam Bujang is the Goddess of wisdom; you can pray to her and you will receive wisdom.

Rinzin

Rinzin is Haa Dzongrab at Haa. He is a 53-year-old married male. While in Haa, the most western district of Bhutan, we went to the district office and asked the Dzongrab if we could talk to him. He is assistant governor of the Haa district. His office was a beautiful traditional room with thangkhas (religious paintings) and he was wearing a beautiful gho and a sword. We were served tea and he gave us all the time we needed.

'I have 5 daughters, all are going to school, and the oldest is a teacher. My wife helps me with my work; she is my assistant. My parents had a farm; I did not work on the farm, my parents had sharecroppers [and] did not work the land themselves. After school (till class 10) I worked for the government in different departments'

'I like to play archery. I like to watch documentaries and Bhutanese movies. I do not really like to change anything in my life. I am almost retired, I enjoy life and I like to help other people with my ideas. When I was young, my mother was the head of the household; today it is [my] father.'

'When I was young, the government chose me and sent me to school in Kalimpong in India. This was for primary education. In that time, early 1960, many children were forced to go to school [in] India by the government. Some parents tried to get their children back by offering valuable items to the government-people who choose the children in the villages for sending them to Kalimpong.'

'At first I was very homesick but later I liked going to school and doing my work for the government. Now I help with the writing of the constitution of Bhutan, I like to give advice to the people. My government job was and is very important to me.'

Who will inherit your assets?

'In case of inheritance, before mostly daughters inherit; but nowadays, all get an equal share. I love going to parties and meeting people. I like helping other people, and if I had a lot of money I would use it to help others.'

What does status mean to you?

'I have status as *Dzongrab*, people come every day to me with questions and requests. If you give respect you get it back, one has to share ideas, make people understand and not discriminate.'

What about power?

'Power means "something that has to be implemented, according to rules and regulations". [It means] maintain[ing] social culture. He enjoys his power.'

Are men and women equal?

'I think now men and women are equal, before it was the women who were the head of the households. Nowadays girls and women work also outside the house and have jobs.'

Religion?

'I am Buddhist. Religion means: "it is the way we [have] been raised as Buddhist". This culture helps us for the future, we are a living culture, living Buddhist. Creation means *"Ta Wa Sum, kon chog sum"* (i.e., God, parents, king – the trinity is God-parent-child). A good county ruled by a good king gives people all opportunities. God is an almighty force.'

Where do people come from?

'I think that people come for the mother, but I do not know where the mother comes from.'

Did you ever want to become a monk?

'When I was young I did not want to become a monk; later, I thought about it, but if you live a life guided by a good heart [it is the same] as being a monk. You have to live your life as a good Buddhist. I do perform rituals and pray a lot. There are still many Bön rituals in Haa. Every year the people of this valley sacrifice an ox to the local deity.'

Do you consult a ngejum or pawo?

'I do not believe in *ngejums* and *pawos*, but they please the deities. They know how to do the rituals and they can communicate with the deities, they know how to respect them. [In] religion [it] is very important to do offerings, like in the morning you burn incense and you give water offerings. This is important for success and to relieve heavy things in life.'

What does knowledge mean to you?

'Knowledge means purity, kind hearted, you have to help the poor, help to create a good atmosphere.'

Have you heard about sustainability?

'Sustainability, this means what has been given to you should be conserved, you have to develop something else which is helpful to all sentient beings. [You should have] respect for mythical beings as protective guardians against all evil. For Bhutan, this means the mythical tiger as [a] protector against intruders, the snow lion as [a] protector of the mountains, [and the] mystical bird and flying dragon [as] protectors of all. Without preserving nature all would disappear.'

What makes nature grow do you think?

'I think the four elements make things grow: soil, water, fire, air. The deities of these elements – everything is made of this-have and these elements have a soul. These are living things.'

Can people help nature?

'People can help nature by having a sweet voice: in the old days, monks told children not to harm or destroy nature. People can help the deities and gods "indirectly by doing *pujas* and spirit possession". Ab Chusum is the deity of Haa; every year the people of Haa offer a yak to him. The government is helping with this *puja*, here Bön and Buddhism go hand in hand. I enjoy nature a lot; it is my living home. I feel very comfortable in nature, I feel safe and healthy while I am in the forest. I only feel threatened by the destruction of nature. I trust nature.'

Are you happy to be a man?

'I am happy to be a man because of a good incarnation. A man that is not good is a lazy man, who depends on others and does nothing. An ideal man is the opposite of this lazy man.'

Do you have wishes for the future?

'My wishes for the future are that I [want] to help others more. Now [...] 60 percent [of the] men [are] working for the government and 40 percent [of the] women; I think by 2020 this will be equal, fifty-fifty. All Bhutanese will be educated, and there will be no difference in gender.'

Do you have a hero?

'The king of Bhutan is my hero.'

Are good relations with other people important to you?

'Good relations with other people are very important, that is why we have *driglam namzha*. It is the basic Bhutanese culture, the basic root for Bhutanese culture.'

Are men and women equal? How about animals?

'Men and women are equal, and animals are equal to humans, we all have blood.'

What does compassion mean to you? Love?

'Compassion is love and kindness. Love is sensations, flowers, and beauty. To go beyond yourself.'

What does wisdom mean to you?

'Wisdom means to think 100 times before action, to do the right thing at the right time and place.'

What do you think of God?

'God to me is peace.'

Tsechu

Tsechu is a 35-year-old male who lives in Thimphu. He is a filmmaker, businessman, and artist. I met him on the street in Thimphu; we started to talk, and he invited me for dinner. In the restaurant, I could talk to him. It is interesting to see that Tsechu has a western way of looking at his wife – his wife is educated and has been studying in Australia – although he thinks men are better in business and better in dealing with daily life.

'I am married and have one daughter. My name Tsechu means that I was born on the 10th day, and this is a very auspicious day.

'I used to do all the chores in the house when I was young.

'I help with the child, I bring her to school [and] play with her if I have time. We have a washing machine for the washing. We live a more western lifestyle, like a nuclear family. I take care of the house altar and perform all the *pujas*. I also take care of the finances.

'My hobbies are photography, [playing] with electronic gadgets, and using [the] Internet. I work at home, but do not like it. The combination office and home is not good, I get too much distracted by the home affairs. I would like to change this. I would like to [rent] an office outside my home, but it costs a lot. I do not have [the] budget to hire staff. I am the head of the household; I make all the important decisions. My responsibilities are earning the money and making sure that everything works. I will make the decisions about my daughter's education. When I was young I could freely choose my profession and studies. I like a lot what I am doing.'

Do you have wishes for the future?

'My wishes for the future are to buy a house of my own to live in. But most important to me [it] is happiness for my family and me.

'I come from a village in south Bhutan close to the Indian border. My mother still lives there and she takes care of the farm. I did not visit her for more than 9 years because it [was] very dangerous to go there. There are Bodo guerrillas from Assam who are fighting against India. Sometimes they shoot at cars and busses. When my mother dies, I will inherit the property, but I do not [want] to become [a] farmer.'

What does status mean to you? And power?

'Status is not important to me; I do not care about it. I am happy with my life the way it is. Power means money, "everything changes with money and you can control everybody with money". I would like to have a position of power, if it means that I would have a lot of money.'

Religion

'I am Buddhist; and I perform two *pujas* per month. Religion means a traditional belief in which everything is connected for the benefit of all sentient beings.'

How do you imagine your creator?

'I cannot imagine my creator. Only high lamas can tell you where people come from, it is the same for everybody.'

Would you like to become a monk?

'I never wanted to become a monk.'

Do you consult a pawo/ngejum?

'Sometimes I consult a *pawo* or a *ngejum* for advice or for good luck.'

What does religion mean to you?

'Religion means that everything is connected. It guides your life and shows you the right way.'

Can women and men reach enlightenment in the same way?

'Women and men can reach enlightenment [in] the same way. There is only one god, and this god is genderless.'

What is a good person to you?

'To be a good person, "one has to help others, taking care and to be nice to others".'

What does knowledge mean?

'Knowledge means "more than learning, everything is knowledge, it is life experience".'

Have you heard about sustainability?

'I [have] heard about sustainability and I am going to make a documentary about the subject. Sustainability is: "To sustain and preserve the forest and the natural resources for the future". The natural activities let things grow and it is very important to work together with nature. We (Bhutanese) take care of nature by doing *puja* and make offerings to nature. I [would] like to help to preserve nature by making [a] film about it. I am grateful to nature and I like to work with her.'

Are you happy to be a man?

'I am happy to be a man, I am proud to be a man, "because as a man one has more freedom". "Women are more gentle and helpful than men, Men do not have this condition, but men need to be nice and helpful, treat people right and taking care [of] other people" – this is an ideal man. I feel very secure as a man and I do not feel threatened by anything or anybody.'

Did you ever take a risk?

'I took [a] risk in my life because I am a businessman. I invested in my own business.'

Are men and women equal? Animals?

'In Bhutan men and women are equal. I noticed that in other countries this is not the case. The difference between humans and animals is only the form.'

What does compassion mean to you? Love?

'Compassion means "generosity towards all". Love means "to be full of heart for somebody or something".'

What do you think about power?

'Power means money. Men and women [do not] have the same power, they depend on each other. "Sometimes a man is more powerful and sometimes a woman, one takes and gives back".'

What does wisdom mean?

'I cannot tell what wisdom is, but wisdom and money are both very important "one needs both". Men are wiser than women.'

What do you think of God?

'God is wise because that is the reason why we are living. God has both genders.'

Kezang

Kezang, a 19-year-old single female, lives in Thimphu. Kezang comes from Mongar, East Bhutan, and works as a receptionist in a hotel in Thimphu. She went to school up to form 9 and came to Thimphu because she knew that she would find work here. She came on her own. Her family lives in Mongar. She is the oldest daughter. Her family is an extended family; her grandparents, and aunt and uncle live under the same roof. I met her in the hotel in Thimphu where she worked. There we talked to each other.

'At home I did all the work like cooking, cleaning, taking care of the cows, laundry, shopping, taking care of [my] grandparents, and working in the home garden. My brother did the same work. I did *pujas* and also helped neighbours and family in case of death. My hobbies are reading, learning English and Dzongkha, watching Bhutanese movies. I like my job in Thimphu.

'At home in Mongar I helped on the farm, I did planting chillies, rice, maize, and wheat. In general the men plough, I do not know why women are not supposed to plough. But men and women both carry dung to the fields.'

Who was the most responsible person in the house?

'My grandmother is the most responsible person in the house, and she is the head of the household and makes all important decisions. She takes care of money matters, [makes] decisions on what crop to sell and what to buy. She made the decision in regards [to] education for the children. My mother will inherit [the] land and house.'

Could you make free decisions about your life?

'I could freely choose my education and work in Thimphu'.

Do you have wishes for the future?

'For the future my wishes are to have my own business like having a hotel.

'Most important for me in life is my family. I will inherit the same as my brothers and sisters, but only one person will take care of the property. Most of my brothers and sisters do not like to take care of the farm. The one who is most suitable will get the farm.'

Do you like to go out and meet friends?

'I like to meet people and friends; I do not like to go dancing. I came alone to Thimphu, but I do not like to be alone or to go alone to places; I like to be with friends.'

If you had a lot of money, what would you buy?

'If I had all the money in the world I would like to buy a car, a house, TV, [and] clothes. I do not need permission to buy something.'

What do you think about status? Power?

'The king has status and *lyimpo* (minister) Jigme Singye, [the] Minister of Health. I would like to have status as a doctor. Power means to be able to give freedom and prosperity to a country.'

Religion?

'I am a Buddhist, and religion is very important. I pray a lot, and the Buddha is an example to humans. People come from the monkey god; this is the creation myth of Tibet. As a child, I [wanted] to be a nun; now, not anymore. I do *pujas* and I go to an astrologer (*tsipa*) if I need advice.'

Why are there so many monks in Bhutan and only a few nuns?

'Every household tries to send one son to the monastery; this is beneficial for the karma of the family. Daughters are needed to work in the house; they inherit the house and land. Women can freely decide to become a nun. Women and men can both reach enlightenment, and there are male and female gods. A good person has to be humble, respect others, [and be] kind, polite, heartfelt, and honest.'

Have you ever heard of sustainability?

'I learned about sustainability in school; it means the environment. Environment means nature resources, and those are important for human life. I think nature lets things grow, nature is there. People can help nature by not cutting trees and planting new trees. People can help the deities and gods in nature by doing rituals. For me, women and men have the same relation with nature. I enjoy nature a lot. Nature gives beautiful things: we get food, medicine, water, and clean air from her.

'I am scared when I am alone at night. I am scared for evil spirits or on the street or of strange men. In nature I feel safe.'

Are you happy to be a woman?
'I am very happy to be a woman. I like being a woman because a woman does not have to work so hard; the man will bring the money to the house.'
What is an ideal woman to you?
'An ideal woman is Kandroma; she is a Buddhist Goddess. Or a Tulku or Rinpoche.'
Do you have a wish for the future?
'My wish for the future is to own a hotel.'
Do you have a hero? Would you like to be one?
'My hero is Pema Lingpa; I do not want to be a heroine – too much hassle.'
Have you ever taken a risk in your life?
'I took a risk to come to Thimphu on my own to look for a job. At home I was fighting with my relatives, and after that I left for Thimphu. If I had money, I would like to invest in a hotel.'
Would you like to have more land?
'In Mongar my family would like to have more land; they could give it out for sharecropping'.
Would you like to be an educated farmer?
'I do not [want] to be a farmer; I [want] to be a hotel owner.'
Do you think that good relations with other people like neighbours are important?
'Good relations with neighbours are very important; [we have] to help each other. But I do not respect other men and women; sometimes I fight with other men and women, only when they respect me [less] than I respect them.'
Do show you anger?
'I have a problem controlling my anger; I show it when I am angry. But it is very important that people are polite to each other.'
Do you think that men and women are equal? What about animals?
'Men and women are equal, and animals are equally important to humans, only animals cannot talk.'
Who is stronger, men or nature?
'Men and women have same power, but nature is stronger than humans.'
What does God mean to you?
'To me God means helping people to find peace.'
And wisdom?
'Wisdom is like God, and wisdom is more important than money. Because money comes and goes, [but] wisdom stays. I think men and women are equally wise and nature is wise.'
What gender does God have?
'God is male and female – both genders.'

Karma

Karma is a 22-year-old female law student in Mumbai (India). She is single and lives in Thimphu. Karma is a beautiful young woman; I met her at a conference on Gross National Happiness in Thimphu. She was helping with the organisation of the conference. Between the sessions, she had the time to talk to me. We sat in the conference's coffee shop.

'I live in Thimphu with [my] parents and grandmother, four sisters, and two brothers, but I am often in Mumbai to do my studies. I am in the middle one of my family.

'At home I help with cooking and shopping, my family has an aid in the house. I like helping my parents in the house. I help to take care of my small brothers and sisters. I take them to school and play with them.

'I perform a lot of *pujas* – me and my family, we are very religious. I always pray and I perform rituals; we often invite monks to perform the rituals.

'My hobbies are sports like basketball, swimming, and reading. But I do not have much time. I have to study a lot. Most the time during the day I have to study. I am very happy with my life; I was born at the right place at the right time. I love my country, Bhutan. In Bhutan, women are more free and more equal than in India for example. Here I am more independent.'

Who makes the important decisions in your home?

'Father and mother both make all the important decisions. Mother takes care most of the time about house-related issues and father makes the decisions about the education of the children. Mother takes care of the financial matters and father about the educational matters within the family.'

Can you choose your studies and work freely?

'I could choose freely my study. I am very happy to study law; it has a lot of scope and it is in demand. For my future, I wish to become a very good lawyer, to make my parents proud of me.'

Do you like to go out?

'I like to go dancing with friends; I am free to go out. But I also like to be with my family.'

What would you buy if you had a lot of money?

'If I had all the money in the world, I would like to buy a monastery for my parents. If I want something to buy, I do not need permission from my parents.'

Who will inherit the property of your parents?

'In my family everybody will inherit the same; I will share everything equally with my brothers and sisters.'

What does status and power mean to you?

'For me, status is more important than money, a person who does good deeds has status. To me, the government officials have a lot of status because they do good work and do not receive a large salary. I would love to have status. Power means authority over people. His majesty has a lot of power. I would like to be in a position of power; this way I can do well for other people.'

Religion?

'I am very religious and I am a Buddhist; religion means life.'

Where do you think people come from?

'I do not know where people come from or who created humans. I heard the story of the creation myth of the monkey god, but I am not sure.'

Did you ever think of becoming a nun?

'I actually would like to be a nun; this way I could lead a "clean" life to accumulate good karma. But I also like what I am doing now.'

Do you consult an astrologer?

'Sometimes I go to an astrologer for advice.'

Why are there so many monks and only a few nuns in Bhutan?

'I think there are more monks than nuns because "in the old days women inherit the land and had to work on the farms. Nowadays there are many more nuns than before, because women can now choose if they want to become nun or if they want to marry".'

We had to stop here, because Karma had to work again.

Provisional reflections based on the ten conversations

In this chapter, I described the conversations I had with people in Bhutan. It was very easy to have long conversations with these people because everybody had time to talk, even during their work. Some respondents invited me for dinner, and we had a very nice time together.

So I ask myself the questions: What did I learn? Or what made me sad, happy or even angry?

I learned about patience – the patience and time the conversation partners had to talk to me.

Meeting with Rinzin in Haa

Rinzin, the Dzongrab of Haa: We went to his office in the Dzong of Haa. Dorji, my translator, asked Rinzin's assistant if it would be possible for us to have a conversation with the Dzongrap. He was a very busy and important man. We were asked to wait, then after a few minutes we were summoned to enter his office. Outside the office, a long line of people was waiting for an audience with the Dzongrap to ask him for favors and advice. He was wearing a *gho* (Bhutanese dress) and a sword, because of his position. (In Bhutan, senior civil servants in official dress wear a large sword on their hip.) His office was decorated with *Thangkhas* (religious paintings) and there was a warm atmosphere.

We entered his office and he welcomed us. Tea and snacks were served and he asked how he could help us. I told him about my research and asked him if I could ask him some questions because I wanted to know his view on my three themes.

He told me that he liked my questions and the themes. He had been thinking about these themes himself before, and was wondering about God, sustainability, and values.

At times during the conversation, his assistant came in to ask him a question or with a message. He said: "Please, I do not want to be disturbed now." And then he looked at me and said: "Do you have more questions? I love them."

We spent about two hours in his office. What I really appreciated was that he explained to me about Bhutanese sustainability. He gave examples of the Bhutanese worldview, and the relation with nature and the deities and gods.

In general, I was surprised about the awareness of people. I talked with them about issues such as gender, sustainability, power, status, and religion. I noticed that people with Western higher education and higher religious education were much more comfortable with my questions than the people with no education – and they even liked them. I realized we had to adjust the questions for the less educated, and sometimes they could not answer them. I also realized that it was strange to talk to certain people about sustainability, because they were living it. It was part of their life. One woman said to me: "I am nature; I am part of nature; we are one." To avoid the word sustainability, For those who were not familiar with the word sustainability, I asked all kinds of questions about nature and the relationship that people have with nature.

I tried to interview a gentleman who was a shaman; he was the mouthpiece of a deity called Ab Chuzum, the deity of the Ha valley. He is totally connected with his environment and has a strong relationship with the mountains and the valley. When we started to talk to him about sustainability and religion, he looked at us and I could see him thinking: What are you talking about? I cannot answer these strange questions? He just replied: "I do not know." We talked about his mediumship and he explained how he became a shaman and his relation with Ab Chuzum. On this subject, he felt comfortable.

I realized that there was not a suitable domain to identify sustainable values in the list of Bilsky and Schwartz.

In particular, the monks are happy to be men and have a chance to dedicate their lives to reaching enlightenment. I did not realize before that reaching enlightenment is so important to Bhutanese people. It surprises me that this is an important goal in life to so many people. There even is a connection between gender and enlightenment. I would never have thought of that before. What made me sad was that "uneducated" women I talked to – in particular the nuns – were not happy to be women because they see women as being lower than men because of menstruation ("dirty"). This reminds me of the story of Wikan in chapter 1. Moreover, nuns do not always have access to higher Buddhist teachings. I realized that, just as with the Western concept of sustainability, gender is a very Western concept, and in Bhutan it has an absolutely different significance.

In my Western perspective, I see the traditional position of women in Bhutan (as I experienced in the village) as strong and independent. As head of the household and as a person who makes all the important decisions, the woman has a lot of power and freedom. The Bhutanese perspective is that village women have a hard life and many attachments (because she owns the house and land), and working in the fields is not good for one's karma (because one kills a lot of bugs while working in the fields, and this is not good for the accumulation of good karma). These two perspectives are very different. In my perspective, nuns have a low status; in the eyes of my female Bhutanese respondents, to be a nun is something desirable because one can lead a "clean" life and be able to reach enlightenment in this life.

Meeting with Neten in Bumthang

"Dorji and I were in Bumthang, in central Bhutan. Bumthang is a beautiful valley that is considered holy because Guru Rimpoche or Padmansambhava meditated there in caves, as did other important Bhutanese and Tibetan holy men and women. The region of Bumthang consists of three valleys: Jakar, Ura, and Tang. In Tang, we heard there was a nunnery, so we decided to go there to talk to a nun.

The nunnery was situated on a beautiful mountain, close to the burning lake. This burning lake is a very important holy place because Pema Lingpa, an important Bhutanese holyman, discovered a *terton* there. His burning lamp fell in the lake and he when he retrieved it from the water, it still was burning. This is considered as a divine sign. Anyhow, close to this important place was the nunnery.

We drove up the mountain to the main building, where some nuns were sitting in the sun. We asked if we could talk to one, and that was no problem. They all were giggling, and more nuns came out the building to look at us. The head nun decided that Neten would be the best person to talk to us. Neten called us to go with her to the main temple, where we could sit and talk. Another nun brought us tea and snacks. We were sitting on the floor, and now and then a nun would come in to watch us talk and to giggle.

Again, the atmosphere was relaxed and we stayed more than two hours. Neten told us that this nunnery was financed by an important Rinpoche (see glossary) and it was one of the first nunneries in which the nuns have access to higher teachings up to the level of Kenpo (equivalent to a Master's degree). Neten was very happy to be there.

In my perspective, the nuns were very warm and open, but it made me sad to see how they regard themselves lower than monks. Also, their main aim in life was to reach enlightenment. The nuns' negative self-image made me angry to a certain degree. I told Neten that, as women, we know best what suffering means and that mothers know best what selflessness means. In most cases, mothers put their children first. So, in my opinion, these two concepts of Buddhism are very familiar to women. In this sense, women must have a higher consciousness and therefore are closer to enlightenment. The nuns' reactions to my comments were, "We never thought of this." They reacted happily to this view that they never had thought of.

What surprises me is that women with higher English medium education are happy to be women and very happy to be Bhutanese. Women with none or lower English education regard being a woman as not good because of the physical suffering.

To most respondents, power and status are not related to money; only one businessman connected power with money. It is interesting to see that he has his own business and money is more important to him than the farmers and the civil servants who earn a salary.

For me as a Westerner, the deep religion people have without being rigid is very interesting. There are so many "do's and don'ts" but they are flexible – there is always a way out. Having a Christian (Catholic) background, it is for me a relief to see that people can be devoted to religion but also live and let live. I was surprised that, in general, many of the respondents indicated such a strong desire to study religious books. They indicated a desire to have more access to Buddhist teachings.

I was also impressed with the fact that most respondents were content with their lives. Nobody complained, which surprised me, as a Westerner, especially as in the Netherlands we have a tendency to complain about many things in life. Interestingly, the answers from old and young people did not differ much; any differences resulted more from people's different levels of education. In Thimphu I talked to people who almost all had some higher education. Those with higher education in Thimphu as well as Punakha, Wangdi, and Bumthang all had modern houses with electricity, indoor plumbing, TV, and radio. Their lives are much more modern than the people in the remote villages, where they live without all the comforts of the modern world. I visited one village where the people still lived in a very traditional house, but they had electricity; however, their way of life was still very traditional. I noticed that the respondents who had been to other countries appreciate Bhutan very much. They are very proud of their country; although their houses are more modern than the traditional one, they are still very Bhutanese and living their lives in a distinctly Bhutanese way – not that different from those in the villages. In the city there may be less elaborate *pujas* than in the villages.

I started to learn from the Bhutanese conversations that we are all connected in a way, and I started to understand the Bhutanese way of regarding my Western concepts of sustainability and gender. In regard to religion, I expected deeper insight of the people into knowledge of Buddhism. In general, what I experienced was that Buddhism in Bhutan, to the general public, is more a folk religion with a lot of rituals that originated from pre-Buddhist times.

In the next chapter I will explore theories as a framework for this research.

Western and Asian Perspectives as a Mixed Methodology

In this chapter I will search for suitable theories as a framework for my research. The central themes and theory of my book are Marx's philosophical anthropology, and theories about Bhutanese religion, gender and sustainability. To obtain an understanding of these concepts I will review the discourse of the themes.

The protection of Bhutanese values is mentioned in many of the development plans and reports. Bhutanese values and Buddhism are pointed out as being the cornerstones of these policies. First, I will delineate the concept of values in Asia in general and specifically in Bhutan. In this book I will point out the Buddhist values on gender and sustainability, and what Bhutanese people find important, good, true and beautiful.

The Bhutanese development discourse is dominated by an interest in preserving the traditional values and culture. According to Marx, the moment a society tries to keep traditions or traditional life, they are gone. With the emergence of a market economy the society is changing. Money undermines the ability of the past labour to obtain the present. Value is given to past labour to future gains. (Marx, 1964) I want to know how these changes have influenced gender relations, sustainability and religion.

Putting the modernisation process of a traditional Buddhist kingdom in a Marxist framework is not an obvious choice. However, Marx's *Historical Materialism* and the concept of "alienation", present interesting assumptions that are relevant to social changes in Bhutan. This book is a reflection on what I see in Marx's historical materialism and the concept of alienation, because in traditional Bhutanese society, people were not alienated and people lived close to nature and nature met people's needs. Money was of minor importance. Social relations and reciprocity were more important.

I will summarise the debate on women in development and eco-feminism. I will explain the theories and put the gender relations of Bhutan into a theoretical framework while connecting the gender debate with eco-feminism, sustainability and religion.

The concept of sustainability will be put in the framework of the "Gross National Happiness"in Bhutan.

Traditional Society and Asian Values

In order to understand an Asian culture, it is important to explore values that are not "economic". Cauquelin (2000) asked: 'how are ancient cultures and traditional values modified by modern developments, for example, under impact of market forces, the consumer culture, and Westernization?' In Bhutan, the people are very aware of values:

> 'None of the religions or philosophies particular to Asia (Confucianism, Hinduism, Buddhism, Islam, Jainism, Animism) draws a distinction between religious and secular values. The religious scriptures contain guidelines not only for worship, but also for correct conduct in everyday life, even including politics, economy and the arts.' (Cauquelin et al., 2000: 3)

Efforts to translate the word "value" show that there is no a single equivalent word in Bhutanese. In Bhutan, there is no semantic distinction among value, religion, way of thinking, belief, purpose or custom. Values are complex and the question is where to distinguish "values" from "codes of conduct". According to Cauquelin et al., 'codes of conduct are the practice or expression of values such as harmony and respect in everyday life. The origins of Asian values can be traced to religious and philosophical texts and traditions; this is likewise the case in Bhutan. However, other factors also have an impact: historical experiences, social development, the rise of a market economy, urbanization and industrialization, geographical and climatic conditions, wars and ecological disasters. (Cauquelin et al., 2000:4)

The debate on Asian values is often connected to economic development and human rights: 'In recent years, Asian values have been touted as the driving force behind Asia's rapid and remarkable economic strides during the past decades. Politicians and scholars have used the concept for a variety of purposes. Some have done so in response to Western criticism of Asia. Others have invoked the concept to legitimize a regime in power and its political system. Yet others have used the term to protect values considered necessary for good government from the decadent influence of the West.' (Han Sung-Joo, 1999:3)

> 'A popular view holds that culture is declining as a determinant of domestic and international politics in the context of globalizing pressure. This process is undermining traditional values and institutions and bringing a convergence of cultures through communication, travel and trade: a fledgling homogenizing "world cultures" as a consequence of increasing shared experiences.' (Inoguchi., 1997[1])

'Whether Asian values exist and, if so, how to define them, has been discussed along with the role of values in respective Asian countries economic development.' (Han Sung-Joo, 1999:3) 'One perspective suggests that Asian values, which were helpful during the early industrialization and pre-globalization stage of development, have actually impeded these Asian countries in adjusting to a new age of interdependence and globalization. A paternalistic state, government guidance and protection of private enterprises, a communitarian outlook and communalistic practices, and an emphasis on social order, harmony and discipline – generally considered to be Asian values – seem to have helped only in the earlier stages of industrialization and economic growth.' (Han Sung-Joo, 1999:4)

Religion and Values

Religious beliefs are linked to values. Do religious beliefs determine values or vice versa? 'The common assumption is that values follow from religion'. (Hofstede, 1998:194) This could be the case, too, in Bhutan. Therefore, to understand Bhutanese values I will first look at religion in Bhutan. 'Buddhism,

---

1   www.unu.edu/unupress/asian-values.html#INTRODUCTION

as one of the world's major spiritual traditions, centres around the pursuit of Enlightenment, and in Mahayana Buddhism this goal is salvation'. (Samuel, 1993:5) In Bhutanese society, values are embedded in all spheres of life. Values are important and Bhutanese Buddhism has a whole set of values which guide life. Bhutan has its own Buddhist state religion.

According to Geertz, 'Religion is a system of symbols which act to produce powerful, pervasive and long-lasting moods and motivations in the people of a given culture'. (Geertz 1973:90) A mood for Geertz is 'a psychological attitude such as awe, trust and respect, whereas a motivation is the social and political trajectory created by a mood that transforms myths into ethos, symbol system into social and political reality. Symbols have both psychological and political effect, because they create the inner condition and deepest-seated attitudes and feelings that lead people to accept social and political arrangements, which correspond to the symbol system. Religious symbols shape a cultural ethos, defining the deepest values of a society and the person in it.' (Geertz 1973:90) First I will look at the core values of Mahayana Buddhism. More difficult to trace are pre-Buddhist values which are passed on by oral tradition. Pre-Buddhism is the religion that was dominant in Bhutan and in the Tibetan cultural area before the 7th century. Sometimes this religion is called *Bon*. Pommaret and Schicklgruber (1999) call it pre-Buddhism, so I will call it pre-Buddhism too. Buddhism and the pre-Buddhist religion still exist in harmony.

Dilgo Khyentse Rinpoche, a Tibetan lama who lived in Bhutan, explained the core values in the Mahayana Buddhist tradition in its Tantric form:

> First, reflect upon the rarity of human existence; this will turn your mind towards the *dharma* (*dharma* means the Buddhist spiritual path). In other words, life is very precious. Second, contemplate death and impermanence; this will make you realize how urgent it is to practice the *dharma*, and will spur your endeavour. Third, there is the law of *karma*, the law of cause and effect, actions and their result. Fourth, Buddhists have the recognition of suffering, the endless wheel of *samsara*, born and reborn again and again. Fifth, free yourself from *samsara* through receiving and practicing the teachings to reach ultimately the unsurpassable level of omniscience, or enlightenment. (Dilgo Khyentse Rinpoche, 1996)

This 5-point *karma* ('action') and the belief in rebirth are commonplace in all Buddhist societies. *Karma* is the effect of actions in past lives on one's present existence and of one's present actions on future existences within the cycle of rebirth (*samsara*).

Mahayana Buddhism places emphasis on the social aspect of enlightenment. Another vital ingredient is "compassion" and the key element being the concept of the *bodhisattva*. A *bodhisattva* is an enlightened being who refuses to go into nirvana unless all sentient beings reach enlightenment (Samuel, 1993). Cauquelin et al. point out that in South Asian culture, the way of thinking is dialectical, circular and holistic, taking the relative rather than the absolute standpoint. This applies to all religions in South Asia.

> 'The ancient Hindu philosophical school of *Samkya* and Tantrism, a religious tradition, which arose in Buddhism and in the *Vaishnava* traditions contributed to Hinduism, as we know it today. Based on a dialectical form, it argues that the static male and the dynamic female are aspects of complementary nature and always exist in combination. The male is seen as the unchanging essence and the female as the power of transformation and change present in subtle and material forms of the world. Tantrism is also holistic and according to its cosmology all manifestations (being, things) are expressions of the divine power.'(Cauquelin et al., 2000:11)

Values in Bhutan

Bhutanese values and codes of conduct are based on ancient tradition and religion. There are different codes of conduct, partly based on Buddhism. Bhutanese social life is guided by *driglam namzha* (code of behaviour or discipline), *tsawasum* (King, the government and the kingdom), *tha damtshig* (loyalty), and *le judre* (karmic action retribution, cause and effect) (Dzongkha Development Commission, 1990). According to Cauquelin et al. (2000), codes of conduct are the practice and expression of values such as harmony and respect in everyday life.

Karma Phuntsho (2004) tests socio-political concepts as *le judre, tha damtsig* and *driglam namzha*, to see if they are religious or what he calls para-religious concepts. In Bhutanese and Tibetan Buddhism, "compassion" and "altruism" are core values of the practitioner.(Karma Phuntsho, 2004) Compassion and altruism have to be connected with "wisdom" and "the practices of the six perfections": generosity, ethics, patience, dedication, concentration and wisdom. Everything must be done in accordance with these six perfections. (Karma Phuntsho, 2004)

Tashi Wangyal (2001) describes a shift in values due to the modernisation of Bhutan in the early 1960s. According to him, 'traditional values have been shaped by Buddhist culture and these values include an individual's relationships with the natural environment and with other people relationships, and incorporate issues of individual self-discipline. Traditional Bhutanese values not only address individual self-discipline and the conduct of interpersonal relationships but also the individual's responsibility to all sentient beings.

'The concepts of *le judre* and *tha damtshig* (loyalty) are central to Bhutanese values. The concept of *le judre* states that good begets good and vice versa. The *tha damtshig* outlines the sacred commitment to others. This is best illustrated in pairing of duty and obligation between parent and child, teacher and pupil, husband and wife and master and servant. Such pairing of duty and obligations reinforces the need for social responsibility. In terms of individual self-discipline Bhutanese values emphasize the *domba nga* or the "five lay Buddhist undertakings": not killing; not stealing; not lying; abstinence from intoxicants and avoidance of sexual misconduct.'(Tashi Wangyel 2001: 107)

Karma Phuntsho (2004) states that '*damtshig* refers to Tantric practices, including a great number of obligatory precepts ranging from obeying one's *guru* (teacher) and loving all fellow beings, to performing ceremonies at the right time. *Damtshig*, as a solemn oath and code of practice for the highly revered and esoteric form of Buddhism, is seen with much awe and fear. The proper observance of *damtshig* rewards the practitioner with swift enlightenment but an infringement of it is said to cause rebirth in the deepest hell. *Damtshig* is a binding force which keeps the community or line of practitioners spiritually pure. This results in an altruistic mind among the Bhutanese people.' (Karma Phuntsho 2004:569 – 570)

'The religious understanding of *damtshig* as Tantric precepts has been extended to several social and moral notions, attitudes and behaviours. Supplied with the prefix *tha,* denoting moral limitations or boundary, *damtshig* acquired a range of social meanings. *Tha damtshig* is more frequently used in Bhutan than in other Himalayan countries. *Tha damtshig*, depending on the context, covers, among others, honesty, fidelity, integrity, rectitude, moral coherence, reciprocal affection, gratitude, and filial piety. *Tha damtshig* can be applicable in a socio-political context, in which people who fail to be loyal to the state and the government are described as lacking *tha damtshig*. Just as there are *tha damtshig* bonds with religious groups, there are also *tha damtshig* ties within families and friends and a political bond is perceived between the people and the government.'(Karma Phuntsho, 2004: 570)

Unlike *le judre* and *tha damtshig, driglam namzha* is not strictly religious. *Driglam namzha* means code of behaviour or discipline according to the Dzongkha Development Commission (1990). According to Whitecross (2002):

'*tha damtshig* means: 'the highest or ultimate vow' and it is based on the word for religious vows (*damtshig*) taken by Buddhists. The term can be taken as simply meaning, respect or returned kindness. *Tha damtshig* is reciprocal and does not mean respect to those senior to oneself or socially higher. It means respect between people who are socially equal and is the moral foundation of *driglam namzha*' (Whitecross 2002:4)

Gender, Sustainability and Buddhism from a Western Perspective

Gender, sustainability and Buddhism are three important parts of this book.

First I will delineate gender theories from a Western perspective, then combine gender and sustainability and finally sustainability and Buddhism. I find it useful to begin by exploring Western theories on gender, sustainability and Buddhism, because with this will make the uniqueness of gender relations, sustainable awareness and Bhutanese Buddhism clearer.

There has been much debate over the words of sex and gender. (Oakley, 1972; Delphy, 1993) According to Den Uyl (1995), within the discipline of anthropology Mead and Rubin called attention to the difference between individual predisposition and social personality and to the social construction of gender. Mead (1947) gives a construction of gender but Rubin (1974) premises the universal subordination of women and to understand this suppression we must examine the sex-gender systems. (Den Uyl, 1995) The original division of the concepts was between that which related to biology (sex) and that which related to social characteristics (gender) (Oakley,1972), although it was quickly recognized that the two ideas could not be kept theoretically separate. (Rubin, 1974) Later writers have argued that sex, like gender, should be seen as socially constructed rather than biologically given. (Delphy, 1993; Butler, 1990)

Mellor (1997) sees embodiment as a material and an historical phenomenon that cannot be "de-gendered" through socialization or counter socialization. Social constructions do not begin from a blank slate. As Mellor (1997) puts it:

'To say that human beings as reproductive mammals are embodied in sexed bodies does not imply anything about sexual identity or sexual orientation of individual people, or even some unified and singular bodily form of the male and the female. Embodiment is a universal human condition, not a determining factor at the individual level. It is also important not to limit discussion to sex, sexuality and reproduction. Human embodiment covers all aspects of human biological needs and developments such as hunger, excretion, maturing and death.' (Mellor 1997:9)

Western Gender Values

Do men and women place different meanings on values? To trace the history of gender differences and values, feminist philosophy is a helpful discipline. Whitbeck (1986) gives a survey of the theories which explain differences between women and men in Western philosophy and science. The survey reveals three general themes or motifs. 'The first of the three motifs, and one which is particularly important in structuring scientific theories, is that of women as partial men. In theories structured by this motif the principal difference between the sexes derives from the supposed fact that women either completely lack, or have less of, some important ingredient that men have. The second major motif identifies two principles in nature and human nature. The first of these principles embodies whatever characteristics are seen as accruing to the conscious self and are taken to be male or masculine. The second principle is defined in contrast to the first and so embodies whatever characteristics are seen as accruing to oneself or to another. It is taken to be female of feminine with the non-rational or even irrational, but this varies with the view of the conscious self. The second motif occurs most often in metaphysical and psychological theories. The third motif holds that the essence of womanhood is defined in terms of men's needs. This motif figures most prominently in religious and mythological literature and in works that explicitly set down norms.' (Whitbeck,1986:36)

Most Western theories are biased against women's nature; men are taken as the norm and women as 'the other'. Most theories about human nature have served a similar function in the Western tradition. Holmstrom (1986) turned to biology, which has the most developed and precise system of classification. She asked the question: are there sex-differentiated natures? In this sense, if women have a distinct nature, then so do men. Her conclusion is that there are significant differences between the sexes. She concludes that the most important determinants of these differences are social and that the usual inference is that men and women do not have different natures, and in the traditional sense of "natures", this is correct.

However, the traditional concept depends upon a contrast between nature and society, which, she argues, is mistaken, particularly in the case of human beings. 'Natures can also be socially constituted. Whether men and women have different natures depends on certain theoretical considerations.' (Holstrum 1986:50) Holmstrom asked why biological differences between the sexes should per se have systematic social implications. The linkage is usually made through psychology. Those who emphasize the biological differences between the sexes as critical to their social roles and their natures usually maintain that the biological differences cause psychological differences and these in turn determine their respective social roles. (...)

Holmstrom wants to find out whether there are psychological differences between men and women, in terms of cognitive abilities and styles and other personality characteristics that suit them in their respective social roles. Holstrom then asked what the source of such differences would be. Social scientists approach the question by looking at the significant differences between sexes in a statistical way but this is not deep enough, according to Holmstrom (1986).

The field of anthropology reveals significant cultural differences in sex roles. If there is any connection between sex roles and psychological traits, then one would expect research to reveal that psychological sex differences vary cross-culturally. In the absence of biological explanation, a variation according to culture strongly suggests that there is a social explanation. By "social" Holmstrom means "not biological". Such factors include family structure, organization of the economy, and innumerable other specific factors. While human beings are undeniably biological beings they are also social beings with a history. Their biological characteristics have evolved somewhat but their social and cultural characteristics have evolved more rapidly and to a much greater extent: a similar distinction to that just made for men and women. The distinction between males and females is a biological one, according to Holstrom; "the nature of women, qua female is biological. However the categories men and women are also social categories, gender. Men and women as social beings might have distinct natures which could explain the sex-related differences in behaviour." (Holstrom, 1986:54)

The Connection of Gender and Sustainability from a Western Perspective

Today in Western and developing countries more attention is given to the interaction between gender and sustainability. The main arguments can be grouped in five main themes: the role of women in environmental changes; women as resource managers; women and population growth; the effect of empowerment on sustainability; and the rural/traditional loci of gender/sustainability issues. (Martine, 2001)

Within eco-feminism, gender, religion and sustainability are coming together to explain the destruction of the earth in terms of "androcentrism". Eco-feminism grew out of the feminist, peace and ecology movements of the late 1970's and early 1980's. More than 35 years ago, Rachel Carson published her book *Silent Spring*. The book was a call for protest against the pollution and degradation of nature (Diamond and Orenstein, 1990) According to Diamond and Orenstein (1990), Rachel Carson was not a feminist, but it was not coincidental that a woman was the first to respond emotionally and scientifically to the desire of human domination over the natural world. Carson's 1962 book prefigured a powerful environmental movement, but the notion that the collective voices of women should be central to greening the Earth did not blossom until the end of the 1970s.

'Eco-feminism is a term that some use to describe both the diverse range of women's efforts to save the Earth and the transformation of feminism in the West that have resulted from the new view of women and nature'. (Diamond & Orenstein, 1990:ix)

Though the term was first used by D'Eaubonne in 1980 it became popular only in the context of protests and activism against environmental destruction, sparked by recurring ecological disasters. 'There are a variety of movements dealing with ecological crises from several perspectives, and within those movements, there are women who make a conscious critique of the movement's androcentrism and seek to show the connection between women's domination and the domination of nature'.(Radford Ruether 1996:2)

There are several views of eco-feminism in North America. Among Northern eco-feminists the connection between the subordination of women and domination of nature is made first on the cultural and symbolic level. One charts the way in which patriarchal culture has defined women as "closer to nature", as on the nature side of a nature-culture dichotomy. This is shown in the way in which women have been identified with body, earth, sex, and the flesh in its mortality, weakness, and sinfulness, vis-à-vis masculinity identified with spirit, mind, and sovereignty power over both women and nature .(Radford Ruether, 1996)

A second level of eco-feminist analysis explores the socio-economic underpinnings of how the domination of women's bodies and women's work connects with the exploitation of the land and animals as sources of labour and wealth. How have women as a gender been colonized by patriarchy as a legal, economic, social and political system? (...) 'From a Marxist-feminist perspective, the cultural symbolic patterns linking women and nature are an ideological superstructure by which the system of economic and legal domination of women, land and animals is justified and made to appear natural: and inevitable within the total patriarchal cosmic vision. Religion comes in to reinforce this domination of women and nature as reflecting the will of God and the relation of God as supreme deified patriarchal male to the "world" that he "created" and rules.' (Radford Ruether 1996:3)

Merchant (1980) has a pessimistic view of science. According to Merchant, science robbed nature of its right to life and spirits, nature is regarded as a machine. In the 16th century with the rise of modern science and technology, mankind's view of nature as a living being changed and nature became a machine to be controlled and dismantled. According to Merchant,

> 'Nature in ancient and early modern times had a number of interrelated meanings. With respect to individuals, it referred to the properties, inherent characters, and vital powers of persons, animals, or things, or more generally to human nature. It also meant an inherent impulse to act and to sustain action; conversely, to 'go against nature' was to disregard this innate impulse. With respect to the material world, it referred to a dynamic creative and regulatory principle that caused phenomena and their change and development. A distinction was commonly made between *natura naturans*, or nature creating, and *natura naturata*, the natural creation.
> Nature was contrasted with art (*techne*) and with artificially created things. It was personified as a female-being e.g. Dame Nature; she was alternately a prudent lady, an empress, a mother. The course of nature and the laws of nature were the actualization of her force. The state of nature was the state of mankind prior to social organization and prior to the state of grace. Nature spirits, nature deities, virgin nymphs, and elements were thought to reside in or associated with natural objects. In both Western and non-Western cultures, nature was traditionally feminine.' (Merchant1980:xxiii)

According to Merchant, before the Scientific Revolution nature and the earth were viewed as a "nurturing mother", who provided for the needs of mankind in an orderly universe. This metaphor gradually vanished as the Scientific Revolution proceeded to mechanize and rationalize the world and gave rise to a mechanistic model of society as a solution to social disorder. In this conceptual framework, scientists became the problem solvers who analysed the world, manipulated it and provided the justification to manage, control and exploit nature. As a result no one considered the permanent insult to the earth caused by strip mining, dumping waste into rivers, clear cutting forest, and draining marshes.

Before the Scientific Revolution, the earth was considered to be alive and sensitive and it was a violation of human values to destroy this source of life. As Western culture became mechanized in 16th century, the female earth and earth deities and spirits were subdued by machines. At the same time, the role of women in society changed. (Merchant, 1980)

Gender Relations in Bhutan and the Nature-Culture debate

During my initial research in the village in Bhutan I saw a community with gender harmony. I will describe what I experienced in Bhutan in terms of the nature-culture debate on gender.

Oliver (1997) has examined the ways in which nature and culture have been defined with relation to the difference between mother and father. 'In the Western world, opposition between nature and culture has been portrayed as a war between mother and father. Not only in philosophy, which traditionally claims to be immune to sexual difference in the quest for universal knowledge, but also in various other disciplines, which begin by recognizing sexual differences. Woman, femininity, and maternity have been associated with nature, not with culture. Women, on the one hand, have been reduced to their reproductive function, which is seen as a natural function. Men, on the other hand, can escape or sublimate their nature in order to perform higher functions.' (Oliver 1997:xi-xviii)

Ortner (1974) tries to explain the secondary status of women in society and concludes that it is universal. Yet the cultural conceptions and symbolizations of women are extraordinarily diverse and even contradictory. The treatment of women and their relative power and contribution vary enormously from culture to culture, and over different periods. In Tantric Buddhism in Bhutanese culture, the female principle and the male principle are equally important. Hence we might guess that maleness and femaleness are equally valued in the Bhutanese culture. Looking at the social structure, however we see an emphasis on patrilineal descent, although we have to make a distinction within Bhutanese society and culture on the macro and micro levels.

I will describe the position of Bhutanese women in relation to that of Bhutanese men according to the three types of data given by Ortner (1974). Ortner asks what it means when women in every known culture are considered to be inferior to men. Ortner says that in its own way and on its own terms each culture makes this evaluation:

'(1) Elements of cultural ideology and informants' statements that explicitly devalue women according to them--their roles, their tasks, their products, and their social milieus are accorded less prestige than men and the male correlates
(2) Symbolic devices, such as the attribution of defilement, which may be interpreted as implicitly making a statement of inferior valuation; and
(3) Social structural arrangements that exclude women from participation in

or contact with some realm where the highest powers of society are felt to reside.' (Ortner1974:69)

These three types of data may be interrelated in any system. Any one of them will usually suffice to establish female inferiority in a given culture. Female exclusion from the most sacred rite or the highest political council is sufficient. Certainly, explicit cultural ideology devaluing women and their tasks, roles, products et cetera is sufficient. Symbolic indicators such as defilement are usually sufficient. Ortner concludes that on all of these counts we find women subordinated to men. The search for a genuinely egalitarian, let alone matriarchal culture has proved fruitless. (Ortner 1974: 70)

Bhutan, though, has traditionally been on the credit side of this ledger. At the village level, women's positions are generally equal to those of men. In some cases women even have a stronger position. One exception I encountered is that women are not allowed to touch bows and arrows (archery is the national sport of Bhutan), but at the state level there is a women's Olympic team in archery.

In Bhutan I saw no difference between men and women. Women and men work together, and their work is equally valued. On a transcendental level women and men are equally important as mediums (shamans) and healers and there is defilement but not only for women but also for men although less so (see chapter 4). Women are not excluded either from the society or from sacral rites. Bhutan does not have a matriarchal culture, but matrilineality and matrilocality do exist.

The eco-feminist view has been heavily criticized, especially for its perspective of women and nature. Many feminist scholars question the relationship of women to nature. The assumption is that women are closer to nature than men. What is the cultural-symbolic view of women and nature? Eco-feminism looks at attitudes and world-views that differ, based on male and female perceptions of life. Whether gender differences are biological or social is still controversial.

Sustainability

A Western perspective
Sustainability is a "buzz" word. In Bhutan it has a meaning that it does not have in the West. First I will give a brief description of the Western sustainability discourse and than I will put the concept into the Bhutanese setting.

Sustainability is often connected with development. This concept is a multidimensional concept and in 1987 the Brundtland Report, *Our Common Future*, alerted the world to the urgency of making progress toward economic development that could be sustained without depleting natural resources or harming the environment. Published by an international group of politicians, civil servants and experts on the environment and development, the report was a key statement on sustainable development, defining it as: *development that meets the needs of the present without compromising the ability of future generations to meet their own needs.* The Brundtland Report was concerned with securing global equity, redistributing resources towards poorer nations whilst encouraging their economic growth. The report also suggested that equity, growth and environmental maintenance are simultaneously possible and that each country is capable of achieving its full economic potential whilst enhancing its resource base. The report also recognized that achieving this equity and sustainable growth would require technological and social change.

The report highlighted three components of sustainable development: environmental protection, economic growth, and social equity. The environment should be conserved and our resource base enhanced, by gradually changing the ways in which we develop and use technologies. Developing nations must be allowed to meet their basic needs for employment, food, energy, water and sanitation. If this is to be done in a sustainable manner, then there is a definite need for a sustainable level of population. Economic growth should be revived and developing nations should be allowed a growth of equal quality to that of developed nations. Arts, et al. (2002) give three different dimensions of sustainable development: ecology, social sustainability, and economic sustainability.

The *Random House College Dictionary* (1984) defines ecology as: 'the branch of biology dealing with the relationship between organisms and their environment'. (1984:481) Commoner (1972) explains ecology as each living species linked to many others. These links are bewildering in their variety and marvellous in their detail. The science that studies these relationships and the processes linking each living thing to the physical and chemical environment is ecology. It is the science of "planetary housekeeping". For the environment is the house created on the earth by and for living things.

Ecological sustainability is not the only goal of sustainable development. Social sustainability, which means the well-being of people and honest division of resources, is also central. Two levels mark social sustainability: one concerns the social-cultural dimension (health, right of existence, access to resources) and the second the institutional political dimension (democracy, accountability and transparency). The third dimension is economic sustainability, which means "producing more with less". In other words, economic growth only happens in a way that could be sustained without exhausting natural resources or harming the environment. (Arts et al., 2002)

The four laws of Commoner and the sustainable dimensions can be seen as Western ecological values. These values are ancient and still alive in Bhutan. These values are intertwined with religion, gender and policy making. In Bhutan this means development based on maximizing gross national happiness, not the gross national product.

However, there is a difference between sustainability and sustainable development. According to Sutton (2001), the core meaning of sustainability is the ability to maintain something over time. One has to make clear what this "something" is: society or economy, or an enterprise, or the environment or a combination. If we use the terms in combination we talk about holistic sustainability or triple bottom line sustainability.

Sutton makes a distinction between sustainable development and sustainability. 'Sustainable development is the change process in society and the economy that enables the achievement of sustainability and the effective pursuit of genuine progress'. (Sutton 2001:1)

'Sustainability has evolved into a post-modern label for everything that is good and wholesome. Treated this way, sustainability becomes a substitute for earlier aspirational goals such as heaven on earth, socialism or progress. It may be appropriate to see sustainable development as a suitable comprehensive goal for society, but it is not appropriate to see sustainability as such a complete goal'. (...)

Sustainability and Buddhism

Sustainability and Mahayana Buddhism go hand in hand. Buddhist worldview is different from the Christian one, which focuses on the domination of men over nature. Buddhism respects all living beings and non-domination of one sentient being over another. According to Palmer and Finlay (2000), the Buddhist view of the world is based on an understanding of nature and origins of suffering. The suffering we experience has its origin in the delusion of perceiving oneself as an isolated independent existing in a world of isolated independent things. Such a sense of separation is the basis for the innate belief that by amassing possessions which one associates with pleasure, one will secure a lasting and stable happiness. This is the assumption from whence greed develops into a habit. Since this greed and selfishness are irrational (although this may be supported by sophisticated rationalizations), undermining it requires spiritual practice. However, although adopting a world-view that sees life this way will help, without committed practice it will have little effect on entrenched ways of behaviour.

Buddhism seeks a middle way between sensual indulgence and the extremes of life, denying asceticism. To lead fulfilled lives, human beings require nutritious food, warm and dry housing, adequate clothing, and medical care. It is only when one is driven by greed to believe that additional *wants* are in fact *needs* that the problem begins.

Buddhism criticizes consumerism on precisely these grounds: that the level of greed is stimulated to a degree that is not only unnecessary to meet one's needs but, contrary to its avowed claim of bringing happiness, it actually increases dissatisfaction, frustration and suffering. Moreover such a lifestyle is damaging to the natural environment, leads to exploitation of the underprivileged, and in the long term is unsustainable. The Buddhist approach places great stress on enhancing the quality of life without damaging either the present environment or the prospects of others. This is not an appeal to poverty, but rather the avocation of simplicity, a quality that becomes increasingly attractive the more life accords to the values taught by the Buddha. (Palmer & Finlay, 2003)

The concept of "Gross National Happiness" was articulated by the King of Bhutan to indicate that development has many more dimensions than those associated with gross domestic product, and that development should be understood as a process that seeks to maximize happiness rather than economic growth. (Jigmi Thinley, 1998) The concept of "Gross National Happiness" is a holistic concept for sustainable development.

About Marx' vision of social change

Firstly, we have to face the question: why using Marx in a Bhutanese context?

I am interested in Marx philosophical anthropology and Marx's vision of social change. According to Marx, before the capitalist production system there was the feudal production system and this can be classified as organic. In the organic way of production labour still is one with production; this organic society is hierarchical organized and its members are dependent on each other and linked with labour instruments, soil and craft tools. The relations are based on personal force, top down. One produces for oneself and there is barter. People still live in the present. (Marx, 1977)

Until 1960 Bhutan can be classified as a feudal society as describes by Marx.

The village were I did research in 1990 had still many characteristics of this feudal society as described by Marx. I choose Marx philosophical anthropology as a method to analyse change in Bhutanese society because of Marx's vision of an Ideal society. The society that I encountered in 1990 in Bhutan was a pre-modern society that lived in the present, to Marx this is an ideal society. To me it was a kind of utopia too, because nature provided all the needs people had and the villagers had only to work four to five months in the fields for their need for rice. The people in the village live close to nature and with their gods and deities. Nature provides the villagers with food and their Gods and deities created the guidelines for right conduct and values with nature and within the community. Marx describes this pre-modern society very adequately in his *Philosophical Materialism.* His description of this pre-modern society in which people live in close relationship with nature fits the society that I do and did experience in Bhutan.

Further I will use Marx's concepts of "needs", "capacities" and "spiritual alienation" as a theoretical framework for the transition of the Bhutanese pre-modern society to a modern society.

Slowly modernisation is changing this pre-modern society. In that respect, I am interested what Marx concept of "alienation" means for the villagers and the other Bhutanese people I interviewed. I like to point out the changes in the traditional values of the Bhutanese people in regard to religion, gender and sustainability.

Secondly, I want to see whether "alienation" plays a part in the interaction of men with nature and with each other. Although for Marx, historical analyses begin with an analysis of "economic" needs and means uses to satisfy such "economic" needs. To me human values and religion are an intrinsic part of human needs, not only economic needs. Although Marx sees values as "economic" values, he only explains values in terms of economic values in regard to material needs.

Marx's Philosophical Materialism

In *Philosophical Materialism* Marx gives his view on the interaction of men with nature and with one another. According to Marx, men do this on the basis of needs and capacities that constitute human nature .(Marx, 1961)

To understand a human society, according to Marx in Elstar (1987), one must examine the relation of the forces of production, the intercourse they produce and the classes developed from such. One must set out from real active men and on the basis of their real life-process to demonstrate the development of the ideological reflexes and echoes of this life process. It is only in examining the material condition of a given person or rather class of persons, that one can understand the relation of people to an economic system that seeks to meet human needs. This analysis which Marx provides for Western-Europe includes not only material productions but also modes of production. The mode of production and how such production is divided up between sexes or classes is determinative of the essence of that person. For Marx, historical analysis begins with an analysis of the needs and the means used to satisfy such needs. The means imply a division of labour, first manifested in the family, which mirrored in the wider civil society. (Elstar ,1987)

Man subjects natural objects to his needs and make those objects his, through labour:

> 'Man appropriates his integral essence in an integral way, as a total man. All his human relations to the world--seeing, hearing, smelling, tasting, feeling, thinking, contemplating, sensing, wanting, acting, loving – in short all the organs of his individuality, like the organs which are directly communal in form, are in their objective approach or in their approach to the object the appropriation of that object. This appropriation of human reality, their approach to the object, is the confirmation of human reality.' (Marx, *Economic and Philosophical Manuscript*. 1977:91)

Marx often refers to the self-expanding process of needs creation, whereby the satisfaction of one need gives rise to another. A mediating element in this process is the development of new human capacities, by which Marx means man's cognitive, creative and productive powers. In *The German Ideology*, Marx, after stating that production is the "first historical act" goes on to say that 'the satisfaction of the first need, the action of satisfying and the instrument of satisfaction which has been acquired, leads to new needs; and this creation of new needs is the first historical act.' (Marx, 1977:161)

The mode of production must not be considered simply as the production of the physical existence of the individuals. Rather it is a definite activity of those individuals, a form of expressing their life, a mode of life. (Marx, *German Ideology*. In: Love, 1984) According to Love (1984), men can consciously control their productive activity and therefore can produce universally and freely. Because men are conscious of and distinct from their life activity, they can express themselves in their appropriations of nature. Marx understands man's labour in terms of material and social relations of production which correspond to expanding productive forces; alienation describes labour under particular relations of production. (...)

Alienation

Cox (1998) pointed out that Marx opposed the common sense idea that humans have a fixed nature which exists independently of their society. Working in nature alters not only the natural world, but also the labourer. 'Thus labour is a dynamic process through which the labourer shapes and moulds the worlds he lives in and stimulates himself to create and innovate.' [...] 'Marx called our capacity for conscious labour our 'species being'. (Marx, 1844. In: Cox 1998:2)

Our species being[2] is also a social being, as Marx explained in *The Economic and Philosophical Manuscript* (1844): 'The individual is also a social being.' People have to enter into relationships with each other regardless of their personal preferences because they need to work together to survive. In *Grundrisse* (1977) Marx stated that society does not consist of individuals; it expresses the sum of connections and relationships in which individuals find themselves. Humanity relates to the physical world through labour; through labour humanity itself develops and labour is the source of human beings relationships with each other. What happens to the process of work, therefore has a decisive influence on the whole of society. (Marx, 1977)

The ability to work, to improve the work and build on successes, has resulted in the cumulative development of the productive forces. One such development gave rise to class society. When society became capable of producing a surplus, it also became possible for a class to emerge which was liberated from the need to directly produce and could live from its control over the labour of others. This process was necessary in order to develop and direct the productive forces, but it also meant that the majority of society, the producers, lost control of their labour. Thus, the alienation of labour arose with class society. (Marx 1977)

> 'The first tool contains within it all the potential future ones. The first recognition of the fact that the world can be changed by conscious activity contains all future, as yet unknown, but inevitable change. A living being which has once begun to make nature his own through the work of his hands, his intellect, and his imagination will never stop. Every achievement opens the door to unconquered territory. But when labour is destructive, not creative, when it is undertaken under coercion and not as the free play of forces, when it means the withering, not the flowering, of man's physical and intellectual potential, then labour is a denial of its own principle and therefore of the principle of man.' (Marx 1996:53)

---

2   The term "species-being"(Gattungswesen) is derived from Ludwig Feuerbach's philosophy where it is applied to man and mankind as a whole. (Marx 1999:31)

In feudal society humans had neither yet developed the means to control the natural world, nor the ability to produce enough to be free from famine and cure diseases. All social relationships were conditioned by a low stage of development of the productive powers of labour and correspondingly limited relations between men within the process of creating and reproducing their material life, hence also limited relations between man and nature'. (Marx, 1977) For Marx, land was the source of production, and it dominated the feudal-manorial system in which men saw themselves not as individuals but in relation to the land. Marx described this in *The Economic and Philosophical Manuscripts*:

> 'In feudal landownership we already find the domination of the earth as of an alien power over men. The serf is an appurtenance of the land. Similarly the heir through primogeniture, the first born son, belongs to the land. It inherits him. The rule of private property begins with property in land which is its basis.' (Marx 1977:79)

Ownership of land depended on inheritance and blood lines: ' "birth" determined destiny. In an early work Marx described how 'the aristocracy's pride in their blood, their descent, in short the genealogy of the body...has its appropriate science in heraldry. The secret of the aristocracy is zoology'. (Marx 1999:252)

According to Cox (1998), this zoology determined life and one's relationships with others. On the one hand, the low level of the productive forces meant constant labour for the peasants, while on the other, the feudal lords and the church officials took what they wanted from the peasants by force. Thus alienation arose from the low level of the productive forces, from human subordination to the land and from the domination of the feudal ruling class. However, there were limits to these forms of alienation. The peasants worked their own land and produced most of the things they needed in their own independent family units.

However, the constraints of feudalism were very different from the dynamic of capitalism. The bourgeoisie wanted a society in which everything could be bought and sold for money and selling is the practice of alienation.(Cox,1998) 'The creation of such a society depended on the brutal enclosures of the common land. This meant that, for the first time, the majority in society were denied direct access to the means of production and subsistence, thus creating a class of landless labourers who had to submit to a new form of exploitation, wage labour, in order to survive. Capitalism involved 'a fundamental change in the relations between men, instruments of production and the materials of production'. (Linebaugh 1993:396. In: Cox, 1998) 'These changes transformed every aspect of life. Even the concept of time was radically altered so that watches, which were toys in the 17th century, became a measure of labour time or a means of quantifying idleness, because of the importance of an abstract measure of minutes and hours to the work ethic and to the habit of punctuality required by industrial discipline.' (...)

'Men no longer enjoyed the right to dispose of what they produced how they chose: they became separated from the product of their labour. By the 19th century, however, wage labour had replaced all other forms of payment. This meant labour was now a commodity, sold on the market. Capitalists and workers were formally independent of each other, but in reality inextricably connected. Production no longer took place in the home, but in factories where new systems of discipline operated. The mechanisation of labour in the factories transformed people's relationship with machines, 'those remarkable products of human ingenuity became a source of tyranny against the worker.' (...) In *Capital* (1976) Marx compared the work of craftsmen and artisans to that of the factory worker: 'In handicrafts and manufacture, the workman makes use of a tool. In the factory, the machine makes use of him. There the movements of the instrument of labour proceed from him. Here it is the movements of the machines that he must follow. In manufacture the workmen are parts of a living mechanism. In the factory we have a lifeless mechanism independent of the workman, who becomes a mere living appendage.' (Marx 1976:460) One of the most important, and devastating, features of factory production was the division of labour. Prior to capitalism there had been a social division of labour, with different people involved in different branches of production or crafts.

With capitalism there arose the division of labour within each branch of production. This division of labour meant that workers had to specialise in particular tasks, a series of atomised activities, which realised only one or two aspects of their human powers at the expense of all the others. In this system workers become increasingly dependent on the capitalists who own the means of production. Just as the worker 'is depressed, therefore, both intellectually and physically, to the level of a machine, and from being a man becomes an abstract activity and a stomach, so he also becomes more and dependent on every fluctuation in the market price, in the investment of capital and on the whims of the wealthy'. (Marx 1975:324) It became impossible for workers to live independently of capitalism: to work meant to be reduced to a human machine; to be deprived of work meant living death. Without work, if capital ceases to exist for him, Marx argued the worker might as well bury himself alive: 'The existence of capital is his existence, his life, for it determines the content of his life in a manner indifferent to him'. (...) There is no choice involved – work is a matter of survival. Therefore labour became forced labour; you could not choose not to work, you could not choose what you made, and you could not choose how you made it. Marx noted:

'The fact that labour is external to the worker, does not belong to his essential being; that he therefore does not confirm himself in his work, but denies himself, feels miserable and not happy, does not develop free mental and physical energy, but mortifies his flesh and ruins his mind. Hence the worker feels himself only when he is not working; when he is working he does not feel himself. He is at home when he is not working, and not at home when he is working. His labour is therefore not voluntary but forced, it is forced labour. It is therefore not the satisfaction of a need, but a mere means to satisfy need outside itself. Its alien character is clearly demonstrated by the fact that as soon as no physical or other compulsion exists it is shunned like the plague'. (Marx 1975:324)

For Marx, the history of mankind had a double aspect. It was a history of man's increasing control over nature and a history of the increasing human alienation. Alienation is a condition in which men are dominated by forces of their own creation, which confront them as alien powers. The notion is central to all of Marx's earlier philosophical writings and still informs his later work, not as a philosophical issue but as a social phenomenon.

To Marx, all major institutional spheres in capitalist society, such as religion, the state, and political economy, were marked by alienation. Moreover, these aspects of alienation were interdependent.

'Objectification is the practice of alienation. Just as man, so long as he is engrossed in religion, can only objectify his essence by an alien and fantastic being; so under the sway of egoistic need, he can only affirm himself and produce objects in practice by subordinating his products and his own activity to the domination of an alien entity, and by attributing to them the significance of an alien entity, namely money.' (Marx, 1964:39. In: Coser, 1977)

'Money is the alienated essence of man's work and existence; the essence dominates him and he worships it.' (... 37). [...] 'The state is the intermediary between men and human liberty. Just as Christ is the intermediary to whom man attributes all his own divinity and all his religious bonds, so the state is the intermediary to which man confides all his non-divinity and all his human freedom'. (...)

Alienation hence confronts man in all human institutions. Alienation in the workplace assumes for Marx an overriding importance, because to him man was above all *Homo Faber*, Man the Maker. 'The outstanding achievement of Hegel's Phenomenology [...] is that Hegel grasps the self-creation of man as a process [...] and that he, therefore, grasps the nature of labour and conceives objective man [...] as the result of his own labour.' (Marx 1964:202)

Economic alienation under capitalism is involved in men's daily activities and not only in their minds, as other forms of alienation might be. 'Religious alienation as such occurs only in the sphere of consciousness, in the inner life of man, but economic alienation is that of real life. It therefore affects both aspects'.(Marx 1964:156)

Alienation in the domain of work has a fourfold aspect: man is alienated from the object he produces, from the process of production, from himself, and from the community of his fellows.

> 'The object produced by labor, its product, now stands opposed to it as an alien being, as a power independent of the producer. The more the worker expends himself in work the more powerful becomes the world of objects which he creates in face of himself, the poorer he becomes in his inner life, and the less he belongs to himself.' (Marx 1964:122)

> 'However, alienation appears not merely in the result but also in the process of production, within productive activity itself. If the product of labor is alienation, production itself must be active alienation. The alienation of the object of labor merely summarizes the alienation in the work activity itself.'(Marx 1964:124)

Being alienated from the objects of his labour and from the process of production, man is also alienated from himself--he cannot fully develop the many sides of his personality.

> 'Work is external to the worker. It is not part of his nature; consequently he does not fulfil himself in his work but denies himself. The worker therefore feels himself at home only during his leisure time, whereas at work he feels homeless'. (:124) [...] 'In work [the worker] does not belong to himself but to another person'. (:125). [...]
> 'This is the relationship of the worker to his own activity as something alien, not belonging to him activity as suffering (passivity), strength as powerlessness, creation as emasculation, the personal physical and mental energy of the worker, his personal life as an activity which is directed against himself, independent of him and not belonging to him.'(i:125)

Finally, alienated man is also alienated from the human community, from his "species- being":

> 'Man is alienated from other men. When man confronts himself he also confronts other men. What is true of man's relationship to his work, to the product of his work and to himself, is also true of his relationship to other men. Each man is alienated from others [...] each of the others is likewise alienated from human life.' (Marx 1964:125)

Man and Nature according to Marx
In regard to estranged labour, Marx (1961) stated that:

> 'Man is a species being, not only because in practice and in theory he adopts the species as his object -(his own as well those of other things)- but –and this is only another way of expressing it- but also because he treats himself as the actual, living species; because he treats himself as a universal and therefore a free being.'(Marx 1961:74)

What does Marx mean by a 'free' being?

> 'The life of the species, both in man and in animal consist physically in the fact that man (like the animal) lives on inorganic nature.: and the more universal he is compared with an animal, the more universal is the sphere of inorganic nature on which he lives. Just as plants, animal, stones, the air, light, etc., constitutes a part of human consciousness in the realm of theory, partly as objects of arts-his spiritual inorganic nature, spiritual nourishment which he must first prepare to make it palatable and digestible- so too in the realm of practice they constitute a part of human life and human activity. Physically man lives only on these products of nature, whether they appear in the form of food, heating, clothes, a dwelling or whatever it may be. The universality of man is in practice manifested precisely in the universality which makes all nature his *inorganic* body-both inasmuch as nature is (1) his direct means of life, and (2) the material, the object, and the instrument of his life-activity. Nature is man's inorganic body- nature, that is , in so far as it is not itself the human body. Man Lives on nature-means that nature is his body, with which he must remain in continuous intercourse if he is not to die. That man's physical and spiritual life is linked to nature means simply that nature is linked to itself, for man is part of nature.'(Marx 1961:74)

Marx's vision on man as a 'free' being is interesting in regard to sustainability. Can we conclude that Marx was a visionary in regard to that alienation (the unfree man) leads to the destruction of the planet?

As we have seen in traditional society in Bhutan, people live with nature and regard nature as part of their life. I will explore this subject in chapter 6.

Reflection

In this chapter, I gave an overview of theories on values in Asia, and Bhutan in particular. I then examined values and religion, gender, and sustainability.

I ask myself: What did I learn from the interviews in regard to the related themes? What happened to my themes? Can I see the interviews now in a different form after studying the theories? Can I use the concepts of gender and sustainability as an way to get a deeper insight toward me meeting the *Bhutanese* other?

Cauquelin et al. pointed out that the religions or philosophies of Asia do not make a distinction between secular and religious values. This is in line with what I learned from the interviews. Also, religious beliefs are linked strongly with values, and Bhutanese values guide daily life and proper conduct. This is important to all the respondents, just like the five-point karma core values pointed out by Dilgo Khyentse Rinpoche.

In regard to gender, I learned from the respondents that Bhutanese people see gender in a different light than do Westerners. In general, the Bhutanese respondents do not consider that men and women have psychological differences. Overall, the Bhutanese view on gender differences is limited to the physical differences of people. Gender is not valued as it is in the West. But, on a religious and mythological level, the essence of womanhood is defined as being less than man, although this is referred to as being a folk belief.

In regard to ecofeminism it is interesting to see that this "movement" is very Western. For the Bhutanese respondents, there is no difference between the genders and their relationship with nature because of the absence of domination of nature and the connection people still have with nature. What I learned is that the concept of "gender" is a Western construction.

Sustainability also is a Western construction, but it interesting to see that the concept of sustainability is known to all the educated Bhutanese but is regarded as a Bhutanese concept. To many Bhutanese, sustainability was and still is a way of life, although this way of life has become a concept known to the world as Gross National Happiness.

What I learned form the respondents is that gender, sustainability, values, and religion still are holistic and intertwined, and form is a cosmology on its own.

However, my findings are that this society is changing.

To learn more about the culture of Bhutan and to obtain deeper insight, I want to explore the history and the religion the country. In the next chapter, I will pay attention to religion and history. In Bhutan, these are intertwined and it is important to arrive at an understanding of the gender relation and sustainability awareness.

In the next chapter I will explore the religion and history of Bhutan.

Bhutanese religion
and history

Religion and history are of vital importance in order to understand contemporary culture in Bhutan. In Bhutan no history exists without religion and no religion without history; these two concepts are intertwined completely.

In this chapter, I will give a brief overview of the history of the country and a brief description of the most important Buddhist schools in Bhutan. I will not go into Buddhism theologically because it is not the subject of this book. I will give a description of religion and history of Bhutan in a way that helped me to understand what I saw and experienced in Bhutan. Also, this is basic knowledge to be able to understand the conversations I had and to understand gender and sustainability as it is in Bhutan.

Next to Buddhism, the pre-Buddhist religion also is of vital importance. This religion expresses itself through acknowledging and respecting the sacred landscape and the many deities who inhabit the earth, sky, lakes, and rivers.

Within Bhutanese Buddhism, many saints play an active and important role in shaping Bhutanese identity, and I will give a brief description of them. Although this matter is rather complex, I will give only a brief description of this area of history since it is not the main focus of this book.

Finally, I offer a description of the Tibetan creation myth based on Buddhism because a significant number of respondents referred to this myth. Bhutan does not have its own overall creation myth, although there are oral folk stories about the origin of the people.

Pre-Buddhist religion and sacred landscape

Bhutan has its own religion, which is a mixture of an ancient animistic belief and Buddhism. This old religion, from pre-Buddhist times (before the seventh century), survived and still plays an important role today. This animistic belief is referred to as pre-Buddhism. According to the pre-Buddhist traditional understanding, every rock and piece of earth belongs to a *shidag* (deity), a non-human owner of the earth. In this context, earth stands for the foundation of human existence in its entirety. (Schicklegruber, 1999; Karma Ura, 2001)

The landscape has been categorized in many ways. From the point of view of sharing the environment with deities and spirits, the most common concept about the structure of landscape and environment is a broad three-tier stratification. There are three layers: an extraterrestrial or heavenly level, an intermediate level, and a subterranean or underground level. At the extraterrestrial level live the *Lha,* at the terrestrial level the human beings, and at the subterranean level the *Lu* (also referred to as Mother Earth). These three levels of existing realms do not fit together neatly; they are a simplification of a more complex distinction. Besides these realms are a whole range of deities, such as the *zhi dags* (lords of territory), *sa dag* (lords of Earth) and *yulha* (deities of settlement). There also are the *duds* (spirits who live in rivers and creeks). (Karma Ura, 2001) Spirits and deities reside in lakes and meadows, inside houses, and in stoves. All these deities and spirits still are realities to the Bhutanese people today. In the village where I lived, these deities ordered the people in their daily lives in regard to what they should and should not do. (Crins & De Graaff, 1990) With the advent of Buddhism in the seventh century and the subsequent arrival of lamas from Tibet in the tenth and eleventh centuries, this old religion mixed with Tantric Buddhism to form the religious practices in Bhutanese society. The specialists in Buddhism are monks and lamas. In the pre-Buddhist local religions, they are called *Ngejums* and *Pawos*.

Ngejums, Pawos and Bon

Ngejums and *Pawos* function as mediums between the world of the gods and man. They are able to communicate with gods and spirits in order to avert and heal illnesses. The invocation of the deities consists of incense, harvest gifts, spirit liberation, and dough image offerings; sometimes even meat and blood offerings are made. These offerings are a synthesis of Buddhism, *Bon* (I will go deeper into the meaning of *Bon* later) and the local pre-Buddhist religion. The oracular mediums wear certain outfits and they become the mouthpiece of the deities they invoke. (Karma Ura, 2001) For example, a farmer whom I visited in Paro and who also is a *Pawo*, was the mouthpiece of the protective deity of that region. He wore a *zhidag gi ringa* (a five-petal crown) in which the five petals were the five goddesses of North, West, East, South, and Centre. He went into a trance by making poetic recitations while holding a small hand drum in one hand and a *drilbu tangti* (hand bell) in the other. The deity in question hears the sound and descends to the place of invocation in response to the invitation. In the village where I lived, my landlady was a *Ngejum*. She had a relationship with a female deity who responded to her invitation. She also was able to help the people in the village who had all kinds of problems, such as losing a cow in the forest. The *Ngejum* could help find the cow by reading rice. She could predict the future or answer questions by shaking the rice in a basket first and then reading it.

> 'The terms *Ngejum* and *Pawo* are possibly derived from the words *Ngejum* (In Sanskrit?: *Yogini*) and *Pawo* (In Sanskrit?: *Vira*). These pre-Buddhist rituals specialists are possessed by local deities and perform a variety of fertility and sickness rituals involving propitiating local divinities. While the majority of the monastic community is state-supported, the *Ngejum* and *Pawos* thrive on the patronage of local households in the village.' (Sonam Chuki, 1994:110–111)

This nature worship is what Westerners call Shamanism or *Bonism*. I do not want to use *Bon* as an overall term since I do not know if these rituals belong to *Bon*. Bhutanese people told me that *Bon* has its own ancient rules and there are rituals in Bhutan that are *Bon* rituals. In general, I will refer to the local pre-Buddhist religion, since every valley has its own deities and spirits. Next to *Bon*, these local pre-Buddhist religions still are in existence today. In the West, these *Ngejums* and *Pawos* are called Shamans, although this term is not correct (since there are many different kinds of mediums in Bhutan, to call them all shamans would not do them justice). Although a single definition of shamanism is complex, I will use the definition of Eliade: 'shamanism is a technique of ecstasy'. (1972:4) Eliade calls it his first definition, since the phenomenon is highly complex. However, I will use the term shamanism as a general term for mediums and esoteric practices that are non-Buddhist. *The Random House College Dictionary* (1984) defines a shaman as "a person who works with the supernatural as both priest and doctor." The definition for Shamanism, according to this dictionary, is 'the animistic religion of northern Asia, embracing a belief in powerful spirits who can be influenced only by shamans.' (1984:1208)

Not much has been written about shamanism in Bhutan. Here is a brief description of what Eliade says about the subject:

> 'The *pawo* and the *nyen-jomo* are mediums, male and female, regarded by the Buddhist as typical representatives of Bon. They are not connected with the Bon monasteries of Sikkim and Bhutan, and 'they seem to be a remnant of the earliest, unorganized Bon as it existed before the so called "White Bon" had developed after the example of Buddhism.' It appears that they can be possessed by the spirits of the death and, during their trance; enter in communication with their tutelary divinities. As for the Bon mediums, one of their chief functions is 'to serve as the temporary mouthpiece of spirits of the death, who had later to be conducted to the other world. The Bon shamans are believed to use their drums as vehicles to convey them through the air. The Bon shaman's cure includes seeking the patient's soul, a characteristically shaman technique.' (Eliade, 1972:432-433)

The *Bon* religion prevailed in Tibet without opposition until the advent of Buddhism. In Bhutan, the saying is, "Buddhism is for next life and *Bon* helps in this life." The shamanic aspect of the Tibetan religion often has been confused with the *bon* religion. *Bon* and *Bon-po* are similar in form and nature to the religious order of Tibetan Buddhism, but claim to derive from the teachings of the *Bon-po* master Shenrab Mibo, which dates from the seventh to the tenth century. This *Bon* religion has shamanic and clerical aspects similar to those of Tibetan Buddhism. (Samuel, 1993)

All the Indian missionaries (Buddhist Tantric priests), such as Guru Rinpoche, Atisha, and others had to engage themselves in the struggle with *Bon* priests so that their hold would be established. All the magical, mysterious Tantric, occult, and other pre-Buddhist exercises were, in fact, symptoms of religious feuds, in which Tantric Buddhism emerged victorious. Buddhism became the religion of the establishment, the regional overlords, and monastic establishment. *Bon* remained the faith of the masses. (Sinha, 2001) According to Sinha, *Bon* and Buddhism prospered and benefited from each other and, in spite of the sectarian feuds, fused with each other, although *Bon* has its own sacred texts and object, which are similar to Buddhism. *Bon* has an elaborate *sham-gyud* (oral tradition), one in which pre-Buddhist folk shamanistic rituals and practices still are followed. This process was reinforced further with the traditions of *terton* (rediscovered texts), along with the *Nyingmapa* sect of Mahayana Buddhism. These texts include *Bon*, Buddhist, astrological, and medical themes.

The Paro and Bumthang districts of Bhutan are known throughout the Tibetan Buddhist world for their "text" repositories, which came to light in the eleventh and twelfth centuries with the help of a number of holy men. (Aris, 1979) The national newspaper of Bhutan, *the Kuensel*, has reported regularly about rituals for protection and healings based on very old pre-Buddhist and *Bon* rituals. In daily life, many Bhutanese consult *Ngejums* and *Pawos* for sickness and safe journeys. These *Pawos* and *Ngejums* work with deities who take possession of their bodies in order for people to communicate through the medium with the deities. All the people I asked referred to these practice as *Bon*. According to Dorji Thinley,

> 'The *Bon* priests are believed to go into a trance, a psycho-physiological state said to be induced by the entry of a deity invoked through ritual offerings and *Bon* prayers. How so powerfully activated the priest's body is during this dreamy state depends not only on the enchantment caused by the deity but also on the priest's own motivation. Hence, the supposedly spiritual tremor is caused simultaneously by the deity's entry and the priest's own impulsion.' (Dorji Thinley, 2005:229)

Pommaret and Schickelgruber, two scholars who specialized on the subject of Bhutan, do not mention the name *Bon*. They give credence only to pre-Buddhists beliefs, animistic conceptions, and shamanistic practices.

Guru Rinpoche

One very important Buddhist saint is Guru Rinpoche, who came to Bhutan in the seventh century and brought Buddhism in its Tantric form. Guru Rinpoche also is known as Padmasambhava, Precious Master, and Ugyen Rinpoche. Padma is a Sanskrit word meaning lotus flower; sambhava refers to born from the lotus flower. He is a historical figure of the eighth century, and Sakyamuni, the historical Buddha, predicted his birth. He is regarded as the second Buddha and had miraculous powers, including the ability to subdue demons and evil spirits. (Armington, 2002)

Guru Rinpoche was a Tantric master from the Swat valley, now known as Pakistan. He is credited with many magical deeds and is regarded as the founder of Nyingmapa Buddhism, also known as the old school. He is one of the most important of Bhutan's religious figures and his visit to Bumthang is recognized as the true introduction of Buddhism to Bhutan. He left an impression of his body on the rock upon which he meditated near the Choskhor valley in Bumthang. There are many places in Bhutan where it is believed Guru meditated and subdued demons. Guru Rinpoche traveled throughout Tibet, Nepal, and Bhutan, manifesting in different guises. He preserved his teachings and wisdom by concealing them in forms of *terma* (hidden treasures) to be found by *tertons* (enlightened treasure discoverers). These *terma* consist of hidden texts, statues of Buddhas, or other religious artifacts related to the Dharma (Armington, 2002). His famous consort was Kandro Yeshe Tsogyal.

Bhutan's state religion is Drukpa Kargyupa Buddhism in its Tantric form. This Buddhist school was established by Buddhist saints such as Milarepa and Marpa in the tenth and eleventh centuries. (Yonten Dargye, 2001)

According to Allen (2000), *Tantra* (Sanskrit) or *Vajrayana* (Tibetan) – also known as the diamond vehicle – is a form of esoteric Buddhism developed from Mahayana Buddhism. *Tantra* drew its philosophy from mainstream Mahayana Buddhism (400 BC) and developed a complex system of rituals, mantras, and *mudras* (hand gestures). *Tantra* focuses on existential problems and emphasizes the use of meditation under the direction of an initiated teacher as a means of achieving enlightenment. Unlike the Mahayana tradition, which attaches most importance to the theoretical aspects of Buddhism, *Tantra* tradition portrays Buddhism as part of the individual. Yogic and meditative methods are used to bring about a complete transformation of practitioners. Female energies and goddesses are worshipped, and demons exert powerful influences. *Tantra* students must be accepted by a recognized teacher and must undergo a long process of initiations and training. The emphasis is to understand compassion through a process of meditation. (Allen 2000, Samuel 1993)

In the study of Tibetan Buddhism, many complexities are resolved by distinguishing between two general complementary components of religious life: the monastic (clerical) and the yogic (shamanic). (Samuel, 1993) The monastic aspects of Tibetan and in this case Bhutanese society are more concerned with the institutional life in which discipline, conduct, education, and power are governed by the monastic disciplinary code and by goals rather than by enlightenment. In contrast, the yogic dimension places its emphasis upon spiritual and societal transformation through yogic practice, relying on views of reality rather than prevailing conventional norms. The yogic dimension also includes many folk elements with pragmatic ends other than enlightenment. In its folk dimension, yogic Buddhism may wish to transform conventional circumstances by extending life, attracting wealth, or averting disaster; or it may seek only the ultimate transformation: enlightenment. It employs a variety of ritual and visionary methods, but its power rests upon direct perception of the nature of mind and reality, which is said in Tibet and Bhutan to be the essence of the Buddha's experience of enlightenment. Monastic Buddhism shares the ultimate goals of enlightenment with yogic Buddhism, but it has other goals, more related to monastic disciplinary codes and the continuity of monastic lineages and education. In Monastic Buddhism, greater emphasis is placed on the gradual path based upon purifying one's karma through accumulation of merit, renouncing virtueless actions, scholastic mastery of texts, debate, and preserving monastic traditions. (Simmer-Brown, 2001; Samuel, 1993) The above delineates, in brief, the essence of Bhutanese society with regard to religion and the relationship between Buddhism, the pre-Buddhist religion, and shamanic aspects.

Nyingmapa

Guru Rinpoche was the founder of the Nyingmapa Buddhist School in the seventh century.

'The Nyingmapa or the 'old school' also is known in the Tibetan world as the red hat sect. It has a loosely constituted hierarchy. This sect also has the unique claim of having maintained its teachings intact ever since they were introduced into a monarchical phase of Tibetan history. This unbroken continuity was achieved in three ways: "by direct transmission of doctrinal text (known as *bka-ma*) from the time of the founder, Padmasambhava; by the rediscovery of text hidden by Padmasambhava (*terma*); and by direct revelation (*dag-snang*) that can perhaps be regarded as another form of *terma*.' (Sinha, 2001:45)

> 'The Nyingmapa were so closely associated with everyday life of the people in their capacity as married Tantric Priests that when rivalries arose it was easy to charge them with being bogus. The strength of their arguments, together with the pervasive practical role of the Nyingmapa in the village and the fact that they never ceased producing saintly figures, are some of the reasons for their continuing survival. The Nyingmapa never wielded concerted temporal power and this was ultimately a source of strength rather than weakness. They remained defused, popular and wholly credible, even if on occasions not entirely respectable.' (Aris, 1979:152)

Another important fact for Bhutan's folk religion is that *pawos* and *ngejums* and other mediums worked together with Buddhist lamas and monks and were not rivals of each other. There are some sub-sects within the Nyingmapa relevant to Bhutan. After the assassination of King Langdarma in Tibet in the year 838, Buddhism in Tibet was persecuted for a long time; many Buddhist monks and lamas took refuge in the Bumthang area in central Bhutan.

Bhutanese saints

One important figure in the fourteenth century was Longchen Rabjampa Drime Özer. He belonged to the important Nyingmapa schools of *Dzogchen* (the School of great perfection), and was one of the greatest scholars of that time. Because of his intellectual and spiritual achievements, Longchen Rabjampa's contribution to the vitality of the Nyingmapa School in central Bhutan was very significant. He also founded several temples. The descendants of great religious figures came to constitute religious nobility known as *Chöjes*. Another important figure was Dorje Lingpa (1346–1405); he was a *terton* (or treasure revealer) and his main field of activity was Bumthang in central Bhutan. Later, his lineage played an important role in central Bumthang. He established several temples in Bhutan. Through their religious prestige, these families were able to assume some temporal power at the local level. These families of religious descent became the local nobility. Pema Lingpa (1450–1521), the most important Bhutanese *terton,* was the first Bhutanese-born religious figure to achieve real fame in the entire Tibetan Buddhist world, and the role he played for his descendants was crucial in the sociopolitical context of Bhutan. The King of Bhutan is a descendant of Pema Lingpa. He became very famous as discoverer of a *terma* in the "burning lake" in Bumthang. (Pommaret, 1999; Yonten Dargye, 2001)

From clans to country

The history of Bhutan is wrapped deeply in the mystery of the past. Bhutan's history is based on an oral tradition, and the Mahayana Buddhist society itself provides a number of ambiguities. Mahayana Buddhism is an unusual mixture of Buddhism, animism, mysticism, Tantric cult, and a battery of practices known as *Bon*. In such situations, historical persons are frequently and intricately linked with supernatural beings, merging themselves into the realm of mystique and sacred. With the establishment of theocracy in the seventeenth century, the clan organizations lost their relevance. Nomadism and migration accelerated this further. The clan and family genealogy was

replaced by an intricate series of reincarnations, in which claims and counter-claims are difficult to sort out. To understand the history of Bhutan, one needs imagination and to be open to spiritual significance. Almost every rock, river, valley, and place contains deities and has stories attached to them (see above), or are places where important events happened that shaped the history of the country. (Karma Ura, 2003; Sinha, 2001; Schicklgruber, 1999)

Buddhism in Bhutan is complicated. It therefore is necessary to outline the different Buddhist schools and pre-Buddhism, which shaped the culture and value system of the country. Tantric Buddhism assimilated the ritual practices, shamanistic devices, and the lore of pre-Buddhist Tibetan religion within its folds – so much so that Tibetan Buddhism took an entirely different form. In the course of time, various monks, reformers, and mystics made a number of innovations as part of their training. They also established a chain of monasteries all over the Tibetan Buddhist world, and an intricate process of reincarnations evolved. The monasteries turned out to be not only the centers of ritual and religious offerings, knowledge, and learning; they also came to be the core of material wealth. Nobility, aristocracy, and commoners supported the monasteries, where a large number of monks and nuns were engaged constantly in religious discourse, debates, production of sacred literature, and other types of sacred performances. Many sects and sub-sects could emerge and were patronized by regional warlords. These sects and religious pantheons were engaged in feuds, wars, and conflicts, not infrequently among themselves. However, by the turn of the twelfth century, all the countries on the cultural map of Tibet had adopted Mahayana Buddhism. Of the entire area which was once the spiritual domain of Tibetan culture and religion, stretching from Ladakh in the west to the borders of Sichuan and Yunnan (China) in the east, from the Himalayas in the south to the Mongolian steppes in the north, only Bhutan seems to survive now as the one resolute and self- contained representative of a fast disappearing civilization. (Sinha, 2001)

According to Karma Ura (2003), a Bhutanese scholar, non-Bhutanese historians assume that the history of Bhutan began only in the middle of the eighth century with the coming of Guru Rinpoche (Padmasambhava). The point of the foreigners was that ethnographic and archaeological research that could expand Bhutan's history still is scant. The account of the coming of Guru Rinpoche, on the invitation of *Sindhuraja* (king) of Bumthang, was recorded some seven hundred years later by *terton* Pema Lingpa (1450–1541). (Karma Ura 2003)

Karma Ura points out that the history of Bhutan was written through the prism of religion and *ter* (hidden and rediscovered text) literature by great lamas such as Pema Lingpa, Tsang Khenchen (1638), Lord Abbot Ngawang Lhundrub, and others. Bhutanese lamas who wrote biographies and other books emphasized a particular point in history if it pertained to religion, and helped record religious strivings or spiritual successes. The record of lineages, either through reincarnations or hereditary succession, became the basis of many biographies and history books. Karma Ura concludes that the historical consciousness of the early period is quite inseparable from Bhutanese religious consciousness. But there is insufficient information concerning the ordinary people in such genealogies, royal chronicles, and biographies. More accessible information about normal life is contained in the accounts left by British expeditions, the earliest of which was led by George Bogle in 1773. (Karma Ura, 2003)

The Drukpa School

In Bhutan the various sects also competed with each other for power. Out of such sectarian wars, feuds, and conflicts, the *Drukpa* theocracy emerged as the national religion and distinct polity of Bhutan:

'Lama Tsangpa Gyarey Yeshe Dorji (1161–1211) discovered a number of esoteric doctrines (*terma*) and founded the monastery of Druk in Tibet in 1189. It is claimed that while the monastery was being consecrated, the "thunder dragon" (the *druk*) resounded from the sky. That is how the monastery as well as its followers came to be known as Druk and Drukpa respectively. [...] Unlike the hermits of some of the other schools, the Drukpa monks developed a tradition of humility, lack of sectarian dissension, and scholastic orientation. Three distinct branches of (*Bar-druk* the middle; *sTod-druk* the upper; and *sMad-druk* the lower) schools emerged from three main disciples of the founder: Yeshe Dorji, its main monastery remaining at Ralung, Tibet, under the control of the Prince abbots, though the school had a network of such establishments in the Mount Kailash region, southern Tibet and Bhutan. All three sub-sects of the Drukpa School started their activities in Bhutan.' (Sinha, 2001:52)

According to Pommaret (1999), 'Phajo Drukgom Shigpo (1184–1251) is one of the most important figures in the history of Bhutan. Phajo introduced the Drukpa Kargyupa School. Its political influence increased as Phajo's descendants gave rise to religious nobility. Since these families carried out temporal as well spiritual duties, they became the most powerful entities in Western Bhutan. In the thirteenth century, four sons of Phajo Drukgom Shigpo settled in the four valleys of Western Bhutan to propagate the Drukpa teachings.' (Pommaret, 1999:184)

Shabdrung Ngawang Namgyel [1]

Another important Bhutanese figure from the Drukpa School was Shabdrung Ngawang Namgyal (1594–1651), the unifier of Bhutan. Shabdrung, "upon whose feet one submits," and the founder of Bhutan as it is today. By the sixteenth century, the political arena still was fragmented between many local chiefs and ruling clans, each controlling his own territory or, as Sinha puts it, 'Shabdrung Ngawang Namgyal turned a frontier community into a vigorous and organized nation'.(Sinha, 2001:54) The Shabdrung (considered an emanation of the Buddha of compassion) was born in Tibet into a family of Prince Abbots. He was installed as the eighteenth Prince Abbot of the Drukpa monastery at Ralung in Tibet in 1606, his grandfather being the highest patriarch of the sect. Ngawang Namgyel engaged in theological and succession disputes in Tibet and was forced to exile himself in Bhutan at the age of twenty-three in 1616. (Incidentally, his father already had been installed as an influential monk house-holder (Abbot) in Bhutan.) But his distracters did not leave him in peace, even in exile. He had to overcome a series of Tibetan invasions in which he displayed strategic planning, leadership in the campaign, and skill in the

---

1   See also Armington, 2002; Sinha, 2001; Karma Ura, 2003; Pommaret, 1999.

aftermath of the conflicts as negotiator of the peace treaties. As a monk-ruler, he built many *dzongs* as strategic forts as well as monastic enclaves. By this time, he had taken a consort who gave him an invalid child.

Shabdrung was a competent war hero and he fought back Tibetan invasions many times. Shabdrung gave Bhutan its own cultural and religious identity, differing from Tibet. He devised many of Bhutan's customs, traditions, and ceremonies. As a revered Buddhist scholar, he had both the astuteness and authority to codify the Kargyu religious teachings into a system that was distinctively Bhutanese. He also defined the Bhutanese dress and *Tsechu* festival (religious folk festivals held on auspicious days in a year). He created a code of laws defining the relationship between the lay people and the monastic community. 'All aspects of social life were regulated by this Code of Laws, which was in use until recently: inheritance, trade, crime and punishment, behaviour of monks and officials, and how lay people have to behave'. (Pommaret, 1999:198-200) One part of this Code of Law laid out by the Shabdrung is *driglam namzha* (a code of conduct*)* that I mentioned in chapter 3. *Driglam namzha* is, according to Karma Phuntsho, not a religious concept but a traditional concept. *Drig* denotes order, conformity, and uniformity. Thus, *driglam* literally means the way or path (*lam*), while *namzha* refers to concept or system. *Driglam namzha* thus is a system of ordered and cultural behaviour, and by extension, the standards and rules to this effect. *Driglam namzha* is not concerned as much with moral or ethical dos and don'ts, rights or wrongs. It deals with more mundane issues of physical and verbal compartments determined as crude or courteous by the specific social and cultural contexts.(Karma Phuntsho, 2004)

Although good manners in the Bhutanese context embody to a great extent Buddhist codes of physical, verbal, and mental conducts that dictate what is proper and wholesome. In particular, the codes of practice, which Shabdrung Ngawang Namgyel introduced to the central monk community and in other monastic and administrative centers, are based largely on the code of etiquette known among Tibetan Buddhist clergy and elites. A system of taxes also was developed: these were paid in kind in the form of wheat, meat, butter, paper, timber, and textile. The people were subject to a system of compulsory labour for the construction of trails, *dzongs,* and temples. (Karma Phuntsho, 2004)

In the 1640s, the Shabdrung created the system of *Choesi,* the separation of the administration of the country into two offices, with the Shabdrung handling the religious and spiritual aspects of the country. Political, administrative, and foreign affairs were handled by the *desi,* the secular ruler, who was elected to the post. Theoretically, the office of the Shabdrung had greater power, including the authority to sign documents relating to important matters within the government. Under the system at that time, the Shabdrung was the spiritual ruler and the *Je Kempo* (chief Abbot) and official head of the monastic establishment. The *Je Kempo* had an equal status to the *desi* and sometimes held that office. The first *desi* who came with the first Shabdrung from the Ralung monastery established an administrative system throughout the country. He formalized the position of *penlop* (provincial governor) in three districts: Trongsa, Punakha, and Dagana. The Shabdrung went into retreat in Punakha Dzong in 1651. He did not emerge again, and his death remained hidden until 1705. When the *Je Khempo* finally announced the death of the Shabdrung, he said that three rays of light had emanated from the Shabdrung's body, representing the *Ku, Sung,* and *Thug* (body, speech, and mind) of Ngawang Namgyel. This indicated that the Shabdrung would be reincarnated in these three forms, though only the incarnation of his mind was considered to be the head of state. Since the position of Shabdrung was one that continued, it was necessary for the mind incarnation to be reborn after the death of the previous incarnation. This structure resulted in a long period during which the Shabdrung was too young to rule, and therefore the *desi* often became the de facto ruler. Because the *desi* was an elected position, there was considerable rivalry among various factions for this office. These factions also took advantage of uncertainty over which of the three incarnations of the Shabdrung was the "true" incarnation. None of the successive incarnations had the personal charisma or political astuteness of Ngawang Namgyel. This all led to internal instabilities, and the next two hundred years were times of civil war, which resulted in the installation of the hereditary monarchy of the Wangchuck (Pommaret, 1999; Sinha, 2001).

The Wangchuck Monarchy

'Shabdrung Ngawang Namgyel and his successors consolidated the Drukpa theocratic regime from the seventeenth century onward for about three hundred years through an intricate process of statecraft. They devised a process in which religious and secular affairs and personnel were intertwined in such a way that the mystic of Dragon policy was accepted universally. Destiny often was in the hands of feuding incarnates and oligarchic functionaries. Perhaps this chaotic system would have continued indefinitely had not the internal and external social forces of Bhutan changed dramatically by the end of the nineteenth century. After nine decades since its establishment in 1907, the Wangchuck monarchy has become a firmly ingrained and most important political institution in Bhutan'. (Sinha, 2001:73)

After the death of the Shabdrung, Bhutan experienced a bleak period not dissimilar to civil war, because his first three secular successors all lacked his spirituality. Old ruling families from the pre-Shabdrung period attempted to seize power again. They often used war-like tactics and many of the monks served them in a less than spiritual way to assert their claims to power. Bhutan came into a dark, warlike period and the farmers suffered a great deal because of the high taxes they had to pay. This lasted until the second half of the nineteenth century, until the *penlop* of Trongsa, Jigme Namgyel (1825–1881), became the most influential man in Bhutan. He became the fiftieth *Druk desi* (secular ruler*)*. He consolidated his position through wars, clever alliances, and by installing relatives and trusted people in key positions. He was a direct descendant of Pema Lingpa, who was perceived to be a reincarnation of Guru Rinpoche. Alongside these descendancies, another deity of Shabdrung Nawang Namgyel, the founder of the nation, came into play, namely Mahakala. The 'Raven Crown" (a crown like a helmet with a raven head on top) is the national symbol of the monarchy of Bhutan. The Raven Crown was the external symbol of the role of the Mahakala. The manifestation of the Mahakala, with the head of the Raven *legön,* Jaro Dongchen represented proof of existence. The wearer of this raven crown was assured of the protection of the fearful deity Mahakala. The son of Jigme Namgyel, Ugyen Wangchuck (1862–1926), consolidated the work of his father and became the first hereditary king of Bhutan in 1907. In this year, members of the clergy and the council of State, local rulers, and representatives of the village communities gathered together in the Punakha Dzong, where Ugyen Wangchuck took the oath of office. The second king consolidated the monarchy. He named the religious head of Bhutan the *Je Kempo* (chief Abbot). He ruled with a central Cabinet composed of four civil servants, and pared down the influence of the *dzonpöns*. In principle, he carried out a reduction of the official apparatus in order to strengthen the power of the monarchy. The third king, Jigme Dorje Wangchuck (1928–72), was the father of modern Bhutan; he started to open up the country and started the modernization of the country by building roads and other infrastructure. (Schicklgruber, 1999; Pommaret, 1999:233)

Nowadays, instead of having regional chiefs (*penlops)* and fort governors (*dzong-pens*), the country has been divided into 20 districts and 196 development blocks (*gewogs).* The administration is run from a central secretariat manned by bureaucrats elected and promoted by the Royal Civil Service Commission under the control of a council of ministers elected by The National Assembly and approved by the *Druk Gyalpo* (Dragon King). Today, King Jigme Singye Wangchuck is the fourth king of Bhutan; he is head of state but no longer head of government. He surrendered part of his sovereignty in favor of the *Tsongdu* (The National Assembly) in July 1998. Now the *Tsongdu* elects the council of ministers to rule the state and even can remove the King by a two-thirds vote.

Today, the king leads a simple life; he travels through the country, meeting people and listening to their problems and wishes. The king is married to four sisters and these four queens are active in supporting him in all kinds of duties. The king is regarded as a righteous ruler, a *bodhisattva* (an enlightened being who, out of compassion, foregoes nirvana in order to aid others), and the protector of the religion. Because Bhutan used to be a theocracy, each king sought legitimacy from the *sangha*. In return, he offered to support their religion. Within Bhutanese Buddhism, even if one reaches enlightenment, the enlightened person will not go into Nirvana but will come back as a *bodhisattva* to help all other sentient beings reach enlightenment. Important people in Bhutan, such as the King, are regarded as *Bodhisattva.*

The Tibetan creation myth

It has been told that Tibet was a land first covered by a large sea, and as the sea receded, it became populated by what is known in Tibet as "non-humans," beings who, according to Buddhist cosmology, belong to the realms of animals and hungry ghost and ogres, wild and ferocious beings who constantly were at war with each other and who destroyed any trace of goodness. Avalokiteschvara, being the emanation of the Compassion of all the Buddhas, saw that it was time to tame these beings and open this vast wilderness to the blessings of the Dharma (the Buddhist teachings, or path).

Having been told by the Buddha himself that he was the One to take care of this land, Avalokiteschvara manifested as a monkey in the jungles of the vast land and took a female companion, an ogress who herself was an emanation of the compassionate Tara (the embodiment of feminine compassion born from the tears of Avalokiteschvara). From this union were born six children, each representing a being from each of the six realms of Samsara (the circle of birth and rebirth). As the waters receded and the land became covered by virgin forest and high mountains, these six children multiplied among themselves and are said to be the ancestors of the six clans of Tibet. Sometimes sources claim they founded four clans, with the monkey-father and the ogress-mother forming two lineages. Those from the father's lineage are virtuous, patient, faithful, and compassionate. Those from the mother-ogress lineage are lustful, angry, greedy, competitive, courageous, active, those whose minds suffer from excess of the five poisons: greed, hatred, ignorance, jealousy, and pride. (Sources: Penjor Rimpoche, 2002; Sonam Gyaltsen, 1996)

Summary of the 56 conversations on religion

Religion, according to the Bhutanese respondents

In this part, I summarize the answers given to the questions related to religious issues I asked during our conversations. I was very curious what religion means to the people I had conversations with, and whether men and women had different views toward religion. In chapter 2, I work out some of the conversations completely.

During my visits in Bhutan, I was amazed about the devotion of the people, but also the fact that Buddhist worldview is very different from my Christian upbringing and worldview. Just the fact that in Buddhism there is no creator made me very curious how the Bhutanese respondents see creation and also, for example, the creation of nature.

In my conversations, I included a list of thirteen questions about religion. I asked the respondents[2]1 what role religion plays in their lives and what religion means to them.

Of all the respondents, one man is Hindu and one woman is a Christian, whilst all others are Buddhist. The majority of the respondents belong to the Drukpa Kargyupa Buddhist School. The two nuns and two lamas I talked to belong to the Nyingmapa Buddhist School. These different schools are not strictly separated, and in both schools the same saints are worshiped. In the Nyingmapa and Kargyupa Schools, religious practitioners are free to marry if they have not taken the vow of celibacy. One lama respondent told me that if a person has reached a high level of spiritual awareness or was born with this high spiritual consciousness, he or she would dream about his future partner, just as Guru Rinpoche dreamt of his consort Khandro Yeshe Tsogyal, who is a role model to many Bhutanese women.

Religion is very important to all respondents, men and women alike; it is seen as guidance for life, and is regarded as a teacher. Many saints, such as Guru Rinpoche and Pema Lingpa, still play an important role in the daily life of the respondents. These saints are called on in times of trouble and sickness, and are seen as role models.

Religion also is seen as a method of reaching enlightenment; in fact, to many respondents, this is the main meaning of religion. Religion also is knowledge, and the identity of Bhutan. For some respondents, it is seen as beneficial for

---

2   I use both the terms respondents and conversation partners (having the same meaning) in this chapter and the coming two chapters, because the term conversatietoon partners is too long for the fluidity of the tekst.

people. For others, religion is a binding force that connects everything. It creates peace in society, and for some respondents, it is a way of life. For some, religion is seen as natural and as something that always is there. Sometimes it is referred to as *Konchog sum* (triple gem, namely Buddha, Sanga (clerus) and the Teachings of the Buddha).

Karma and incarnation are very important concepts in the life of the Bhutanese. Everything is related and connected due to *karma* and incarnation. This reflects the answers people give to many questions about life, the meaning of life and creation. Altruism and doing good to others is in relation to *karma* very important to most respondents. Doing good and helping others is a way to reach a better incarnation in the next life. This vision of religion is identical for men and women I interviewed.

I also studied the differences in answer patterns between man and woman. All men were happy to be a man. To some, this was due to their fortunate incarnation that they were born as a man; they had been good in previous lives and this resulted in the fact that they had been born as a Bhutanese man. Other men were happy because of their physicality; they had less pain than women because of their physical bodies, or they regarded themselves as more religious (because they can be monks and dedicate their life to religious studies). To some men, it meant more freedom; a man can do what he wants, has more freedom than women, and more possibilities. Another answer was that men can help others more. One young man said to me: 'To be a man means that I have been reborn 80,000 times; this means that I have a big responsibility in this life to be a good person.'

From the women: four of the 26 women were not happy because of their incarnation as a woman. One woman was not happy because of her poverty, another woman because of her sickness. One woman would like to have a better job, and one said she 'had no choice in being a woman.'

In relation to the previous question, I wanted to know who or what an ideal woman or man was. The women gave answers such as: "A woman who is strong and independent." "A woman helps others." "Kandroma (Dakini) or a female holy person is an ideal woman." "An ideal woman is a woman in the city with a career who can balance career and marriage." Other single answers were: "A woman in a high position," "a beautiful woman," "all women," "a free and single woman," "a mother."

When I asked the men the same question they replied, "an ideal man is a man who is honest and good," "a man who helps others," or is "the King of Bhutan." "Religious men" are ideal or "a man with a lot of knowledge," "a polite man," or "a man with status and power."

About Creator, Creation, and creation myth. In regard to the meaning of religion, I was curious as to how my conversation partners understood the term creator. Besides, I wanted to know what the answers would be to the question: "How do you imagine your creator?" although in Buddhism there is no such concept. To phrase the question about the creator in a different way, I asked: "Where do people come from?" With regard to the question about the creator, I also wanted to know if there were creation myths.

To the first question, the answers were quite diverse. For one respondent, a man who is Hindu, the creator is Krishna, and for the Christian lady, the creator is not imaginable but it is great and powerful. To the majority of the Buddhists, a creator is seen as the Buddha, something mysterious, a powerful saint, father, and mother, an omnipresent force, and seven respondents regard the creator as *karma* and incarnation. Seven respondents did not know an answer to the question, and three said that there was no creator. Two respondents said "I am my own creator," or it is *karma*. A minority of respondents referred to God as creator.

All respondents, men and women, saw God as a genderless mystical force. I asked what God means to the respondents, and the answers were very diverse. Most respondents, men and women, said, "a mystical force that takes care of you." Other answers were: "it is in ourselves," "powerful and invisible," "deities," "enlightenment," "everything," "the life giver," "like mum and dad," "giving peace," and something "omnipresent," nature. A common belief for people is that *karma* and incarnation are the source of creation. Due to *karma* and reincarnation, one becomes human. This also was a common answer. Some respondents referred to the myth of the Monkey God as the origin of humans. The Monkey God was a popular answer and refers to the Tibetan creation myth as delineated below. *Karma* and incarnation also was a frequent answer. One farmer gave a practical answer by referring to the male sexual organ as the creator of humans. Those with more education gave scientific evolution as the explanation for the existence of humans. One studied lama gave cause and condition as answer: "When the cause meets the right condition."

Another question was: "Do all respondents perform *pujas* (rituals/prayers) and do both women and men perform *pujas*?" To all respondents, performing *pujas* is very important in maintaining good luck and harmony with the deities, and many have an altar room at home with many different Buddhas and Saints, such as Guru Rinpoche and Shabdrung. Local deities are worshiped just as the Buddhist saints. This is much in line with the sacred landscape as delineated above and the awareness that deities are all around and have to be respected and worshipped. This pre-Buddhism is just as important as Buddhism, although there is a difference in attitude toward visiting a *ngejum* or *pawo*. Of all the respondents, half do not consul a *pawo* or *ngejums*, the main reason being that *pawo* and *ngejum* are regarded as not being Buddhist but as belonging to the *Bon* religion. The ones who do not visit these shamans are monks or nuns, or those with a higher education. One respondent said that *Bon* is beneficial for this life and Buddhism for the next life. One respondent was a *pawo* himself. He is the mouthpiece of Ab Chuzum, the protective deity of Paro valley. He is an old man and the villagers consult him for different problems, such as sickness and for safe travel. He became a *pawo* when he was young, in his twenties, after he had suffered from a mental disease. After he had been cured, he realized he had the gift of healing by communicating with his personal deity, Ab Chuzum.

Although pre-Buddhism, *Bon,* and Buddhism are intertwined, it is interesting that some respondents were different as they did not consult *pawos* or *ngejums.* In most Buddhist *lhakang*s (temples), there also are shrines for the local (pre-Buddhist) deity. There are beautiful small special shrines for the water and earth goddess, *Lu*, who some Bhutanese call Mother Earth. Every Buddhist Bhutanese has a special relationship with the deity that belongs to the house where the person was born, one respondent told me. I also asked the respondents about the gender of all the deities and all the answers were that there are male and female deities.

I asked all the respondents whether they ever had any aspirations to become a nun or a monk. I interviewed two nuns and four monks. Twenty-two respondents thought about becoming a nun or a monk. It is mostly women who once in their life had the desire to become a nun, but could not do it for several reasons. The reason why they had wanted become a nun was that as a nun you could live a "clean" spiritual life and work toward enlightenment. As a lay person, one has too many attachments. Some female respondents still have the desire to become a nun when they are older, to create a better *karma* for their next life.

In Bhutan, there are many monks, many of whom are supported by the state, but there are only a small number of nuns and nunneries, although a large number of women among my respondents had had or still have wishes to become a nun. I asked all the respondents why this was. Most answers given were that for men it was compulsory to become a monk, or at least for one male from each household. This was good *karma* for the family. Women were free to choose, and in most cases women inherited the family property. Also there were answers such as: "women have more attachments for the reason they can have babies." Some respondents regard men as more religious than women because of the physical build of women. Two respondents said it was a rule made by the Shabdrung that men had to become monks. All the respondents said men and women could reach enlightenment. Some respondents (with little or no education) and nuns said that a woman has to be born nine times to become a man, and it is much easier for a man to reach enlightenment.

Meditation and prayer is an overall goal for the people in Bhutan. Respondents, in particular those older than thirty-five, aspire to the idea of praying and meditating more in the future. For them, it is an important preparation for the moment of death. It is very important to die in a proper spiritual way. The *Bardo* (death rituals) are time consuming and elaborate and date back to the times of Guru Rinpoche. To do the rituals in a proper way is important for a better incarnation in the following life. There are lamas, but also lay people, who meditate for three years three months three weeks and three days. There are many caves in Bumthang, central Bhutan, and other places where lamas, monks, nuns, and lay people meditate. One young woman said to me: "if I had a lot of money, I would buy my parents a monastery, where they can meditate and prepare for their next life."

To all the respondent men and women, religion is very important in their lives and religion gives the respondent a Bhutanese identity. For the people who had higher English medium education (four men), religion has a different meaning: it is "just a belief." For the other conversation partners (men and women), it means traditions and philosophy to guide the country.

The doctrine of *karma* and incarnation is very important to all the respondents, as is being a "good" person, as said before. But I wanted to know what qualities a "good" person has; in other words: "what is a good person?" To the respondents, a "good" person is a person who is compassionate, which is an important Buddhist concept. Next to compassion, being "helpful," "trustworthy," "generous," "kind," "religious," "humble," and "polite"' were the main answers. Another answer is, "a good person does not gossip." Gossiping can be an issue in a small community, as there are many such communities in Bhutan. Finally, I asked the respondents about *Driglam Namzha*: How important was *driglam namza* to them? *Driglam Namzha* is very important to all respondents. It is seen as a true Bhutanese concept that guides people through life and shows them how to behave in relation to other people. *Driglam Namzha* is important in daily interaction with other Bhutanese. It starts with the proper greeting, drinking tea, talking, eating, sitting properly, and so on. Bhutanese society is a hierarchical society. So, one needs to know one's place and the right conduct to use when dealing with people in superior standing.

Reflection

In 1990, in the village, I had my first encounter with this deep religious country where everything was different than in my Western world. At first I could not understand the religion and it was a total blur to me: so many deities, Gods, and Buddhas, so many do's and don'ts. After being in the village, I started to study Tibetan Buddhism just to be able to understand what I experienced in the village. During my later encounters with Bhutan, I realized that history and religion play a very important part in the daily life of the people, and to be able to understand Bhutanese culture and to interact properly with the Bhutanese "other," it helps very much to have a basic knowledge of the religion and history of the country. Many age old concepts still play an important role today as many Saints from the past do for the people of Bhutan.

For example: once I visited *The Centre for Bhutan Studies* in Thimphu with my translator. I was invited to have lunch with the staff of the Centre. I asked my translator, "please come and join me with having lunch." She replied: "This is not possible." I asked: "Why?" She replied: "It is *Driglam Namzha*." She meant that due to the proper etiquette, she was of lower rank and thus not supposed to eat with us.

Later, I realized in many encounters with Bhutanese people that they are much more at ease with me, because I know some of the etiquette and I understand certain jokes and stories related to historic and religious figures and happenings.

For me, coming from a Western country, it was as if I had landed in a fairy tale. Especially my time in the village was sometimes very surrealistic. All the do's and don'ts! All the deities in the air, fire, rocks, trees, and earth!

My landlady was a very religious person and she was a medium/healer. Because of that, and because of all the magic around me, I tried to build a wall around me not to be affected by it, because it was too much for me to comprehend. Bhutan's landscape, its forests, its buildings like houses, temples, and chortens is like a fairy tale. Many houses have huge phallusses painted on them, and on every corner of the roof hangs a phallus as protection against evil. For someone from the West, this is very strange to see those male body parts painted in every detail on a wall from a house. But for the Bhutanese, it was a protection coming from a saint called Drukpa Kunley, who could chase away evil spirits with his divine phallus. Other important saints are Pema Lingpa and Shabdrung Ngawang Namgyel. The King of Bhutan is regarded as the incarnation of Pema Lingpa (he also is regarded as a boddhisatva) and Shabdrung is the founder of the country now known as Bhutan and the Bhutanese identity. In general, the upper classes of Bhutan claim to be descendants or incarnations of important religious figures from the past. Many of the old traditions, dating back to the times of Guru Rinpoche and Shabdrung Ngawang Namgyel, still are flourishing and have remained part of daily life until today. *Driglam namzha* is an example of this.

Driglam Namzha still is important in daily life. Almost all interaction between people is guided by *Driglam Namzha,* although this interaction is not rigid or stiff. My experience is that, interestingly, the first encounter with superior people is very formal, but after the sharing of formalities, the sphere becomes informal and warm. There even is a department for the enforcement of *Driglam Namzha* within the government of Bhutan. *Driglam Namzha* also dictates the national dress for all Bhutanese to wear in formal situations, such as work or festivals. In the 1980s, a growing concern about the decline of Bhutanese customs and the need to strengthen *Driglam Namzha* culminated in a royal decree. These years marked the beginning of a systematic promotion of *Driglam Namzha*, particularly by the enforcement of national dress, *Gho* and *Kira*. Within the upper strata of Bhutanese society, there is concern for traditional values and customs to be maintained since the development and modernization process and Western influence has increased. Ironically, it is this group, trained in foreign countries and who are the least familiar with the *Driglam Namzha*, who urge the maintenance of it. To the people in the rural areas, it always has been their way of life. Changes that I noticed in the last 17 years of my visits to Bhutan in regard to religion is that people told me that their *chokus* (rituals) are not so extended as they used to be. For example, a yearly house *choku* could last for several days, with many monks to perform the prayers and many people invited to eat and drink. Nowadays, this *choku* only will be one day or even less, with fewer guests and fewer monks.

Since my first stay, I learned a lot about the religion and history of Bhutan. I got used to the fairy tale of Bhutan and learned to look beyond the fairy tale:

there is a real country with a lot of magic in its daily life, even today in the twenty-first century.

Reflecting on religion in Bhutan, I have to be self-critical and ask if I have not lost my foothold in my European post-rational positive way of thinking. Because I do not have a religion anymore (I was raised as a Catholic, but that is a very different story), I have to address the relationship between religion, gender, and sustainability. As we have seen in this chapter, religion in Bhutan is on top of the world. Religion is the place where everything is constructed. As I am walking on the bridges of religion, gender, and sustainability, the bridges are connected to the place I am coming from – but do they bring me to the place I want to go? The place I came from had a very natural distinction of the topics of religion, gender, and sustainability. In my world, these three categories are separated and exist next to each other. They do not form a holistic system.

Coming back to the answers the respondents gave about religion, we can see that, for the Bhutanese, religion is a total cosmology. So, can we conclude from the answers that religion is as omnipresent as nature? Does this mean that religion is nature? And what does this mean for the gender relations and sustainability as Western categories? This is so different than my Western perspective.

In the next chapter, I will go into gender relations. I explored literature on the subject, and I tried to explore why gender relations in Bhutan are as they are, because they are very different than in surrounding countries. I will explore gender in relation to religion and sustainability.

Bhutanese Gender
Relationships

In the previous chapter I examined religion in Bhutan. In this chapter I will focus on contemporary gender relations and point out how the Bhutanese people experience them. I will try to explain the history of gender relations, the role of Buddhism on gender relations and how they have been shaped during time.

I will try to depict values on which gender relations are based. I also wanted to know if men and women have the same values, and did these values change due to the rise of a market economy?

First I will focus on gender relationships with regard to history and religion. As stated before, this book is a pioneering work and I have a limited number of Bhutanese sources on which to rely. However I am relying what I learned while living in a village in northwest Bhutan (Crins & De Graaff, 1990), an explorative research conducted in 2000 (Crins & Wangdi, 2001), the interviews I collected in 2004, and a small body of literature. I will describe gender roles and gender identity.

In order to understand gender relationships it is helpful to pay attention to the division of labour division, Bhutanese social organisation and to the position of women and men. During my stay in the village I encountered a society in which gender relations- in my eyes- and on a political strategic level were equal: Both men and women did almost all the same work except for ploughing and bringing dung to the fields. In this stage of my research, I wanted to know if this labour division was characteristic of Bhutanese society as a whole. During my interviews I explored this subject and I was curious if could detect a change in the labour division and/or gender roles as a result of modernisation.

Gender Relations in Bhutanese History

In order to gain insight into the position of women in Bhutanese Buddhist society, we must return to early Buddhism. According to Horner (1989), 'Siddhartha Gautam, the Buddha, was born around 563 BCE and died around 483 BCE. Shortly after his first Teachings, there was a rapid growth in the number of religious orders of monks and nuns. This was a strange phenomenon for Indian society since participation in religious affairs was limited to the Brahman, and to men. During the life of the Buddha, religious orders flourished. An increase in the number of monastic order was successful at first and women were eager to take part: the times were characterized by greater freedom and reverence for women than had previously been the case. Women were allowed to enter the orders, 'subject to the same ceremonial regulations as had been made for monks, and subject to certain other disciplinary measures drawn up on their admissions'. (Horner,1989: xxii-xxiii) Buddhism gave women the possibility of choice; should they not marry, they could still have a respectable life as nuns. In this way, they were in control of their life. However, 'After the Buddha's death, the upward mobility of the women diminished, hostility to women became active within Buddhism. The Buddhist texts were written down by lamas only 200 years after Buddha's death, these lamas were all men. In these texts, women are shown as inferior creatures, someone with a weaker character then of men'. (Brauen, 1994:80-81)

'Many mystics and famous female saints are beautifully depicted in bronze or plaster but very few in real life forms compared to those of men. For thousands of years the embodiment of God was exclusively the domain of men. This can explain why there are so few female *trulkus* and why *rinpoches* (reincarnated lama) can be married.' (Pommaret 1999:264) A few female saints were active in Bhutanese society. According to the Bhutanese writer Kunzang Choden,

'Bhutanese women drew their inspirations and guidance from the exemplary lives of well-known Buddhist women such as Khandro Yeshe Tshogyel, Ashi Nangse and Gelongma Palmo, the early parts of the lives of Khandro Yeshe Tshogyel and Ashi Nangse coming from a background of unhappy familial circumstances and marriages were easy to identify with'. (Kunzang Choden, 1997:254)

She describes how women in Buddhism see themselves. 'The strongest factor in women's self-image was the female body. For centuries, there was been a belief in the biological inferiority of women. Women's bodies have been associated exclusively with procreation, and pregnancy is a cause of suffering. Because these biological realities affect the psychology and therefore women have a tendency to associate them selves with suffering. Buddhist scholars have claimed that nowhere in Buddhist texts or manuscripts were there references to the biological inferiority of women. They said that this belief could have been perpetuated just to create a stigma'. (Kunzang Choden, 2001:9) According to a Bhutanese folk saying, a woman is nine incarnations below a man. The number nine refers only to the idea of plurality and not to any mathematical truth. (Dorji Thinley, 2005)

Makley (2002) conducted her study in the Labrang area in Tibet. She found that the possibility for social and karmic mobility or transcendence was associated with the masculine. Meanwhile, the feminine was associated with that which is immanent to the body, to place, to households, and to the mundane. In contrast to the male, the adult female body was more corporeal and thus more impure because of its "extra" sexual characteristics: vagina, breasts, menstruation, and pregnancy. In the Buddhist idiom often invoked by Labrang men and women, the male body is inherently more morally pure and thus karmically auspicious, while the female body is morally impure and thus an inferior rebirth. Makley points out that morality, the interplay between good and bad deeds and their consequences, was literally embodied for Tibetans. Understandings of ritual-social propriety were most generally expressed across discourse and contexts, in an idiom of corporeal cleanliness and filth. Ordinary people, both lay and monastic, tended to conceive of all practices for self-improvement in terms of bodily and mental purification, whether they were directed at one's karmic status for future lifetimes or one's social status in this one. Thus ritual and everyday efforts to control dangerously contagious corporeal pollution indexed the sacred and social boundaries of the community. The most potent substances and the most potentially offensive to deities and humans were the effluvia associated with bodily functions: urine, faeces, bad breath, menstrual blood and semen. For Tibetans (and the Bhutanese) the body was inherently unclean, and men and women could be polluted and polluting through inappropriate or bad deeds. (Makley 2002)

Goddesses in Tantra Buddhism

Mahayana Buddhist religion and philosophy are dominated by men, characterized by a large and complicated pantheon of Buddhas and Gods. Women play a role as Goddesses, but to a much lesser extent than men.

> 'The early texts of the Tantric Buddhist philosophy can be summed up as follows: The Gods and Goddesses are symbols of Buddhist concepts (representations) of the four elements and the five constituents of being. The earth is represented by the goddess Locana, water by Mamaki, fire by Panadaravasini and the air by Tara. The five constitutions of being are represented by the five Dhyani[1] Buddhas. Creation is due to the Sakti or female energy of the Adi Buddha, and as such the adepts should realize that the female sex is the source of all'. (Bhattacharyya, 1977:210)

The ancient Tantra school is based on a dialectical form. It argues that the static male and the dynamic female are aspects of a complementary nature and always exist in combination. The male is seen as the unchanging essence and the female as the power of transformation and change present in subtle and material forms. This principle is reflected both in the Hindu pantheon and in the Mahayana Buddhist pantheon where bodhisattvas and Dyani Buddhas have female consorts. (Bhattacharyya, 1977) Tantra Buddhism offers a variety of ideas about the role and philosophy of the female, both in terms of the position of women within its theocracy, and the esoteric meaning of being female.

Campbell traced several distinctive aspects that have their roots in ancient times. She characterized this theme under the heading: 'Early religious influences and the shamanic component, and the waning power of the Great Mother and the Steps of Tantra'.(Campbell, 2002:36) Campbell, too, refers to the introduction of *Bon* in Tibet. It is believed that *Bon* came to Bhutan through the Duars and the Tibetan and Bhutanese passes. *Bon* was a form of Buddhism brought to Tibet from Zang-Zung, an area that bordered on what is now Pakistan. *Bon* texts confirm the existence of Indian Tantric thought as well as the basic tenets of Buddhism and pre-Buddhist beliefs. In earlier days both in *Bon* and Buddhism devotion to the Mother Goddess were maintained in different forms. Particularly important was her form as the central figure representing female energy. In Sanskrit she is known as Dakini whilst in Tibetan and Bhutanese her name is Khandro, which literally means "sky-goer". Her dynamic presence is a particular feature in the biographies of all famous practitioners of Tantra, appearing as she does to help the acolyte on the path by clearing obstacles, challenging an intellectual approach, and engaging in sexual union with the male practitioner in order to realize the highest truth. Her association with charnel grounds links the Dakini with several ancient Goddesses whose powers over life and death are described in the texts of many traditions. (Campbell, 2002)

In an insightful essay on the *Sin-mo*, the mythical Tibetan demonesses (who had to be subdued in order for Buddhism to become established in Tibet (and in Bhutan), Gyatso (1987) proposes that her supine presence in art and in literature are actual forces which had to be set under control so that the patriarchal imperatives of Buddhism might prevail. 'Her femaleness was necessary, because the subjugation of the land as Mother Earth was inevitable, social patterns of matrifocal and matrilineal customs had to be wiped out and the early patriarchal view of that which is uncontrolled and threatening as feminine had to be established'. (Gyatso1987:47) Campbell is convinced that 'the Sin-mo does not primarily represent women, but rather a religion, or more accurately a religious culture and world-view that is being dominated'. (Campbell, 2002:44) Campbell's point could explain why female shamans, matrilocality and matrilineality could survive in Bhutan. In Bhutan there are two *Lhakangs* (temples) from the time that the demonesses were subdued. However, in Bhutan social patterns such as matrilineality and matrilocality were not wiped out by mainstream Buddhism. Shamanism, or better, pre-Buddhist mediumship, performed by women is still very much alive. This might be due to the tolerant attitude of the Nyingmapa and Drukpa Kargyupa School to the local shamans and mediums. (Crins, 2003)

Monks and Nuns

There are *dzongs* all over Bhutan, built by the Shabdrung in the 7th century. These *dzongs* are impressive fortress-like buildings with a triple function: monastery, temple and a management centre. These *dzongs* were originally the centre of power and knowledge and a bastion for men. Although the position of women in society is strong in Bhutan, within Buddhism the monasteries are the domain of men. In Bhutan about 5000 monks are supported by the state.(Ministry of Planning, 1997) There are only a few nunneries and some of them are under the supervision of male monasteries. Monks also perform all official rituals. Within the monasteries a hierarchy of monks and lamas exist. The lamas hold the highest positions, often *tulkus* and *rinpoches.* Since the introduction of Buddhism in the Himalayan region, monks and lamas have made themselves indispensable to the population by helping them, ensuring that they receive payment, and controlling the elements of nature. In addition to these activities, they were engaged in the practice of Buddhism.

However, Bhutan is a country based on agriculture and despite the rapid development of the capital and a few other cities, the majority of Bhutanese live in rural areas. In these parts of the country women play an important role as *Ngejum* or shamanistic mediums. They are held in high esteem, but also feared for their knowledge and supernatural power.

Religion and Gender Values

In Tantra Buddhism the principle of the male and female dialectic is very important. In theory, Buddhism recognizes equality between men and women so both sexes are charged with the duty of following the *Dharma*. Through time the scales have been tipped in favour of males, but Bhutanese Buddhism has developed its own unique understanding of gender, though in a context different from the contemporary concerns of western culture. According to Makley, from a Tibetan perspective 'the body is the temporary, moral outcome of a confluence of human and nonhuman actions, subject to ongoing intervention and thus capable of changing, in all its biological aspects, for better or for worse'. (Makley 2005:587)

Simmer-Brown (2001) describes gender relationships in Tibet before the Chinese occupation; her descriptions are similar to what I saw in Bhutan. In Tibetan society questions of personal identity and gender are considered a contemporary western phenomenon. As in Tibetan society, in the Bhutanese culture every detail of life is infused with religious concerns such as the appeasement of obstructing spirits, accumulation of merit, and the attainment of enlightenment. Tibetan concepts of "feminine" and "masculine" have been important only to the extent that they reflect this ultimate dynamic in ritual and meditation. Gender has been understood to be beyond personal identity, a play of absolute qualities in the experience of the Buddhist practitioner. For Tibetans, the "feminine" refers to the limitless, ungraspable, and aware qualities of the ultimate nature of mind; it also refers to the intensely dynamic way in which that awareness undermines concepts, hesitation, and obstacles in the spiritual journey of female and male Tantra practitioners. The "masculine" relates to the qualities of fearless compassion and actions that naturally arise from realization of limitless awareness and the confidence and effectiveness associated with enlightened action (Simmer-Brown, 2001).

This sacred view of gender does not necessarily reflect Bhutanese women in religious life; nuns and women in the villages regard themselves as less religious than men because of their attachments to the farm and to children. (Crins & Wangdi 2000)

According to Campbell 1996 ; the way in which human identity is constructed is through relationship with a grander theme which pertains to the evolution of religious thought. In the case of Tibetan and Bhutanese Buddhism, one would have difficulty in arguing that gender was of no significance, because in Bhutan just as in Hinduism, one finds at its core exalted images of sexuality acting as symbols of transcendence. 'Futhermore, at the intersection between belief and social custom, one finds a communal project between the theocracy and the lay community that pertains to a belief in divinity, and results in the creation of a mystical infrastructure in society. Both these aspects concerned with two important universal preoccupations, sexuality and parenthood. No one could deny that the Tantric representations of 'father-mother' deities engaged in the sexual act , convey anything other than an extraordinary arena of significance through the medium of what can only be described as a transcendental 'primal scene'.' (Campbell 1996:x-xi)

However, in social life, women in Bhutan enjoy more prestige and freedom than in many other Asian countries. In many cases women own land, houses and assets, and the inheritance is matrilineal. Husbands move in with their wife's family (uxorilocality). Women have power in trade, in nomadic herding, the management of large farms and families and as *Ngejum* (shamanic healers). Men help in with the domestic chores and raise children, and in many cases it is the women who are making the important decisions. (Brauen,1998; Crins, 2004) Traditionally women have not been active in public life and decision-making, although they have participated in village meetings. Most of the time these meetings were attended only by women because the men were away. (Sonam Kinga, 2003)

Lineage and Inheritance

The fact that the Bhutanese have no female or male names and no surname, makes it difficult for outsiders to trace someone's familial lineage. Most names have religious meanings and are applicable to men or women and some people are named after the day that they are born.

Bhutanese society is roughly divided between nobles ("big bones") and commoners ("small bones"). 'This notion of bones resembles the Tibetan concept of *sha* and *rus*. *Sha* is flesh and stands for the female gender. *Rus* stands for bones, the male and royalty'. (Stein, 1972:107) In noble families, the family line follows the father. The families of commoners have their lineage go through both parents, although inherited possessions go through the mother. Along with noble families, there are prominent families who are descendents of holy people or incarnations of historical figures. Most Bhutanese trace their ancestry through the father and mother. For example, in a case where the father comes from Paro and the mother from Bumthang, both families are important. However, in the upper strata, the descendants of noble families follow the father's line of descent. The right of inheritance follows the mother's line. Among commoners, both the mother and father's lineage are considered.

Consensual polyandry and polygamy were common practices. According to the CEDAW report (Department of Planning, 2003): 'Polygamy and polyandry are socially acceptable. However the law requires that if this occurs it must have the consent of the spouse. In many cases multiple wives are sisters and multiple husbands are brothers, or they are persons closely related to the first spouse'. (Department of Planning, 2003:6) This form of sororal polygyny is centuries old and can be traced to Tibet. According to Stein, 'this was reserved exclusively for the rich and noble, and the reason behind this practice is that it serves as a manner of taking in the surplus of women who would be without husbands since many men joined cloisters'. (Stein, 1972:97) An example of sororal polygyny is that of the king of Bhutan, who is married to four women who are sisters, all of whom are queens. Fraternal polyandry is originally a Tibetan tradition. It also occurs in Bhutan, especially in Merak Sakteng, but it is rare. In the village were I lived, there was one household in which the husband's brother lived in the house and helped with the housekeeping. In another example, a brother helped his sister-in-law during her child's delivery because the biological father was absent, although he was somewhere in the village. Just a in Wikan's story in chapter 1 where the nun got pregnant from the brother of her partner.

Bhutan may be the only country in Asia where, in most cases, the right of succession stemming from the mother has survived.

> 'The country places high value on taking care of the family and has it enshrined in the inheritance laws. Overall 60% of rural women hold land registration titles: in urban areas 45% of women hold property titles. Any citizen of the country can inherit property according to the Inheritance Act, 1980. The Land Act and the Loan Act of 1981 also have provisions on the rights of women and girls'. (Department of Planning, 2003:8)

The matrilineal system varies from valley to valley. A patrilineal system is dominant in the southern part of Bhutan where most of the residents are descendents of Nepalese and Indian migrants and predominantly Hindu. According to Bhutanese law,

> 'In Bhutan all persons are equal before the law. All individuals are entitled to equal protection without discrimination. Any person whether a man or a woman, can institute court proceedings if she or he believes his/her rights have been violated. Traditional customs favour women in the area of inheritance. In the matrilineal family system in western and central Bhutan land is inherited through the mother'. (Department of Planning, 2003:6)

In 1999, I conducted an explorative research on the position of women in Bhutan. I interviewed fifty Bhutanese women from different backgrounds and regions of the country. Most of the families of the women had a matrilineal heritage system and most women found the matrilineal system worked best. The matrilineal system not only exists in the villages, but also in the city. Stores and businesses can be bequeathed to the owner's daughters. Women manage many large hotels, and, in addition, a large construction company is headed by a woman. Women are industrious and like to be independent from their husbands. This is especially true in cities where men and husbands are salaried workers while women want to start their own business in order to guard their independence. (Crins &Wangdi, 2001)

There is not a "dowry system" in Bhutan and there is no stigma attached to widows who remarry. (Pommaret, 1998)

Households

'Household is the basis unit of Bhutanese society. It is the basis of family identity'. (Sonam Kinga, 2003:57) Family bonds are very strong and members support one another in times of illness, death and other adversity. The average size of a household is estimated at five to six. The extended family numbers seven to eight people. The older women usually nurture the family and take care of the younger children. (Department of Planning, 2003) in the size of Bhutanese households can vary. In urban areas, the family composition is primarily nuclear. In rural areas, households are made up of extended families; several nuclear families along with grandparents and aunts and uncles all live under one roof. Households could also comprise a mother and children, a father with children and other family members or friends who temporarily reside with the family. (Crins & De Graaff, 1990; Pommaret, 1998; Sonam Kinga, 2003)

Every member of the family is registered in the ancestral household. All properties such as land, cattle, house, forestland, are registered in the name of the household, not as independent properties. Incomes earned by individuals are household assets, and used to purchase household provisions or spent on collective necessities. Households are still the unit of taxation in rural areas. All taxes are paid as a household, not by individual members. Voting is also done by the household and not by the individual members. It is the process of decentralization that resulted in the empowerment of the household, and not through individuals in terms of decision-making by voting or arriving at consensus. (Sonam Kinga, 2003)

Den Uyl gave the following definition of a household: 'it forms the key unit based on familial organisation. Female and male labour production and the production relationships are not only interwoven, but what is more, where exchange between male and female work takes place'. (Den Uyl, 1995:35-37)

In Bhutan, rural economic units are based on the family. Every member of the household had his or her tax bill based on his or ability to accomplish. This meant that an individual who had studied in a monastery would be exempt from doing heavy physical work on the land. He would help indoors with the mending, using a sewing machine, taking care of the small children or maintaining the domestic altar. There is hardly any mention of a strict distribution of labour. Teams of men process the wood and women bring the manure to the fields. Other activities in the field and in the home are done together.

In central and eastern Bhutan weaving of cloth is the domain of women, and weaving is integral to a woman's gender identity. Bhutanese men also produce textiles, but in general they do not weave. (Myers, 1994)

In the village community I visited, reciprocity plays an important role. In the village family, members or members of the same nuclear family help each other without expecting anything in return. Among families who are not members of the same lineage, reciprocity is important and strict rules apply to the way people interact. (Crins & De Graaff , 1990)

Most Bhutanese living in the urban communities still maintain ties with their rural traditions. Most of them have inherited property in their villages. Lands are looked after by cousins or relatives and sharecropping is practiced at the end of the harvest. In most cases, at the end of the year (mostly winter months) people from urban areas contribute to the annual *chuko* (a ritual which lasts for three days conditional upon the financial situation of a household) by providing money and edibles such as meat, oil and sugar. The people in the urban areas also provide financial support for their rural cousins or families. While the men and women are busy in the field and with domestic work, children help their parents by looking after the cattle, collecting firewood and manure. The grandparents or the elderly help by looking after the younger children. In times of illness, death or even during the *chuko*, relatives from other households help the family. (Crins & De Graaff, 1990)

In urban communities, it would be very unusual if no relatives from the village were living with a family. In most cases, rural children are sent to school in the cities, as their parents believe that education there is better. Parents and/or grandparents also live with their families in the urban areas although it is sometimes a large financial burden. Elderly relatives, in turn, contribute by looking after their grandchildren when the parents go to work. With modernisation and development, the traditional kinship in the urban communities has not broken down, although some adaptations have been made. (Pommaret, 1998)

Gender Roles within the Society

One characteristic of the high level of gender equality in Bhutan is the fluid marriage system, in which people can live together (without performing a ritual) and divorce is relatively easy. According to Pommaret (1998), this marriage system and the freedom for couples to live together might be attributed to the fact that in Buddhism, marriage is not a sacrament and to the belief that everything is transient. I think a much older value system from pre-Buddhist times has shaped gender relations in Bhutan.

'Another reason for the fluid marriage system could be that women inherit in the same way as men, and keep their inheritance for themselves. The fact that women do not surrender their property to the man when they marry makes them financially independent. Because of these two factors divorce has always existed in Bhutan and it is not a social problem'. (Pommaret, 1998:18-19)

According to Kunzang Choden, 'In principle, both men and women have equal status and opportunities. There are no sharply defined male/female domains. At household level women are neither subordinate, nor is their access to resources limited.' (1997:254)

The situation of Bhutanese women today is summarized in the report of the Convention on the Elimination of all Forms of Discrimination against Women:

'There is no formal gender bias at home and in the workplace, women in general are regarded as homemaker, wife and mother. The perception that women are physically weaker and sexually more vulnerable has greatly influenced their access to educational and employment opportunities. Women's own perception of themselves seems to be based on these two factors. There is no division of roles in the most rural areas between men and women. The head of household is also not a gender-specific domain, usually the more capable person-often the wife or the elder daughter-assumes this responsibility. Women are generally in charge of the finances. In the urban areas men are the primary earners'. (Department of Planning R.G.O.B., 2003:5)

Men significantly outnumber women in all sectors of paid employment. In 2003, 15,050 people were working in the civil service, of which 26% were women. Still, a majority of women are concentrated in the lower levels. Within the judiciary, there are six women lawyers and eight female law students. More than hundred women have joined the police force in recent years. The secretaries of foreign affairs and finance are women, and it is expected that these women will eventually become ministers. In the Ministry of Labour and Human Resources, 49% of the staff is women. (Ministry of Planning, 2003)

Traditionally, women were have not participated in the decision-making bodies of the government. Today the government of Bhutan tries to recruit equal numbers of men and women in the higher levels of the bureaucracy. The key factor in this inclusiveness is education. (Sonam Kinga, 2003)

Bhutan's development is moving along rapidly. In 1997, the government began its eighth five-year plan, whose primary goal was the preservation of Bhutan's cultural identity. This emphasis on identity is important for the Bhutanese because it offers security in times of great change. In 1999 the country started receiving TV transmissions and connections to the Internet. The country's two largest cities, Thimphu and Phuntsholing, are changing quickly and because of this, a gap is forming between the cities and the countryside.

The rural areas are still very traditional; religion continues to play a large role in everyday life. Particularly for the young people of Bhutan, rapid development is confusing. In addition, tension is developing between modern education and the traditional lifestyle. This tension surfaces, for example, among young people who are having difficulties reconciling what they learn at school with their belief in the world of Gods and spirits. In this traditional world, the woman has a strong and important place. Although women in the rural areas say that their lives are difficult compared to the city counterparts. (Crins & Wangdi, 2001)

As Bhutan develops, modernisation is putting great pressure on its traditional way of life and equality of the sexes. Women in Bhutan like to be independent. Many women will try to start their own businesses. The businesses range from bars, restaurants and stores to large travel agencies, construction companies, or hotels. City life is becoming more modern; salaried work is increasing and private enterprise is becoming an attractive career option. When couples marry or live together it is mostly the men who are engaged in salaried work. The women usually stay home and care for the house and children if no relatives live in the area. The women who want to combine work and motherhood look to their parents and family members for assistance. Yet there are working women who remain unmarried because there is no one to whom they can delegate their responsibilities. (Crins & Wangdi, 2001)

Summary of the 56 Conversations on Gender

Gender relations according to the Bhutanese respondents

An important part of our conversations was about gender relations. I wanted to explore gender relation in greater depth and I asked the respondents about gender roles. In this part I will highlight their answers. In chapter 2 I worked out some of the conversations completely.

I started the interviews by asking fifteen questions about labour division within the household. I wanted to know if work activities were carried out by both genders or if some tasks were done only by women or men. I interviewed eight farmers, four of whom were males still living in the traditional household. The respondents said that they performed household chores and all the farm work but the women did not plough and in the western parts of Bhutan men did not carry dung to the fields. However, Bhutanese men from the eastern part of the country did carry dung to the fields. I asked why women are not supposed to plough and the answer was: 'If a woman touches a bull, the bull will incarnate as a cow in his next life'. In addition, more practical reasons were given such as 'a bull is too strong' and 'a woman cannot handle an animal like that'. In the village, however, I saw many women handling large bulls so it was not necessarily a problem.

In some villages in west Bhutan men are supposed to plough and women carry the dung to the field. The farmers I interviewed told me that only women carry dung because of their "uncleanness". This was not the case with the respondents from central and east Bhutan, where men also carry dung. Most men help with the household chores: preparing food and taking care of their children. It is only in the cities, where people have full-time jobs, that their lives resemble the western style. Either the wife is a housewife or if both people are working they have an aide, or both help. The respondents who grew up on a farm (and about half of the respondents had done so) told me that they helped with all the chores and farm work at home. The only taboos women faced were that they were not supposed to plough and that they were not allowed in the Mahakala *Lhakang* (temple) when they were menstruating or in the *dzong* at night, although there are no strict rules. If there are, these rules can be changed as needed. For example, a female architect had to restore a Mahakala Temple. According to the monastic rules she was not allowed to enter the temple, and the workmen believed that she were to break the rules, misfortune would befall them. To make it possible for the architect to enter the temple and do her work, lamas performed rituals to make the temple accessible to the architect and safe for the workmen.

While I was living in the village in 1990, time was a different concept from the one to which I was accustomed. There were no week-ends and no "free" time (see chapter 1). I was curious as to whether or not the respondents had considered "free time" and if so, how they spent it. Some respondents, both men and women liked playing sports, reading, listening to music and going to the movies. Praying, meditating and socializing were also important. Archery is a popular activity amongst the men. I interviewed an older man sitting outside with his wife on the lawn in front of their house. He told me that his main hobby was drinking wine and chasing women. He said that his greatest wish was to be young again and being able to go out with women dancing and drinking. It struck me that he and his wife enjoyed talking about these passions and escapades.

With regard to the labour division, I wanted to know if the respondents would like to change anything in their lives, and if so, what it would be. I wanted to know if the Bhutanese were content. A third of the respondents (both male and female) were happy as they were. Others expressed an interest in "praying or meditating more or to be more religious". "To study more" was a popular answer; some men wanted to stop drinking or change certain bad attitudes.

I asked 25 general questions to identify general ideas on gender, world-view and opinions. The first question was who was the most responsible person in the house. I also wanted to identify the head of the household. Half of the respondents responded that father and mother, or those with spouses who took joint decisions as head of the household. Respondents who lived with their family and who were not married (almost one-fourth) said that father was the head of the household; another fourth said it was the grandmother, mother or sister who was the decision-maker. One male respondent told me that inside the house it was the mother who made important decisions whilst outside the house it was the father. But in general both heads of households took the major decisions.

Another question I asked was whether the respondents, men and women alike, were free to choose their work and education. Only a small group of respondents were not free; six men had been sent to a monastery or boarding school and three women had been sent to school by their parents. I asked them whether they liked their work or study. Only a few respondents (two men and one woman) did not. The woman was a police officer and since the government had paid for her education, she had to stay in the job for five years before she would be allowed to choose another job. She did not like her work.

There was no big difference between men and women with regard to these answers. The respondents who were from the eastern part of Bhutan had even less labour division according to gender than in the western part of the country. In the eastern part more women were considered head of the household.

I asked all the respondents whether they were happy as men or women. All the men were happy, only four women were not; the women who were not happy said that it meant lots of pain because of menstruation and childbirth. In addition, the women were more limited in their freedom because they had to take care of the farm and household. Another factor is that men are regarded as more religious; they can go to the monastery and have no attachments. Women are seen as dirtier because of menstruation. The other 22 women who were happy to be women said, 'women are simply better than men'. Some women liked being housewives and some said they were happy because they could have babies. To a few women their gender was not important. They did not really care. Other women said that women are more attractive and it is just nice to be a woman, although women have more physical pain.

Some men were happy with their fortunate incarnation; they believed that they had been good in previous lives and this resulted in their birth as Bhutanese men. Other men were happy because of their physicality. They had less pain than women or they regarded themselves as more religious. To some men it meant more freedom, a man can do what he wants, has more freedom than women and more possibilities.

I was curious if men and women were afraid of anything. Five women felt vulnerable at night and in the forest, they were afraid of men at night and of wild animals; all of the other women felt secure. Of the men two did not feel secure, one was afraid when he is in India and the other man felt insecure in some situations. Another question I asked is if people felt threatened as a human being and if so, by whom or what. The minority of the respondents did not feel threatened at all. A few respondents two men and two women were afraid of wild animals, or ghosts and deities.

I asked the respondents if women and men were capable of doing the same things. The majority of the respondents said, 'yes, but there is a physical difference'. To a few women, 'women are more clever and mentally stronger'. According to a few respondents, men were stronger. According to a lama, 'in Mahayana Buddhism, gender is an illusion [this is in line with the concept of gender in Tibet according to Simmer Brown as mentioned earlier], we are all human beings, we look different but we have the same ability to reach enlightenment and become Buddha's.' Some respondents (mostly nuns and uneducated farmers or less educated men and women) regarded women as inferior to men. According to them a women has to be reborn nine times to be able to be born again as a man. For highly educated people this is a folk belief. In the folk belief a man has more potential of reaching enlightenment because he has fewer attachments, e.g. he does not bear children, does not inherit the farm and assets. He is considered cleaner (no menstruation), less vulnerable to rape and therefore has more freedom to travel.

While I was living in the village, the oldest woman in the household took all the important decisions; she was the head of the household. I wanted to know if this was also the case with my conversation partners and if there had been a change.

Half of the women interviewed claimed that they made the important decisions, or with their partner or older sister. To some women it was the father, the mother, or the husband. For the younger women it was the parents. Half of the men said they take decisions with their partner. To a few young men, it is the father or the mother. One man identified his daughter.

In regard to living with other people and because compassion is a very important concept in Buddhism, I wanted to know what compassion means to the respondents. To the women, compassion means: 'helping other people', 'understanding others', or 'to be good to all sentient beings', and 'to be good to animals'. Other single answers are: 'to be generous', 'self-sacrifice', 'to save life', 'loving', 'respect others is important' and 'thinking well of others'. To the men, it means 'to be good to all sentient beings', 'to be good to animals', 'to understand others' or it means 'to treat people equally'. It also means 'to be loving'. Other single answers are: 'being friendly', 'empathy', 'respect others', 'self-sacrifice', 'generosity' and 'just doing good'.

In this connection, I wanted to know what love means to the respondents. To the women, it means 'caring for others', 'children mean love'. 'Love is connected with *karma*' and 'love means helping' and 'not gossiping'. Other single answers are 'love means worrying about others', 'to be kind to someone who not deserves it', 'sound relations with other sentient beings', 'to have feelings for others', and 'to return love when loved'. To the men, it means 'finding a good wife', or 'caring for others', 'love for all sentient beings'. Other single answers are: 'full heart for others', 'everything between humans and animals', 'love is connected with *karma*', 'respect', 'love is a ladder to climb on', 'empathy', 'love is an illusion', 'a universal gift', 'sensation and beauty beyond yourself', 'there are two types of love, to parents and girls'. Other answers are: 'children are love', 'something that creates life', 'love is lower than compassion', 'a universal gift' and 'faith in each other In general men and women feel free in making choices for their lives and there is freedom of movement for both genders. It is interesting to see the high level of awareness people have in regard to worldview, aspirations for the future, and as citizens of Bhutan. In general, the respondents are content with their lives and feel safe.

Reflection

Gender reflection

The household is the basic unit of Bhutanese society; this reflects the answers given by the respondents with regard to family values. Family is very important and within the household there is hardly any strict labour division; men and women do all the chores except that men do not weave, (although men used to weave for religious purposes) and women do not plough. In the traditional setting, women are often the head of the household and take the important decisions about farm, shop, house and money matters. Nowadays, in cities and among educated respondents who are married and living in a nuclear household, important decisions are taken jointly. In rural households where the father is more educated than the rest of the family, he is the head. However, in general gender relations are very relaxed. Rules can be adjusted if needed.

Although family and household are important and a strong binding factor for people, men and women have much freedom to make their own choices. In general men and women have a lot of freedom to do what they like and have a great deal of mobility.

With regard to their vision of gender equality, the majority of respondents do not regard women as weaker but as equal to men. The interrelations between the genders are marked by a "relaxation" where, in daily life, strict male and female domains are absent. In mental capability men and women are considered the same. Although nuns and uneducated women regard themselves as religiously inferior to men it is because of their biological differences, not their mental capacity.

The more-educated respondents regard men and women as equal in all ways, including religion. In the city it is the highly educated people, who have studied at Western universities, and who are more inclined to adopt a Western lifestyle. They form nuclear families; have cars and TVs, and ensuring that their children receive a good education is very important. In general, most respondents value education. The reason the respondents give is that education will develop the country; working for the government means a good salary and status.

The majority of the respondents freely chose their education and profession, whereas others were sent to school by their mother or father or by the government. Some had to choose between two professions because the government needed them. The altruistic mind in Bhutan reflects the answers given to the questions about wishes for the future. Respondents' wishes are dominated by the desire for self-improvement through education. In educating oneself, one helps the country. But also, through more religious education, in order to attain a better "afterlife", and better education for children, and helping the poor. The altruistic mind is imbedded in the psychology of the Bhutanese people. Within Bhutanese Buddhism, even if one reaches enlightenment, the enlightened person will not go into Nirvana but will come back as a *bodhisattva* to help all other sentient beings reach enlightenment. Important people in Bhutan, such as the King, are regarded as *Bodhisattvas*[1].

To summarize, according to our conversation, what is important to people is, first of all, the family, followed by education for oneself and family, and lastly religion and personal freedom. It is interesting that the respondents who are involved in their own business enterprise are more interested in money and material things than are the respondents who are civil servants or farmers who choose for the family, offerings, building temples and *stupas,* and helping the poor.

Although gender issues are important in Bhutanese development policies, women seem to be at a disadvantage. There has been a shift from the female head of household to the male. More and more men are engaged in wage la-

---

1   Enlightened beings

bour and women are staying at home to be homemakers. Bhutan is losing its traditional ways of gender interaction. The overall opinion is that the country is developing and that gender relations are becoming more equal. It would seem, however, that the opposite is more the case. With an increasing market economy woman are losing their traditional position as head of household, and influences from India and other countries are changing the views and expectations of boys and girls.

If we come back to the question on which values gender relations are based, we find specific Bhutanese answers in the data. To start with, family values are very important as is improving oneself through education, religion and helping others. With regard to the basic values upon which gender relations are based, we can conclude that these values are equal for men and women. The answers that men and women gave to the interview questions are identical. The answers given by men and women to the questions grouped according to the eight domains are identical, too.

As an educated Western woman I felt very connected with the nuns and the "non-educated" women. As a woman I always find it unfair that we women have to suffer so much due to our physicality. I find the Bhutanese women's view in this regard very interesting; it reflects exactly how I felt after I gave birth to my child. I felt I was not free anymore. In this sense I feel very close to the village women and the nuns, even though we come from very different worlds. In the village, I witnessed a strong relationship of the people with the environment. The environment belonged to the gods and deities; those gods and deities were male and female and both equal important. The mouthpiece of the deities and gods were female and male shamans, depending on the gender of the god/deity. In this sense, in pre-Buddhism, there is a stronger gender balance than in Buddhism. To me, that was an eye opener.

Coming back to the respondents' answers, what values can we elicit in this gender discussion? Further, I have to ask if gender should be discussed on a Western level. I like to reflect on Flax's (1999) view on gender relations: Flax defines "gender relations" as a category meant to capture a complex set of social relations, to refer to a changing set of historically variable social processes. They are not universal, but determined by local social processes. In the West, the naturalized articulation of gender posits a dualistic structure, man and woman, based on physical sexual differences. This conception of gender allows one to dominate the other. The category "man" is the normal, while "woman" is the exception, the deviant. Both men and women are prisoners of this system, though men benefit more.[2]

---

2   See previous chapter.

I addressed in this book what I consider the high level of gender equality from my Western perspective. I addressed it from a political strategic level, but do I do justice to this matter? Can I address gender in Bhutan from my Western perspective?

For example, for many Bhutanese, gender is not an issue to begin with; this is a value as such. Also, the whole historical, social, cultural, and philosophical frame of Bhutanese society is so different from my situation as a Western woman. As we have seen in the previous chapter, gender in Buddhism and pre-Buddhism is not regarded as two separate sexes; in Buddhism, it is regarded as the female and male principle within every human being. This is very different from the Judeo/Christian tradition of my upbringing, in which the bias is on the male side. In the context of Bhutan, we can detect values such as karma, incarnation, altruism, and compassion and the absence of domination by one sentient being over another sentient being as basic important Buddhist values. In this, there is a connection of gender with religion and sustainability.

I have learned that I should be aware not to judge gender from my Western perspective in terms of equality. Equality is a powerful term and, as we have seen in this chapter, women are not equal at all levels of Bhutanese society.

To obtain deeper insight into gender in the Bhutanese setting, it would be very valuable to have Bhutanese feminists analyze gender relations in Bhutan in a way that they articulate feminist viewpoints within the social worlds in which they live.

The next chapter is dedicated to sustainability in Bhutan and the connection of sustainability with gender and religion.

Bhutanese sustainability

In this chapter I will use the Western concept of sustainability again as an instrument to obtain deeper insight into this concept. As we have seen in the previous chapter, sustainability still is a way of life in Bhutan and not a concept as such.

I experienced the animist / Buddhist religion that determines that life is experienced entirely in the present and where spirituality is everywhere and immediate. In Bhutan, this experience is identified (explicitly) with "sustainability." Experiencing Bhutan has revealed to me that "sustainability" is not a partial quality of politics, economics, or of society as we see it in the West; sustainability is either a total ontology (as in Bhutan) or it is self-contradictory. In a fragmented lifeworld, as in Western (post)modernism, the holism characteristic of traditional Bhutan culture is just what is lacking (and what will continue to be lacking in Bhutan as it modernizes).

I will address the meaning of sustainability in a Bhutanese setting and explore how my conversation partners value sustainability as it is seen through my western eyes? Is there a connection between gender values and the values of sustainability? To understand sustainability in Bhutan it is important to consider Buddhism and pre-Buddhism.

In the West sustainability is a "buzz" word with many meanings. Sustainability in the Bhutanese setting is connected to the country's development policy and an important guideline of "Gross National Happiness" (G.N.H.), the main development concept in Bhutan. Norbu Wangchuk uses Priesner's vision of G.N.H.: 'Priesner labels GNH as one of the last truly indigenous development approaches, it is not an intellectual construct detached from practical experience, but rather the translation of a cultural and social consciousness into development priorities'. (Norbu Wangchuk, 2003:1) I will connect the definition of G.N.H. with the Bhutanese understanding of knowledge in regard to values and worldview. I will examine sustainability as a Western concept. Lastly, I will reveal the answers to the questions I asked during the conversations.

Sustainability as a way of life in Bhutan

'When he goes out into the farm, he is armed with a walking stick. While walking between the apple trees, he cannot restrain from talking to some of them. He overtly expresses approval to some of the healthy trees: "You have improved this year; your blossoms are turning into fruits. You have not wasted my hard work". He consoles other weak and infected trees. "You are impervious to care. Medicine has been sprayed. Compost has been applied. Everything has been done. Yet you are sick." He murmurs while he prunes a shoot. Amused students overheard him talking to apple trees, as a rational interaction between an anxious and ardent farmer and its living subjects. Any kind of farming has it negative aspect: its leads to conflict with the life of a lay Buddhist. He is remorseful that insect control is unavoidable in his apple farm. His orchard used to be sprayed with insecticide, which took the life of both harmful and harmless insects. Spraying has set heavily on his conscience in spite of the profitability of his farm. Only a few years ago, did he find a way out of it. He has now taken up EM. EM technology is a Japanese technology that uses friendly micro organisms, which are beneficial for human beings. EM is sprayed on trees; the insects live on EM liquid without destroying the trees. EM technology is a valuable tool for a pacific Buddhist farmer'.(Karma Ura, 2002:216)

This story is an illustration of farming in Bhutan. It shows how Buddhist farmers feel about the dilemma of farming and working with nature. To the Bhutanese, Buddhism and sustainable values are very important. Buddhism respects all sentient beings; one sentient being should not kill another, even if it is a worm or a fly. The ethical, cultural and aesthetic role of biological diversity is very important. The basic principle is to restore to nature what has been taken away and to respect all forms of life. Thus, in Bhutan, the ethical and aesthetic role of biodiversity is an integral component of the culture. (Ministry of Agriculture, 2002)

Accompanying this Buddhist view is a pre-Buddhist view of the sacred landscape as (chapter four). 'Deity beliefs were particularly important in mediating relations between humans and the natural resources'. (Allison, 2003:537) Everywhere in Bhutan there are deity habitats or "citadels" in the landscape, which humans avoid. According to Allison, 'While some might be quick to dismiss the deities as the ancient superstitions of uneducated villagers, the deities play exceptionally important social, spiritual and environmental roles. In the lived experience of the Bhutanese villagers, the deities are as 'real' as the crops that feed them and the animals that roam the forest'. (Allison, 2003:555)

According to Pommaret (1998), sustainability in Bhutan is the field where the traditional values imparted by religion meet the new Western concepts: respect for the environment. This respect derives from religious beliefs that relate to Buddhist and to pre-Buddhist principles . Pommaret points out that the environmental awareness of the rural population is not conscious. It is their way of life; like people in other rural societies the Bhutanese depend on their natural resources. This is reflected in a careful management of the environment: rotation of the crops in the fields, management of pastures, and preservation of the forest and animal species. Buddhism enhances this aspect with the precept not to kill any living being .(Pommaret, 1998) The Bhutanese farmer sees deities everywhere, and the farmer is part of the environment. He or she does not look upon the land as a commodity to use as he or she wishes. There are strict rules about placating the deities that inhabit the land, river, air and rocks. In this way the farmers live in a sustainable way, and nature provides food and shelter. The deities are the guides to sustaining this system.

Their belief in the power of the local deities guides Bhutanese farmers and teaches them to respect the environment. (Crins & De Graaf, 1990) Local deities date from pre-Buddhist times *(Bon)* and are incorporated into Buddhism: they are associated with rocks, mountains, rivers and soil, and the most important is the deity of the valley or region, the *Yul Ha*. (Karma Ura, 2001) The whole environment is deified and therefore sacred. If properly worshipped, these deities bring good luck, health and fortune, as well as fertility. If angered, though, they can inflict misfortune and illness on people and cattle. They can also bring catastrophes such as droughts, floods, hailstorms and, death. The deities must not be disturbed in their habitat, or if they are, proper rituals have to be performed to appease them. This means that the Bhutanese farmers are reluctant to touch parts of the land, which are the abodes of these deities, and the result is that their environment has been preserved. (See also: Crins & De Graaff, 1990; Pommaret, 1998; Karma Ura, 2001; Allison, 2004)

This respect for the living landscape and all living beings is an important part of government's development policies. In this way Bhutan has taken a unique development road that reflects the Bhutanese values and worldview.

An article in *The Kuensel*, the national newspaper of Bhutan, describes the relationship that the people of the country have with their environment and its deities:

'Bonism and Shamanism: An integral part of Bonpo culture (cursive text added, RC)

> *The people of Bongo, a remote village under Chukha dzongkhag, are optimistic that this year too, their crops will be bountiful, natural calamities will be less and there will be no sickness in their village. The villagers as usual, invoked their Yul-Lha (local deities) and believe that their year round hard work will not go to waste. A five-hour walk from the nearest road head in Meritsemo, lies the village of Bongo where "Bonism and Shamanism" which involves animal sacrifice is still very much a part of daily life and are an integral part of the Bongop (people of Bongo) culture.*
>
> *Every year, the 52 households of Bongo come together twice a year and conduct the invocation recital for good heath, to dispel misfortunes and to usher a good harvest. The invocation recitals of Yul-lha are the most auspicious annual event in Bongo. It is observed during the 10th day of the second and 10th month of the Bhutanese calendar. It is called Sochoed (spring ritual coinciding with the crop sowing season) and Serchoed (fall ritual coinciding with the harvest season and offering of first harvest to the deities). Invocation of deities and spirits begins at 5.00 in the morning and concludes three hours later with the feast offering or animal sacrifice to their Yul-lha, Am Yangtam and Yangchum (two sister deities,) at the Neykhang located above the village.*
>
> *During the rituals people worship, offer Nyendar (cash offering) and pray to the sister deities. A symbolic environmental cleansing through purification rites of incense burning is done before invoking the deities. They also summon other deities and spirits residing in mountains, valleys, lakes, forests, streams and cliffs invoking them to assist and protect people from misfortune, rivalry, contempt, ailments, epidemics and to ensure a bountiful crop.*
>
> *It is not known when and how the tradition came to be. "It is an age old tradition*

established by our ancestors and we should maintain it", says 67 year-old Bonpo Pema Wangchuk. "If we do not conduct the ritual, misfortune would befall us and our crops would be destroyed". Animal sacrifices during public ceremonies like Sochoed and Serchoed are usually small as compared to private ones where a large numbers of animals, mostly poultry birds, are sacrificed to appease the local deities. Household sacrifices are usually performed to cure sickness and drive away spirits.

A Bonpo (a bon priest) who performs the ritual is entitled to a portion of the animal sacrificed and seven dres (one dre equals one and half kilogramme) of grains from each household for conducting the public ritual. "Until last year a village sacrificed about 300 poultry birds, pigs, goats and bulls in a year," Ap Phub Sithub, 75, told Kuensel.

But in recent years, the rituals have undergone a change. The tradition of animal sacrifice (marchoed) during the invocation recitals has been discontinued following a kasho (edict) issued by His Holiness the Je Khenpo (Head of the sangha). Today the local people offer animal products like eggs and cheese known as karchoed. The lam of Bongo lhakhang, Pasang, said that offering of animal products had replaced animal sacrifice in the seven villages of Bongo, Damji, Ketokha, Toktokha, Jungley, Zamsa and Phasuma, all under Bongo geog, where Marchoed was widely prevalent. "This has helped in saving the lives of hundreds of animals," says Lam Pasang who added that the people were convinced that karchoed was a good substitute.

The people were further convinced after the statues of the two female deities were installed at the Bongo lhakhang, where an invocation through the rolling of the holy dice indicated that the deities were happy with the change. "We consulted the villagers and drew up an agreement to discourage killing," says Bongo gup, Nim Gyeltshen. A committee comprising the gup, chimi, tshogpa members and the village lam was also formed to monitor slaughtering of animals. According to the committee's rules, a violator will be fined Nu. 5,000 and a repeat violator would be charged in court.

The practice of animal sacrifice still prevails in various regions around the country. It is a sect of animistic shamanism, a pantheistic cult embracing the belief that all beings in the universe have souls.

It is believed that Bonism came to Bhutan from Tibet where it prevailed before the advent of Buddhism in the eighth century. According to a legend of Bonism, it was created by Tenpa Sherab, a contemporary of Buddha, in a mystic region known as Tazi in Tibet. The Bonism followers believed that at the very beginning of the creation, there were two eggs, one white and one black. The two eggs burst and from the white egg came out deities and humans and from the black egg came out parasites, demons and spirits.

Although animal sacrifice is being discouraged, the Bongops still continue to sac-rifice at least one animal a year. Each household slaughters a pig during their an-nual ritual, Choesung that is performed to appease their protective deity, Gyem Mani Naap, also known as Pekar. "Meat is indispensable to invoke our deity and it is not possible to cease practicing this tradition," says Tshering Dem, 50. For the sacrifice the Bongops select and identify a piglet which when in adulthood is sac-rificed to appease Pekar. "The pig offering should be clean," says 70-year old Dorji from Zamsa. "Normally we do not buy pigs from Phuentsholing because they are not clean". In Baikunza under Bongo geog, animal sacrifice is still rampant.'(See: Rinzin Wangchuk, 2005)

To the people in Bhutan, sustainability is a way of life, not an abstract concept. More than 85% of the Bhutanese are farmers who live in remote villages in the valleys. They are subsistence farmers with a barter economy. (Ministry of Planning, 1996) According to the Bhutanese National Environment Strategy (N.E.S.) Task Force, there is no single definition of sustainable development. Each country, with its own historical and cultural heritage, unique geographic and physical characteristics, and social and political systems, brings its own meaning to the term. The N.E.S. came up with the following definition for Bhutan: 'The capacity and political will to effectively address today's development and environmental problems and tomorrows challenges without compromising Bhutan's unique cultural integrity and historical heritage or the quality of life of future generations of Bhutanese citizens'. (N.E.S.,1998:28)

Prior to the 1950s, any visitor to Bhutan had to travel for more than five days by horse or mule from the Indian border to the capital, Thimphu. , This was a trip through dense jungle and over mountains of pine forest. Thimphu was noth-ing more than the *dzong* surrounded by hamlets and villages. Until the 1950's the country had not changed for many hundreds of years. The roads were mule tracks and footpaths connecting the *dzongs* and main villages. People lived in hamlets and villages in harmony with nature and were self-sufficient. Con-struction materials consisted of wood, bamboo, mud and stones and most ma-terials such as wood for fuel and vegetables were collected from the forests. The main activity was working the land for crops and trade was done through bartering with neighbouring villages. (Karma Ura, 1999; Pommaret, 1999; Crins & De Graaff, 1990)

Today it takes five hours by car to reach Thimphu from the Indian border. Development is happening very fast in Bhutan, although the country's own de-velopment approach is different from its neighbours. The Royal Government of Bhutan is committed to sustainable development, as reflected in the Paro

Resolution, which recognizes that Bhutan's natural resource base is central to a sustainable and prosperous future. It acknowledges sustainable development does not imply a stagnant society. The Royal Government of Bhutan (R.G.O.B.) is aware that society changes and evolves; it is a challenge to use the resources in a sustainable way. Chhewang Rinzin (2003) from the Royal Institute of Management reflects this commitment of the R.G.O.B. 'to the approach to development, and its awareness of possible negative impacts on environment, social- economic structure and Bhutan's traditional cultural values. This implies that Bhutan's approach to development must be in harmony with its environment, its fragile mountain ecosystem and its cultural value system'. (Chhewang Rinzin, 2003:4)

Bhutan's development policy continues to be guided by the traditional value system, which is essentially Buddhist and pre-Buddhist. With the introduction of modernisation in the 1960s, Bhutan's environment, socio-economic structure, and traditional value system is changing. The Bhutanese are aware of the impact of modernisation and the rapid changes that it brings. However conservation of the traditional values and respect for the natural world has led to a development strategy that suits the Bhutanese style of life. Bhutan has chosen the "middle path" of development. The "middle path" is a Buddhist phrase that means development can happen, as long as it is moderate and gradual. Bhutan chose to develop the country but in a careful way with respect for tradition, religion, values and ecology. According to Lyonpo (minister) Kinzang Dorji, 'The Middle Path-National Environment Strategy for Bhutan aims to highlight issues, potential problems and constraints, and choices that our country has to make in order to ensure the conservation of our natural resources while pursuing economic development'. (N.E.S., 1998:13) This development strategy resulted in a unique Bhutanese development approach: "Gross National Happiness".

Gross National Happiness in relation to sustainability

Gross National Happiness (G.N.H.) is a strategy for social and economic change in Bhutan. As Mancall stated, 'in the decade since the fall of Communism, many thinkers and authorities have been attempting to define a "third way" between neo-liberal free market capitalism and now defunct Communism. The attraction of GNH outside of Bhutan lies in this search'.(Mancall, 2004:11)

Happiness is an important value in western and eastern philosophies. The concept of G.N.H. was introduced in 1998 as a means of placing the Buddhist and traditional values at the heart of life, replacing the conventional measure of a nation economic activities: the Gross National Product (G.N.P.).

'The concept of Gross National Happiness was articulated by the King of Bhutan to indicate that development has many more dimensions than those associated with Gross Domestic Product, and that development should be understood as a process that seeks to maximize happiness rather than economic growth. The concept places the individual at the centre of all development efforts, and it recognizes that the individual has material, spiritual and emotional needs. It asserts that spiritual development cannot and should not be defined exclusively in material terms of the increased consumption of goods and services. GNH is founded in the belief that human happiness is a composite satisfaction of both the material and the non-material needs. It rejects the view that there is a direct and unambiguous relationship between human happiness and economic growth. Blind consumption and wealth accumulation do not necessarily enhance happiness'. (Bhutan 2020, 1999:45)

In the kingdom's long development strategy, G.N.H. has taken the form of five main guidelines ((R.G.O.B. Planning Commission, 1999).). The first is human development: to maximize the happiness of the Bhutanese people and to enable them to achieve their full and innate potential. This is to be achieved within the framework of traditional values and ethics, and through sustainable improvements in the standard of living, the quality of life, and well-being.

The second objective is culture and heritage: awareness and appreciation of the country's rich cultural heritage and a continuation of its social philosophy. Meeting spiritual and emotional needs and maintaining a distinctive Bhutanese identity and in cushioning the Bhutanese from some of the negative impacts of modernisation.

The third objective is balanced and equitable development. This objective ensures that the benefits of development are shared fairly among all income groups and regions.

The fourth objective is good governance. Institutional development must embody a commitment to the principles of morality in government and of ethical behaviour in the conduct of public affairs. It must also promote transparency and accountability, and be supported by the force of law that gives tangible expression to the distinctive features of Bhutanese culture and society. (R.G.O.B. Planning Commission, 1999)

The last objective is environmental conservation: the protection of the biological productivity and diversity of the natural environment.

The central idea of G.N.H. is to encourage a rethinking of what is important in people's lives: should the success of a nation be judged by its ability to produce and consume, or should it be based on the quality of life in that country, the happiness of its people, however difficult that might be to measure in practice? The concept of G.N.H. has yet to mature. However, the National Environment Commission of Bhutan has a definition of G.N.H.:

'Gross National Happiness: According to both Buddhist and pre-Buddhist philosophies, the mountains, rivers, streams, rocks and soils of Bhutan are believed to be the domain of spirits. Pollution and disturbance are believed to be the cause of death and disease for those spirits. The Buddhist respect for all living things has led to the development and adoption of ecologically friendly strategies – a solid base upon which a national environmental strategy can be built. This coupled with the Buddhist tenet that the acts of this life will be rewarded or punished in the next, provides a powerful motivational principle for sustaining Bhutan's natural resource base.

Historically speaking, economic development has generally been dedicated to improving the quality of life. In western cultures, this has usually meant the satisfaction of the population's material wants. According to this conventional definition, a country could only be called "developed" once it reached a certain level of material consumption. On an individual level, this translates into consumerism and materialism.

Compounding the waste and excess inherent in these attributes is their essentially progressive and competitive nature. Not only do individuals want to be better off than they were last year, they also want to be better off than their neighbours, who also see their material fortunes improving. Given that the vast majority of these material acquisitions are derived from nature, this geometrically rising pattern eventually exceeds the ability of the surrounding resource base to regenerate itself. Unless consumption patterns are altered or foreign resources can be brought in to fill the gap, the inevitable result is unsustainable development. This dynamic is only accelerated if individually increasing "needs" are compounded by collectively increasing populations.

In Bhutanese culture, however, the original definition of development was based on the acquisition of knowledge. Those who possessed greater knowledge were considered to be more developed. In a similar vein, the process of communal enrichment was based on a dynamic in which those who possessed superior knowledge imparted that knowledge to others. In the Buddhist religion, this concept of personal development was refined even further to entail overcoming the delusion arising from ignorance, aggression and the desire for consumption and acquisition.

The notion that gross national happiness is more important than gross domestic product is thus inherent to the Bhutanese value system.' (National Environment Commission, 1998:19)

As we have seen here, sustainability in Bhutan has its own unique meaning. This meaning has resulted in a development strategy that fits Bhutanese traditions and worldview . In the words of Pankaj:

> 'The development strategy of Bhutan seeks to strike an appropriate balance among social, economic, political, cultural and environmental goals. The development strategy places human development at the centre stage. A holistic approach to development has been designed to take care of material as well as the spiritual needs of individuals. Health and education have been considered as priority areas for basic capacity development towards the generation of human capital. This is to be achieved within the framework of traditional values and ethics so that the "society in transformation" keeps on taking inspiration from the nation's cultural heritage.' (Pankaj, 2003:115)

Pankaj views Bhutan's development strategy as a holistic one since it takes all elements of society into consideration. He does not give an alternative definition of holism, but we can conclude that in Bhutan's development approach economic development is not the single main aim. The holistic view of Bhutan's development approach comes into consideration in the Bhutanese interpretation of the Gross National Happiness index instead of the G.N.P./G.D.P. It is clear that G.N.P. is inadequate as the general index of national well-being and measure of economic growth.

Environmental economists and eco-feminists are now looking at ways in which natural capital can be included in an overall indicator of national wealth, which could also include social measures such as infant mortality, male and female literacy, and life expectancy. Indicators of measuring welfare are needed here to capture the full value-added through the effort of an aware society. Various approaches of G.N.P. have come to be used as the primary macroeconomic indicator of welfare and progress in modern society. These have been pursued to find alternatives to the most deficiencies of the G.N.P. For Bhutan it is the G.N.H.

Knowledge, worldview and sustainability

As we have seen in the N.E.S. definition of Gross National Happiness, the accumulation of knowledge is more important than the accumulation of wealth. But what does knowledge mean in the Bhutanese context? N.E.S. does not give a definition of knowledge in Bhutan, but Chah (2003) gives a description of knowledge in a Buddhist way. In Buddhism, knowledge is also spiritual knowledge. Experienced knowledge and knowledge from outside are different from direct knowledge and indirect knowledge. (Chah, 2003) The following quote will give an illustration of the meaning of knowledge in a Buddhist setting:

> 'Like the Buddha, we too should look around us and be observant, because everything in the world is ready to teach us. With even a little intuitive wisdom we will be able to see clearly through the ways of the world. We will come to understand that everything in the world is as a teacher. Trees and vines, for example, can all reveal the true nature of reality. With wisdom there is no need to question anyone, no need to study. We can learn from Nature enough to be enlightened, because everything follows the way of Truth. It does not diverge from Truth.' (Chah, 2003:79)

Only a few decades ago, monastic education was the only way for the majority of Bhutanese people to educate themselves. 'Monastic institutions, which for centuries were the only centres of learning, have lost their monopoly since the 1960s, when Western education was introduced on a large scale'. (Pommaret, 1998:20) The Western scholarly tradition is very young in Bhutan, and Ueda (2004) points out that monastic education in *Choekey* (Tibetan script) and *Dzonkha* used to be the hallmark of being well educated. Today, people see Western (English medium) education as the means to success. English has become an important language among the well-educated Bhutanese. The meaning of success has also changed with socio-economic conditions. According to Imaeda, 'Before development activities started, almost all the population lived largely on subsistence farming with limited trade between neighbouring valleys through barter. This meant that there was little change in a person's social position. Success came rarely, and was usually restricted to the small number of officials who worked for the king, who might be given the rank of *Dasho*'. (Imaeda, 1994:228 In: Ueda, 2004) Although changes are happening, the development in Bhutan is still characterized by Buddhist mystic tradition and philosophy. According to Priesner:

> 'Buddhist philosophy lacks a period such as the European Enlightenment resulting in the schism of science and religion. Economic thinking and all other indigenous sciences are an integral part of Buddhism. As such, the overreaching goal of every aspect of life, including economics, is not seen in the multiplications of material wants, which can be satisfied by consumption, but in the purification of the human character. The objectives of market economics, i.e. increasing consumption and accelerating growth, are thus only relevant as means to an entirely different end- human well-being. Buddhism turns the for-

mula of Western economic thinking which views all pre-and non-capitalist values as instrumental in either impeding economic growth, on its head. Besides, Buddhist moral philosophy provides a definition of happiness, suggesting that well-being is to be drawn from the harmonization of spiritual and material aspects of life.' (Priesner, 1998:37)[1]

Buddhist philosophy provides strong arguments for the adoption of an environmentally sensitive development strategy. Priesner put it this way: 'The Buddhist concept of *sunyatta* holds that no subject or object has an independent existence; rather it dissolves into a web of relationships with all dimensions in its environment'. (Priesner, 1998:50)

To Priesner, these relationships are non-hierarchical, since Buddhist moral philosophy does not differentiate between humans and other living species. Secondly Buddhism perceives reality as circular and not linear as in the Western worldview, with human life regarded as a stage in an eternal cycle of reincarnations. This means that sustainable development is in one's self interest. Next to the Buddhist philosophy, self-imposed isolation, a difficult, inaccessible terrain, and delayed development are the main reasons why the ecology in Bhutan has been so well preserved. This view is clear as Pankaj (2003) formulates it, according to the National Environment Conservation Strategy:

'Bhutan's environmental conservation strategy is deeply rooted in the Buddhist philosophy and religion which Bhutanese people have cherished and nurtured over centuries. In rural Bhutan, for example, nature is interpreted as a living system rather than just a resource base to be exploited for material gain. People consider themselves as a part of the whole of the living system. This kind of outlook is the result of the fusion of Tantric Buddhism and animistic *Bonism*, which is further assimilated into the mainstream beliefs and values.' (Pankaj, 2003:115)

The Bhutanese government makes a clear statement that it not only respects nature, but also confers on it a living mysticism. Places are identified with deities and spirits, and a large part of the landscape is mapped in such terms in the minds of Bhutanese people.

---

1   This stands in sharp contrast to utilitarianism, which was frequently criticized for failing to define happiness (Priesner, 1998).

Sustainability as a Western concept

As we have seen, for many people in Bhutan sustainability is a way of life. In the West it is a *concept*. There are many definitions for the concept of sustainability in the Western world. One definition is:

> 'A concept and strategy by which communities seek economic development approaches that benefit the local environment and quality of life. Sustainable development provides a framework under which communities can use resources efficiently, create efficient infrastructures, protect and enhance the quality of life, and create new businesses to strengthen their economies. A sustainable community is achieved by a long-term and integrated approach to developing and achieving a healthy community by addressing economic, environmental, and social issues. Fostering a strong sense of community and building partnerships and consensus among key stakeholders are also important elements.' (www.ci.austin.tx.us/zoning/glossary.htm)

Sustainability is very often connected with development, hence the term sustainable development. This is a multidimensional concept and is recognized in the Brundtland Report, *Our Common Future*, which alerted the world to the urgency of making progress toward economic development that could be sustained without depleting natural resources or harming the environment. (Bruntlandt, 1987)

According to Van Dieren, 'Present patterns of Organization for Economic Cooperation and Development per capita resource consumption and pollution cannot possibly be generalized to all currently living people, much less to future generations, without liquidating the natural capital on which future economic activity depends. Sustainability thus arose from the recognition that the profligate and inequitable nature of current patterns of development, when projected into the not too distant future, lead to biophysical impossibilities'. (Van Dieren, 1995:99)

Van Dieren continues to describe sustainability as the "maintenance of capital" or non-declining capital. Natural capital is our environment, and is defined as the stock of environmentally provided assets (such as soil, atmosphere, forests, water, wetlands), which provide a flow of useful goods or services. The flow of useful goods and services from natural capital can be renewable or non-renewable, and marketed or non-marketed. In this way sustainability means maintaining environmental assets, or at least not depleting them. (Van Dieren, 1995)

To Newton (2003) 'the perspective of environmental sustainability requires that we ask ourselves how each interaction with the natural environment will affect, and consequently be judged by, our children in the future'. Newton uses a Native American tradition as an example: 'A Native American tradition requires those who would use scarce resources to consider their actions from the perspective of those seven generations from themselves. That seems to be a convenient benchmark'. (Newton, 2003:1)

Summary of the 56 conversations on sustainability

Here I will summarize the views of the respondents on sustainability and the meaning of nature. I raised seventeen questions about sustainability in relation to nature. My first question was whether respondents had heard about sustainability. A majority of the respondents had heard of sustainability, mainly at school and through the government. Those respondents, who did not know the concept, were uneducated.

Sustainability had different meanings for the respondents. It means that one has 'to take care of nature, not destroy it but to preserve it for future generations'. It also means 'sustaining the Bhutanese way of life': traditions, culture, spirituality and ecology. Other single answers are: 'It is the development approach of Bhutan'. 'It means continuity in interconnected development and long-term investment in development programmes of the country'. Other answers were: 'Gross National Happiness, a holistic developmental approach' and 'Sustainability is a system of capacity to manage the development of the country in a holistic way'. Or it meant 'self-sufficiency', 'eco system', 'being self-sufficient' and 'preserving nature'. To one respondent it means 'taking care of flowers because flowers are an offering to the Gods'. To three respondents it means 'nature' and one respondent said: 'it is nature and nature is part of me'. Other respondents could not tell or did not know how to express the meaning for them the best.

I wanted to know if there was a God concept attached to their image of how nature is created. Therefore, I raised the question about what they think things make grow. A Nyingmapa lama said: '*karma* and incarnation'. I asked him to explain this to me. He clarified: 'if a river is doing bad things, he will become a waterfall. If a tree is not behaving well, it will be reborn on a rock with so it will be difficult for it to reach its food and water'. Other respondents assumed: 'humus and fertility let things grow', or 'it is the elements that make things grow'. Or 'the forest God makes things grow'. Others answering *karma* and incarnation, meant to say that 'your karma results in the way you will grow'. Some answered: 'It just grows' or 'one has to take care of nature to let plants grow,' or 'if causes and conditions are met'. Three respondents said 'God' one of whom was Christian, one Hindu and one Buddhist. Other answers were: 'nature is God'; 'emptiness is God because everything is a dream'. Seven respondents did not know how to answer this question?

Next I wanted to know: 'Can people help nature?' Here almost all of my respondents agreed: 'nature can be helped by taking care of it, not destroying it and by making offerings to the gods'. In response to the question whether people can help the deities, only a few said 'no' or 'did not know', whilst the majority said 'yes they could, by praying, doing *pujas* and by offering to the deities'. One respondent told me that every year in one valley in west Bhutan an important ritual is performed by killing an ox and offering it to the deity of the valley. The respondent referred to this ritual as a *Bon* ritual: the ritual ensures that all the inhabitants of the valley will prosper and remain healthy. Another respondent told me a story about a holy lake high in the mountains above Thimphu. This lake belongs to a deity. If you visit the lake, one has to be respectful to the lake: it means no shouting or use of abusive language, nor polluting it by throwing things in it. A few boys went to that lake and had a party there; they were not respectful and perhaps they polluted the lake. The story goes on: when the boys wanted to go home they got lost. Two became very sick, and all were not able to find their home again, and so they ended up in a valley for away from Thimphu. Although the lake was a few hours hike from Thimphu, it took the boys days to be able to reach home. People said that the boys had got lost because they disturbed the deity of the lake.

Then I wanted to know whether women and men have the same relationship with nature. To the majority of the respondents they indeed have. However, according to a few respondents, women are gentler and more caring. Only one woman made the connection that women are closer to nature because of their ability to give birth.

Sustainability is regarded as a holistic concept by the respondents who are familiar with the term. The answers of the respondents reflect the relationship that the Bhutanese have with the environment. This relationship is delineated above and is characterized by respect and being part of one's life.

Just as in the gender chapter I asked questions about the relationship of the people to the environment. I derived the questions from some of the research of Bilsky and Schwartz (1987). Regarding the first enjoyments domain, whether people enjoy nature, all respondents said yes. Another question was what nature means to them. To most respondents, 'nature is a provider, it means beauty and peace'. Other answers were: 'it means happiness', 'it means everything' and 'it means life'. Some answers were: 'humans cannot make it' or 'nature is human', or 'it means a soul, and it means karma and incarnation', and 'the impermanence of life'. One man said: 'he is part of nature and it has a mirror image to him'.

Regarding the second, security domain, I asked whether my respondents felt secure in nature. Some respondents are afraid of wild animals, so they do not feel very secure. A few respondents are afraid in the jungle and one man is afraid of the results of environmental destruction. All others feel safe. Other questions in this domain were: 'Does nature provide your family with food?', and 'Do you trust nature to provide you with food?' A few respondents said that they did trust nature, but that they have to work in order to let nature provide their food. All other respondents agreed. To the second question everyone said yes. One respondent added that he did not trust nature anymore due to climate changes. I asked whether the fields are fertile enough. A minority of the respondents did not have fields; almost half of the respondents said yes. A few respondents said it could be more fertile and one has to put dung on the fields.

Two questions I asked are from the fourth self-direction domain. I asked whether people would like to have more land. Half of the respondents said yes, but only if there were enough people to work on the land. My next question to the farmers was whether they would like to be an educated. I raised this question because farming is not very popular among the people as it is hard work and not very beneficial for *karma*. The majority of the respondents said 'no'. Respondents who were interested in becoming educated farmers, were only interested if the government was willing to provide training, tools, seeds and land.

About the fifth restrictive-conformity domain, I formulated the question: "Do you respect your natural environment?" All answered yes. Nature is seen as something very valuable and a living entity which should not be harmed.

Concerning the sixth pro-social domain I asked: 'Are humans and animals equal?' The majority of the respondents said yes, the only difference being that animals cannot speak or animals do not have any religion. Other answers were: 'No, humans are higher' or 'animals are our forefathers', 'animals have less mental power'. One woman said: 'What is the difference "they live downstairs and we live upstairs"...'.

About the social-power domain I asked whether they think humans have power over nature. The majority of the respondents responded that 'nature is stronger'. Exceptional answers were: 'Man can destroy nature, or humans are stronger because they can work the land'.

Regarding the seventh maturity domain, I wanted to know whether they thought nature is wise. Almost everyone said 'yes'. I wanted to know what knowledge and wisdom in general mean to the respondents. In Buddhism, knowledge is also an important concept. Especially because of the definition of the G.N.H., I wanted to know whether knowledge and wisdom are important. To some respondents both concepts meant everything, to others both meant 'compassion'. To some 'religion is knowledge and it meant receiving teachings from a master or an education to understand life'. The answers were all different, but the general understanding of knowledge is that with knowledge one is able to understand life, to help oneself and others and taking care of others. For them, knowledge means wisdom. Then I asked what wisdom means to the respondents. Some did not know, other said 'it is knowledge with a good heart'. 'God is wisdom', 'knowledge of things', 'wisdom is religion', 'compassion and knowing yourself' were the main answers. To most respondents, wisdom and knowledge are more important than money. They said: 'wisdom and knowledge stay', 'you cannot lose it whereas money comes and goes'.

Reflection

The conversations show that compassion and serving others applies not only to humans but to all sentient beings. It seems with the absence of any domination by one sentient being over any other sentient being. Here there can be seen a connection between gender values and values of sustainability. According to the answers given, one can conclude that men and women share values and world-view with regard to the environment and to other living beings.

To me, the natural environment is breathtakingly beautiful in Bhutan despite the changes, especially in West–Bhutan where more roads are being constructed and the cities Thimphu, Paro, Punakha and Wangdi are growing. It will be a challenge for Bhutan to find the balance between economic growth and to sustain the environment as it is today. To almost all the respondents, protecting and respecting the environment is an intrinsic part of the Bhutanese culture and society.

Sustainability in Bhutan and in the West have different meanings. Sustainability in the West is an (abstract) *concept*. For Bhutan it seems that sustainability is a natural *method* or way of living, embedded in the values, culture, spirituality and tradition of the country. Buddhism and pre-Buddhism are religions that value sustainability. Taking care of nature, performing rituals and protecting nature are the main answers to the questions with regard to the natural environment and how to treat nature. Nature is not seen as something "out there" but as embedded in and inseparable from one's daily habitat. In Bhutan, the sacred landscapes, the habitats of the deities are not supposed to be disturbed. Respect for all sentient beings, is deeply rooted in the mind of the people and is an important value. Sustainability is not only seen in regard to nature and ecology; it is also seen as sustaining the Bhutanese way of life. Sustainability in the Bhutanese setting is holistic and this means that in daily life, all aspects of life are connected and not separated by time or function. Spirituality is omnipresent, gods and deities are part of every action and area. This connectedness is also present in Bhutan's development strategy, "Gross National Happiness". According to the National Environment Commission, the definition of G.N.H. is closely connected with knowledge and wisdom as Bhutanese Buddhist concepts. To my respondents also, knowledge and wisdom are highly valued. One understands that improving one's knowledge and wisdom can lead to a better life. One can be a better person and as a result incarnate to a better next life.

I can conclude from my findings that sustainability is the prime religious principle in Bhutan. With this finding, I can conclude that gender and religion are elements of this cosmology. It is a basic ideology that is so different for me to grasp. I realize that I am from a totally different (fragmented) world in which everything is categorized, and I realise that I use these categories to try to understand what I experienced in Bhutan. I am walking the bridge of sustainability; I know where I came from, but I do not know where I am going to. I realize that sustainability in Bhutan is not what it is in the West. It is not the definition of the Bruntlandt report or triple bottom line (people — planet — profit) or any other Western definition. It is a whole cosmology as such, where religion, nature, and gender are related.

In the next chapter I will draw conclusions from my research and explorations.

Meeting the "Other":
Conclusions

In this chapter, I will draw conclusions of the explorations and experiences that I have presented in the previous chapters. In this book, I sought answers to several questions I had: about what it means to do research in a humanist, self-reflective way while reflecting in and on interactions? I will address the questions: How and what kind of insight is produced when I, a Western researcher, meet the other? Did it change me, did I find otherness in myself, becoming "other"? How can I contribute through the development of reflexive arguments to an understanding of gender and sustainability in the Bhutanese setting? Because of my many years of experience with Bhutan, I seek to reflect on what kind of change I witnessed due to capitalism that came into the country?

I also want to point out how this research influenced my methodology and the methods I used? My answers to these questions are my interpretations of all the conversations I had with Bhutanese people, my meeting with the "other." In my reflections on studying "the other," it became crucial that I have started to under-stand my own feelings, interpretations, observations, methods, and prejudices.

My meeting with Bhutan

I went to Bhutan for the first time 18 years ago. I left as a student of cultural anthropology to be part of an irrigation project in Bhutan. I stayed six months in a village. During this stay, my first encounter with Bhutan, I was fascinated by the complex cultural factors around gender, sustainability, and Buddhism, and about what I could learn from them.

Being in the village, I realised that the society was marked by a deep Bud-dhist religion but, in daily life, the religion was marked by a tremendous respect for the natural environment. I was impressed by the relaxed gender relations in the village. Almost all the households had the oldest women as head of the household; marriage was not the norm and divorce was easy. Men were car-ing and helped with household chores and took care of babies. Women could change from partners and it was the women who had the last word with impor-tant decisions. I realise now that this first visit raised many questions originat-ing from my Christian, Western, academic upbringing. In reading literature on Bhutan, I became conscious that not much was written about the country; this gave me the incentive to become a kind of pioneer on Bhutan.

After this first encounter, I visited the country several times, and in 2004 I managed to get a research visa for Bhutan. Then, my aim was to learn more about the gender relations, sustainability, and influence of Buddhism on these concepts. I wanted to know what people value in regard to these concepts. I knew that if I wanted to do research on gender, I had to taken religion and sustainability into consideration. I knew that these concepts were connected somehow, but I did not know how exactly. I knew that in Buddhism there is not a creator as in the Christian tradition. I wanted to know how people see crea-tion. I starting interacting (sometimes by translator) with Bhutanese men and women and raised a lot of questions in many conversations.

What did I understand having conversations with many Bhutanese for a long period? I realised that the society was marked by deep religious belief. Most Bhutanese belong to the Drukpa Kargyupa and Nyingmapa Buddhist schools. It took me some time to understand this complex religion. Bhutanese Mahayana Buddhism in its Tantric form is a complex mix of Buddhism and pre-Buddhism, and it has its own distinct identity. In the whole country, numerous deities and gods animate skies, earth, fire, mountains, lakes, rocks, trees, and houses. And all these deities and gods have to be taken care of. Buddhism as it is can be identified with animism: The whole world is animated with numerous deities and gods, beneficial and not so beneficial for humankind, but all have a significant meaning to the people. So Buddhism, as I understood it, can be seen as a complex form of animism. In daily life, the Bhutanese religion is more animistic than it is pure Buddhist. Buddhism is celebrated in the monasteries and the temples, and even there, Buddhism is intertwined with the animated world.

This pre-Buddhist and Buddhist religion, the belief in the sacred landscape and the historic socio-geographical conditions, plays a significant role in the value system in Bhutan. High mountains and dense jungle isolate the country. The low population density and the semi-nomadic society have shaped the country's evolution over the centuries. Colonialism and modernisation could be kept at bay. Although Tibet played an important role in establishing the culture and the religion of the country because of the many important religious figures who fled Tibet and came to Bhutan for shelter, Bhutanese have developed their own identity. In daily life, the religion is marked by a tremendous respect for the natural environment. Bhutanese identity is related strongly to nature, and the natural environment can be seen as a way of life and is approached in a holistic way, i.e., Bhutanese are relating to or concerned with whole or complete nature rather than analysis of dissection into parts, or of fragments of the natural environment. I will refer to this way of life as a holistic cosmology.

But, it was not the only shift in religious understanding that I experienced. Another category I tried to explore in Bhutan was gender relations. I approached gender from my Western point of view and the way I experienced gender in my own life. In Western tradition, gender differences are derived from the supposed fact that women are less than men in all walks of life. Based on my experiences in the village and later during my other visits in Bhutan, Bhutanese gender relations are marked by a high level of gender equality. Now, at the end of this journey, I realise that my understanding was dominated by my Western mindset, which could not approach the gender relations in Bhutan. The Bhutanese cosmology is so different, and approaching this cosmology with the Western concept of gender turned out to be totally unsuitable. In Bhutan, I experienced relaxed relations in which gender was understood as a form of compassion for life, in which the differences and conditions of the sexes were regarded as almost value free and related to the specific natural conditions surrounding people. The consequence, as I experienced in many interviews and in the village, was that many households had the oldest women as head of the household, marriage was not the norm, and divorce was easy. Men were caring, helped with household chores, and took care of babies. Women could change from partners and it was women who had the last word with important decisions. Again, this understanding is in line with the holistic Buddhist/animistic worldview and value system in which all forms of life are valued equally.

I also recognised another shift in attitude. As a Westerner, I hoped to ana-lyse natural environmental developments in Bhutan by introducing the West-ern concept of sustainability. The interviewees did teach me that nature in Bhutan has to be understood as a core value and that is encompassing and a holistic principle or cosmology. As said earlier, I started by thinking of reli-gion as the absolute main principle in Bhutan. Now, at the end of this inquiry, I have to adjust this finding. By looking deeper into the meanings of religion and nature, I come to the conclusion that those two categories are one. Or, even better, in Bhutan nature as a holistic cosmology is a prime cause and religion is a result of this. This means that everything becomes nature: sustainability becomes nature, life becomes nature; and as a result of this, we can conclude that even gender becomes nature. Because of this insight, gender as a Western conceptual apparatus is collapsing. In Bhutan, nature is top of the world and the absolute principle.

To summarise, during the interviews, I realised that my Western concep-tions of gender, Buddhism, and sustainability had a completely different mean-ing than they had for Bhutanese. I had to adjust these concepts; the result was that, as a start, I had to adjust "sustainability" into nature. As a result, nature became "religion"; what I thought was that "Buddhism" actually was animism and finally "gender" became nature because there was no value distinction between men, women, and animals. In Buddhism, these are called sentient beings: all sentient beings are equal. So the Western concept of gender can be understood as compassion for life, and for nature.

But, in the course of my writing, my understanding shifted another time. The country is making the transition from a pre-modern society toward a mod-ern society. There I found another Western misunderstanding. Even economic development as a Western category does not fit the Bhutanese cosmology. The King of Bhutan is aware of the vulnerable cosmology of the country; he uses a Bhutanese concept for economic development that fits and tries to protect this natural cosmology of Bhutan. Instead of Gross National Product, he intro-duced the Bhutanese concept of Gross National Happiness, a holistic Bhuta-nese approach toward development that is embedded in the values and tradi-tions of the country and in which nature is a guiding force.

In other words, while I walked (as a Western researcher) the bridges of re-ligion, gender, and sustainability (all Western concepts), I realised during the interviews in Bhutan that the bridges were starting to fall apart under me. I know where I came from (Europe), but these Western concepts did not bring me to the place I wanted to go (Bhutan). At the end of this journey in words, I realise upon further research and analysis that gender and the animist/Buddhist cosmology of the Bhutanese people are embedded and related to the natural environment they have compassion for. All are as a coherent cosmology. In the Western world, we are happy to be able to understand processes and these processes are disconnected from the context; we see them as fragmented entities in the development of knowledge. In Bhutan, phenomena and reality are regarded and understood as interconnected and coherent. The consequence is that it is hard to build bridges to Bhutan based on Western concepts, which do not take in consideration Bhutan's holistic cosmology.

What about Bhutanese holistic cosmology when global capitalism enters the country?

If I try to compare this cosmology, these "vivid keys" into Bhutan, with my own Western perspective, I realise that I am a product of the rationalist, analytic, modern, and post–modern "cosmology" of my society, which I felt much stronger during my experience with Bhutan. I realised that my meeting the "other" is a meeting between someone from the Western world with someone from a different Bhutanese world; my perspective was differing from a Bhutanese perspective. As a consequence, I can draw the conclusion now that Western concepts do not work because Bhutan is a coherent cosmos.

I learned from my meeting with Bhutan to appreciate better certain values as compassion, non-domination, politeness, and patience. I learned to look "deeper," and that beyond horizons there are more horizons. I learned to be aware of my own prejudices and my own ethnocentricity. In this regard, I learned from Wikan's shocking story about a woman's life in Bhutan, not explaining anything about Bhutanese society. I think we can learn a lot from the holistic cosmology perspective still active in Bhutanese society: respect for nature, respect for all forms of life that results in an economic model — Gross National Happiness.

The big question is: will Bhutan be able to keep following the line of Gross National Happiness now that global capitalism is coming in? I have experienced the country for many years and I witnessed a slow change. In 1990, I encountered a pre-modern society that existed in the present. This society still was very traditional. During my stay in the village in 1990, I witnessed a society in which reciprocity in work and barter was more important than money, and the people lived on the rhythm of the seasons.

Bhutanese society was a kind of ideal society for me, because nature provided everything that the villagers needed; they only had to grow and harvest rice for four to five months. Vegetables and herbs were collected in the forest.

The people in the village live close to nature and close to their gods. Nature provides the villagers with food and their gods and deities created the guidelines for conduct and values.

One disadvantage of the traditional society was the absence of health care. Access to health care was difficult and people suffered from and even died of preventable and curable diseases.

Marx (1977), from a Western perspective, would classify the village society where I stayed in 1990 as organic, hierarchical, and one whose members are dependent on each other. Bhutanese society was hierarchical in status and possession of land. All households owned enough land to be self-sufficient. The shortage of labour, however, was expected to increase because after 1990 children had access to schools and most young educated people left the village to find employment in the city.

In 1990, Thimphu was a small town with one hotel and one public telephone, a small basic health unit, and an estimate of only 10.000 inhabitants (this is an estimation of people who lived in Thimphu; a census was not undertaken then).

In 2004, Bhutan was in transition from a medieval society to a modern society, with its own distinctive identity as a Buddhist Himalayan Kingdom. This is expressed in the Bhutanese economic model of Gross National Happiness: Bhutan is a kind of a welfare state in South Asia because of free health care and education. The government is a large employer and controls many fields. Soon, a new generation of Bhutanese will take over and the question is: will they continue on the same path as the government today?

Bhutan faces many challenges. City life is becoming more modern and popular; the number of salaried jobs is increasing; private enterprise is being stimulated and is becoming attractive for many people. Until very recently, men in the city predominantly were engaged in salaried work. When a couple "marries" or lives together, the woman often stays at home and cares for the house and children if no relatives live in the area. Women who want to combine work and motherhood look to their parents and family members to mind the children.

According to my findings in 2004, Bhutan is losing its old ways of gender interaction. The overall opinion is that now that the country is developing, gender relations are becoming more equal. However, with an increasing market economy, there is a tendency for women to lose their traditional position as head of household. The influence from India and other countries, especially through TV and films, changes the view and expectations of boys and girls. Boys expect girls to be housewives and homemakers and girls like boys to be the money earners. The influence on young people of these Western and

Indian role models from TV, literature, tourists, and travel is growing. More awareness of Bhutan's social history in schools could be very beneficial for the future.[1] But today, values such as caring, sustainability, long-term planning, patience, helping, gentleness, and compassion still are valued highly. In this regard, the natural environment is cherished as a living entity that has to be treated with respect and care. These values can explain the government's policy of sustainability and the government attitudes toward everything living. It is the connection inside Bhutan of gender and sustainability in a general context inside Bhutan that could be a crucial area for further exploration outside Bhutan. Perhaps this link could provide information in greater detail on issues like respect, compassion, and sensitivity to social and environmental surroundings. An exploration of the fields of shamanism in connection with gender and sustainability could be very interesting and valuable.

In 2004, Thimphu was growing; a market economy was emerging, especially for the urban population and the tourism industry. More and more shops, restaurants, and hotels were being built. Thimphu's population had reached 100.000 and there were discos, restaurants, bars, and small shopping malls.[2]

Since 1999, Bhutan has had TV, Internet, and mobile telephones. Although times are changing, religion still is important in urban and rural areas. Mythology and legend still play an important part in daily life. Next to the Buddhist monks and nuns, *ngejums* and *powas* are still the shamanistic pre-Buddhist specialists. The Bhutanese government and clerics officially recognise the ancient belief in the sacred landscape; there are *stupas*, prayer wheels and prayer flags, at almost every bend of the road and on the high mountain passes. All these places have mythical stories.

Driglam Namzha, the guideline from the seventeenth century, is used in daily life. For all my conversation partners, *Driglam Namzha* was important, particularly among the upper strata. There was concern for preservation of traditional values and customs in light of modernisation and Western influence. Ironically, it is this group, trained in foreign countries and the least familiar with the *Driglam Namzha,* who urge its preservation. Just as *Driglam Namzha* is regarded as important, some of my conversation partners with medium Western/English education want it to be modernised and to become less hierarchical. The views of religion between the medium-educated Western/English respondent and the

---

1 Indian nationals and members of SAARC countries are free to enter Bhutan without a visa. Other people need a visa and have to travel to Bhutan trough a Bhutanese travel agency. A tourist visa can cost between $180 and $240 per day but it includes lodging, meals, and transportation. Some Bhutanese have a "quota," which means they can invite foreigners without paying the tourist visa. To be able to work or to do research in Bhutan, one needs a work/research visa from the government.

2 See: http://en.wikipedia.org/wiki/Thimphu

non-Western-educated respondent differed significantly. The former regard them as Buddhist but would like to modernise the monastic institutions. They are very concerned with keeping the Bhutanese traditions but in a way that fits the contemporary way of life. These people are afraid of losing the distinct Bhutanese religious traditions. It is interesting to see this contradiction between wanting to reform the old institutions and keeping them because of the changing times. This vision of the conversation partners has more to do with their education than with living in the globalised capital or in the countryside. The people who had the advantage of higher education are aware of the changes of the traditions and culture. At the same time, they are more alienated from those traditions and religion, so they question them and do not take them for granted.

Many young people like to work for the government; this means a steady income in money and many benefits. Many Bhutanese prefer this to being a farmer. Becoming a civil servant means security; being a farmer is risky, and it is not so beneficial for one's *karma*. Bhutan will face many challenges in the areas of employment, increased birth rate due to improved medical care, and finding sources of revenue to be able to pay for the "welfare state."

Although change is happening, there is a strong awareness from the government but also from the Bhutanese people in general that their culture and way of life is unique, and that it is worthwhile to protect its vulnerability. Here lies the challenge: whether the model of Gross National Happiness in the end is able to protect this Bhutanese holistic cosmology.

Meeting the Other, becoming Other

As an anthropology student in the 1980s, I had problems with the fact that not much attention was paid to the ethical code of the researcher when studying another culture. I resented the arrogance of the Western academic approach to non-Western cultures.

In this book, the themes are explored and written in a post-modern humanistic tradition, in which an ethical code is maintained and in which self-reflection is a guideline. I asked myself how I could contribute to the development of reflexive arguments in order to understand gender and nature in the Bhutanese setting. In my reflections, studying "the other" is crucial; by studying the other, I can start to understand my own feelings, interpretations, observations, and prejudices. In other words, what can I learn from this experience; how did this experience in Bhutan change me?

I like to reflect upon my actions as a Western researcher in Bhutan.

Why am I writing this essay on Bhutan instead of on my country or one closer to me? When I first had the chance to go to Bhutan, I had no idea what to expect.

I was sent to a country that was closed to foreigners and about which not much had been written. For me, this was a tremendous challenge. I always dreamt of how it must have been for the explorers of the nineteenth and twentieth centuries to go to far-flung places, where nobody had gone before. I welcomed the chance to experience this.

Did my first stay in Bhutan change my life? It did, indeed. Through my experiences there, I learned more about my own country and myself. During this first trip, I learned *not* to judge too soon and to be aware of my own ethnocentricity. "Things were not always as they seem to be." I realised that what I saw was "my image," "my view," and therefore was biased. Crapanzano (2004) points out that we construct horizons that determine what we experience and how we interpret what we experience. There and then, I understood what he has meant. During my stay in a small Bhutanese village, I encountered a fascinating society. I wanted to learn more about it; I had many questions about what I saw.

The first visit to Bhutan and stay in the village was a deep experience. At first, everything was alien to me. In the first month of my stay in Bhutan, I suffered from culture shock. After the first month, I adapted, and the alien world was not so alien anymore.

My second visit, nine years later, was not very different from the first. The second visit was like a homecoming. Arriving in Bhutan and smelling the familiar smells, hearing the beautiful Bhutanese language again, felt so familiar. Bhutan became almost like a second home. I felt that way in all my subsequent visits.

During this second stay, I realised that I wanted to do further studies on Bhutan. I talked to many Bhutanese about how to proceed. Karma Ura and the Centre for Bhutan Studies helped me to obtain a research visa. The Bhutanese government was suspicious of Western researchers who come to their country. During the 1980s, cultural anthropology did not pay much attention to self-reflection in the field and in ethnographic writing. More attention was paid to the hardships an anthropologist has to endure during fieldwork in a non-Western setting and in the remote corners of the world. Very limited attention was paid to the interaction with "the other." The anthropologist had to stay objective and find an answer to the research question.

During my own fieldwork, I realised the impact of my presence in the village. In the first two weeks, people asked us what we were doing there and if we were from the government. We also noticed that the people complained about the hardships of daily life. After they had become accustomed to us, this attitude changed. I learned to observe and to listen; I really did learn that it was very important to interact with the people. I learned to help them when help was needed, and to be compassionate in times of trouble.

The people in the village started to trust us and they came many times to ask for help in cases of sickness and injury. One day, a village monk gave us Bhutanese names and a family adopted us as their daughters. During my many other visits to Bhutan, I encountered openness, trust, and friendship. I realise that I still was seeing this non-Western culture through western eyes.

What do I mean by that? The concept of time in Bhutan, and especially in the village, was very difficult to understand. In the beginning, people did not greet or say goodbye to each other. I thought that this meant that we were not welcome, but the opposite was the case. I learned that much later, after I discovered that the Bhutanese people live in the present. I also had to get used to the presence of the many deities and gods that had to be pleased; all the do's and don'ts were very complicated for me. What also was very hard to comprehend was to not show any anger, frustration, or impatience; by showing any of these, one loses face, and this would shock Bhutanese people.

Bhutanese and Western people have different ways of interacting. It took time to learn how the Bhutanese communicate and to understand them at least a little. I learned to be more patient, because this is a very important value.

I realised what observations can be deceptive. There are layers and multiple realities to be discovered. I realised that being an objective researcher is a challenge, and the interaction of other humans a strange and mechanic concept that is not appropriate in the interaction with humans and cultural analysis.

I realised that the Bhutanese cosmology is very vulnerable, and the Bhutanese people are aware of this. Bhutan is the last bastion in the world that has not been ruined by modernisation. In the 1990s, Bhutan still was exotic. Today, the country is opening and development is progressing rapidly.

Can we conclude from these changes that the country is in the process of ruin and cultural decay? I think not. What do the Bhutanese think? There will be change and maybe we Western researchers will not like this, but it will be a challenge to see what these changes are bringing: new possibilities for an old culture.

This thesis is an essay about *my* 17-year meeting with Bhutan. When writing about Bhutan, I have an obligation to write about "the other" with respect. People in Bhutan are very proud of their country, and my experience is that I can write about everything, as long it is not in an insulting or confrontational way. To judge another culture is a dangerous thing to do. There are layers of realities and, as Crapanzano says, "when an author does not distinguish between his own view and native's views, readers tend to forget that the author's voice is the only one they hear in the writing." Therefore, readers assume that a text is transmitting an objective reality. Another point Crapanzano makes is that anthropologists generalise about the whole population of a society. For example, based on his experience with a group of informants in his research, Geertz wrote: "the Balinese never do anything in a simple way when they can contrive to do it in a complicated way" [...] and "the Balinese are shy to the point of obsessiveness of open conflict" (McGee & Warms, 2004:603). Crapanzano argues that this kind of generalisation is commonplace among anthropologists. Anthropologists tend to separate themselves from the population they are studying. Crapanzano claims that Geertz separated the "anthropologist" from "his Balinese" (McGee & Warms, 2004:603). "Anthropologists, and all social scientists have to be wary of hear[ing] the voices of those we study, not only what they have to say about themselves but also what they say about us." (Crapanzano, 2004). For the methodological consequences of this sentence, I refer to the next paragraph.

In my conversations with Bhutanese who lived in the capital, I realised that their daily life is similar to mine. The greatest difference is the connection between religion and worldview on sustainability. Doing research in Bhutan is very easy, because people are hospitable. All my interview partners had time for me and it seemed that they enjoyed our talk. With Dorji, my translator, I drove to different places. What surprised me was that Dorji knew so much about the Western world. We had long conversations; she liked the music of the Dixie Chicks. Dorji has never been outside Bhutan but she knew what was going on in the world.

Coming back to becoming "other": Bhutan broadened my horizon. I learned that there are different worlds, that one can try to understand that other world and one can adjust to the other world; this is meeting the otherness, but becoming the other in a total sense is something different. Sometimes, I encountered the "Asian or Bhutanese" way of interaction that I did not understand at all. I realised that there are layers of values, hierarchy, and etiquettes that are profoundly different from those in my world.

At the end I did not become Bhutanese. I realise my condition is very Western. But I learned to understand the Bhutanese worldview and the Buddhist values; the latter (I think) could be very suitable for a highly developed capitalist country as The Netherlands, in which money of prime importance.

I think we can learn a lot from Bhutan. In our developed world, we are facing many sever problems because of our relation – or lack of relation – with nature. The result we all know. More and more scientists claim that we have to approach the world in a much more holistic way, because we are realising that we all are connected. To be able to heal people and to heal the world, a holistic approach is of vital importance, and in this sense, we can learn from Bhutan: Having more respect for nature, protecting nature by making laws that really make a difference. And by nature, I mean people, animals, and flora. In this, I became the other. By meeting the other, I became other; by learning from the other, my life became richer and I learned to be compassionate.

Reflection on methodology

The research for this book has not been planned; this book came into existence organically. The research for this book consists of three forms: The first form was anthropological research in the village in Bhutan in 1990; the second consists of social conversations conducted in 2004; and the last form is self-reflection.

In the prologue I gave a description of my first encounter with Bhutan, my stay in the village. Here, I would like to reflect on the interviews I conducted in 2004:

Gender and natural environment according to the respondents

As we have seen, Buddhism in Bhutan's daily life is strongly animistic. Bhutanese religion never has abolished female mediumship or shamanism. It respects and worships female saints, who are protective deities within nature. The feminine part in Buddhism and in pre-Buddhist religion is respected as much as the male part. However, there is a contradiction in regard to women in Buddhism. Nuns, farmers, and women with less education regard themselves as spiritually inferior to men. This view of inferiority is physical, not intellectual. As we have seen above, I came to the conclusion that gender is nature, and in this sense in Bhutan, there is no value judgment attached to the gender or even to animals. All sentient beings are regarded as equal and can be regarded as a value tool that is very different from my Western value system. Just as Dilgo Khyentse Rinpoche noted in chapter three, in Buddhism, all life is precious and this life is a result of previous lives; this is related to karma and incarnation, the law of cause and effect. All sentient beings are suffering because of the endless wheel of being born again. This value domain in the Buddhist setting is reflected in the conversations I had. Another important value in Buddhism is compassion; it also is important to all my conversation partners.

In regard to natural environment, the Bhutanese government has chosen an encompassing and protective path for the country: 60 percent of the country still is protected dense forest and national park. The country is investing in hydroelectricity, using the mountain streams for the generation of electricity. This is the main source of income for the country. Tourism also is an important source of revenue and is much regulated; only a certain amount of people are allowed to visit the country per year.

But in regard to the gender relations, influence from outside has a great impact on Bhutanese gender relations. These gender relations are changing the traditionally strong position of women, as we have seen in chapter five, and little is done to create awareness about the uniqueness of the traditional gender relations.

For example, my Bhutanese conversation partners took gender equity for granted. The Bhutanese who have been living abroad are more aware of the presence of gender equity in their country because they have been to countries where it was not the norm. The influence of the Western world and neighbouring countries like India on gender relations is increasing. To the younger people I talked to, the male (father) is the head of the household, for example, and the women have to stay at home to be housewives. When I asked about their grandparents or even father and mother, they replied that the grandmother or mother was the head of the household and she had the last word in decision-making. But today, men are educated and they have to make all the decisions. Coming back to my conclusion that gender is nature in Bhutan, we can conclude that everything still is nature.

What happens if capitalism comes in? How does this affect the natural holistic cosmology of Bhutan and, as part of this, the gender relations?

The gender relations are changing under pressure of the increase of a market economy, but the culture and developmental paths of Bhutan still are much in line with its traditions. Bhutanese traditions and values seek harmony in all circumstances: community, family, authority, and decision-making. Values are part of the harmony of nature, not external to it; this is reflected in the answers to most of my questions. For example, losing one's patience or getting angry is seen as losing face, and by expressing these negative feelings, one attracts "negative energy" that is best avoided.

This way of thinking is dialectical, cyclical, and holistic, not circular and dualistic as in the West. Some Bhutanese told me: "There is not good or bad. For example, you think you do something good for someone but at the end for this person this deed can be received as not good at all, so it is a question whether this action was good or bad?" The intention was good and that was what counts. In the circular view, everything is connected and changing, even though things stay the same. The law of *karma* is an expression of this circular feature and *le judre is* an example.

According to the circular view, time is fluid. Patience is a virtue. One cannot force things to happen; they happen if the time is right. This concept of harmony, circular view, and holism reflects the outcome of the inquiry on values in Bhutan.

One concept that was dominant in the outcome of the inquiry was that of the "altruistic mind." This means that one has the duty to serve others; this is related to the selflessness that is a key Buddhist value. In Buddhism, it is seen as a major achievement for a sentient being to be born as a human; due to good deeds performed in previous lives, one has the chance in this life to escape from the circle of death and rebirth by reaching enlightenment. Only humans have the ability to reach enlightenment. This is extremely valuable and brings with it the responsibility of leading a good life. This is central to Bhutanese life and worldview. It means respect for all forms of life, and thus also for the natural environment. Nature is a holistic way of life and to most respondents it means protecting the Bhutanese way of life. This is the core value.

This nature as core value is translated by the King of Bhutan into a unique Bhutanese concept: Gross National Happiness. This concept is a holistic approach of preserving and developing the distinct Bhutanese society, a society in which the Bhutanese core value of natural environment is primary. Although traditions and values are cherished and important to the overall Bhutanese development strategy, traditions and values in regard to gender are neglected in contrast to nature. This is in line with my finding that gender is regarded as nature and part of nature. But to me, the gender relations as I experienced them, gender in the sense of how women and men interact with each other, are very interesting and worthwhile describing.

The Bhutanese government could benefit from studying gender relations and by designing a gender program for the future that will preserve Bhutanese gender values: a kind of "Gross Gender Happiness." This could take the form of a program to ensure that Gross National Happiness extends equally to both genders. I believe that Gross National Happiness is possible only if there is Gross Gender Happiness. Gross National Happiness is a natural outcome of Gross Gender Happiness, and it is here that the gender values and values of sustainability come together. This would be an interesting topic for further research, especially now that capitalism is coming into the country and the whole cosmology is changing.

Reflection on the value domains

In regard to the eight domains of Bilsky and Schwartz (1997), my findings during my research in 2004 are that certain value domains are more important than others. The answers given to the questions I asked in 2004 are related to certain domains and a reflection of which domains are valued most; they give insight into what the conversation partners find important. The first domain, the enjoyment domain, is highly valued. In general, the conversation partners are happy with their lives. In the security domain, the restrictive-conformity, pro-social, and maturity domains are valued highly; the respondents are secure in their country and with nature. Family values also are very important, as is education. Becoming more religious and being able to help others more are the most popular achievements.

Although all conversation partners feel free to make choices for their lives, important decisions are made jointly or with a partner, mother, older sister, or father, depending on the composition of the household. Obedience, politeness, cleanliness, and self-control are important values for all respondents. Being helpful, forgiving, loving, and to honour equality are important values, too, and most respondents even regard animals as equal to humans. Moreover, compassion is very important. Almost every conversation partner had a different definition of love. Love is not as important a value as in the West. I was surprised that my respondents had problems answering my question about love.

The social-power and achievement domains are not recognised by the conversation partners. Social recognition is power, and is regarded as freedom to do what one wants. Only a minority of men and women see money as a means to power. Being able to help others, friendliness, and self-control are forms of power. Leadership, authority, and status are regarded as something that must be earned and that comes with a great amount of responsibility.

As said before, these value domains of Bilsky and Schwartz are very American and this theory has its weak points, but as a start it helped to point out certain values that people find important. The domains are designed for a Western culture, although Bilsky and Schwarz claim they are applicable universally. For Bhutan, they are shortcomings, and I realise that Buddhist and pre-Buddhist values are dominant in the answers about how people value religion, gender, and sustainability. I deduce from the interviews that values like non-domination in relation to other sentient beings, compassion, altruism, harmony, and being non-judgemental are core values. The human realm and the natural realm are regarded with equal respect, the only difference being that as a human, one has the ability to reach enlightenment and to become a bodhisattva to help other sentient beings reach enlightenment. Deeper study on values of this Bhutanese culture based on nature would be another interesting topic for further research, since there are not many countries left in the world where this is still alive.

Comments on Wikan

Finally, as a consequence of my reflections, I developed a comment on Wikan's article on the nun. *What is my comment?* Wikan took the nun's story out of context and her story highlights an unpleasant aspect of Bhutanese life. It is easy for women to be raped in a country in which most people live in remote areas and are surrounded by dense forests. Footpaths connect most villages and women travelling alone are vulnerable. Even in Thimphu, the capital, it can be very dark at night, and the national newspaper reports cases of rape. Is this different from any other country? Rape always has been a threat to women everywhere.

Wikan used a sentence in her article that insulted many Bhutanese intellectuals. This became clear during a conference on Bhutan studies in 2003 organised by the Centre for Bhutan Studies. Wikan cites a Bhutanese saying, "let those who have less suffer more" (Wikan, 1996:281) in relationship to the suffering of Grandma.

What Wikan describes is the hard life of *one* woman in Bhutan. Why did *Wikan* decide to tell this one story? What were the experiences of other women? This story presents a very different Bhutan. In the story, the anthropologist depicts Bhutan as a country where rape, even by monks, is commonplace. What about the role of the *government*? This institution takes everything away and leaves grandma with nothing. Does Bhutan have a government that takes from its people? Today, Bhutan is known as a "welfare state." Education and health care are free, and when I was in the village, the Bhutanese government gave land to families who did not have any. This is in contrast with Wikan's story.

Wikan's perspective is very Western; she tells an extreme story and emphasises only the suffering of Grandma. She gives the impression that women in Bhutan are oppressed and have no freedom of choice. Did Wikan learn anything from her experience in Bhutan? She does not elaborate on this.

The concepts on which Wikan *focuses in her work* are civil society, gender, and social ethics, and she uses reflexivity in her encounters with that society to defend what she finds important. She should have elaborated more on the Bhutanese society as a whole to give the reader a wider context of the story of grandma. Or she should have given a Bhutanese perspective on the story in contrast to her Western perspective. This would have been very valuable and it would have been a very interesting gender study.

My view of Bhutanese society is very different; even my Western perspective on Bhutanese society is very different than Wikan's. During my research in the village, I noticed that the women had a strong position as head of the household. Inheritance went from mother to daughter and, in general, parents preferred daughters to sons. What impressed me most was the freedom women had; they could travel wherever they wanted, and even young girls did not need permission from their parents. Village women are free to have romantic relations with men and a couple did not need to marry if they wanted to live together. Divorce or separation was easy and not stigmatised. Monks and nuns, if they did not made a vow of chastity, can have sexual relations or they can live together. And as we have seen, in Bhutan it is socially accepted that a woman can be married to two brothers or a man to two or more sisters, as in the case of the king of Bhutan

My experience is that men were very gentle and helpful; in the village, men cooked, sewed, and took care of babies and children. Later, I asked many women in Bhutan about what it meant to be a woman. To my surprise, my feeling of being a woman in a Western world was the same as that of the "uneducated" women in Bhutan. Women in the village did not like to be women because of the physical pain of menstruation and of giving birth. Women were not free to travel because they had to take care of their children. Bhutanese women do not see themselves as inferior to men, but they have to suffer more. I shared this view with the women in Bhutan.

So my inquiry is different than Wikan's. Hers is a life story of one woman in Bhutan who endured many hardships, and it is written down in her words. It would have been interesting to know what the nun would have said about this story if someone had read it to her. Just as in Wikan's story, there are many horizons or beyond of the picture of grandma. It is just what we want to see or what "freezes our view."

Wikan took the story of grandma out of any context, and it is written in Western grammar, without any deeper reflection on Wikan's side.

This is an example of my own experience in the field that "froze my view." One household was building a new house and had hired a group of carpenters. The carpenters were guests of the family that hired them and had to be treated very well. They were given good food, plenty of *arra* (an alcoholic drink made of rice), and lots of betel nuts. The family told me that the head carpenter had to be born in the year of the snake because this would symbolise a stable foundation for the house. On the day that the roof was to be put on, there was a big party. Everybody in the village was invited and the party started at six o'clock in the morning.

I went to the house around eleven and most of the villagers were there. There was singing and dancing. In Bhutan, the women sometimes dance separately from the men. To my surprise, I saw one of the carpenters dressed like a woman! This went on for the whole day. At that time, I did not have a good translator; I had a young boy who was not very skilled and I asked him why this man was dressed like a woman. The translator replied: "This is Bhutanese custom!" This was a very unsatisfactory answer. I wondered if the man was a transvestite? I found out later that this was my Western interpretation.

Later, when I had a better interpreter, I asked the villagers why this man had been dressed like a woman. I discovered there had been an unlucky number of female guests; one more was needed, and so they asked the carpenter if he would be willing to be a woman for one day in order to "satisfy the gods." I never would have thought of this! In Bhutan, auspicious numbers and days are very important and everybody tries to live up to them. The people find many ways to get around these rules when necessary. At first, I thought that this story could give a deeper meaning to gender, but then again, I did not see women behave as men in Bhutan. Could it be an example of a religious play comparable to one in Europe during medieval times in which men played women?

Still, the fact that a man was willing to be a woman for one day struck me as very unusual; but for the Bhutanese, it was perfectly normal. The horizon behind this story is sense-making and gender in Bhutan, or can we conclude that gender is not an issue at all? Behind this story, there are many more stories and meanings. It helps us, as Westerners, to look past our own interpretations and prejudices.

In my writing, I tried to let the "other" speak as much as possible, and I checked my assumptions with my Bhutanese counterparts. In addition, I tried to use as many Bhutanese sources as possible to confirm my findings. This does not mean that one cannot be critical, but to criticise a different world or "the other" is possible only if one has a deep knowledge of the "other" and if one knows the background of what is being criticised.

There are some aspects of the Bhutanese culture that I do not like, but these are a part of the Bhutanese reality. While in the field, I could identify the "multiple realities" that had been pointed out by Marcus and Fisher. Life in the capital city of Thimphu was different from life in a Bhutanese village. Thimphu was developing as a modern globalised capital and many Bhutanese are leading a more Western lifestyle, although the culture still is distinctively Bhutanese.

Another reality that I saw was that of the life in the monasteries and nunneries. I had long talks with nuns and monks around Buddhist scriptures, meditation, and the rules inside the monasteries, with the goal of reaching enlightenment or at least a better incarnation in the next life. I realised that the life of a farmer in Tsachaphu, the village that I described in chapter one, has its own reality, just as does the businessman in Thimphu and a nun or monk.

Because of my long stay in the village, I learned about village life, which is the root of the Bhutanese culture. Not long ago, Bhutan consisted only of villages and hamlets. Thimphu is becoming more and more globalised, with Internet cafés, restaurants, and shopping malls, but next to this reality is a different one.

The farmers, monks, and nuns have a different life. The life of the farmers and the clerics has not been changed much the last hundred years. Although change is underway by means of infrastructure (electricity for the villages and more roads to connect the villages), schools and hospitals are available to everybody. People are exposed to TV and the Internet and the world is becoming bigger. People know that Bhutan is a small Himalayan kingdom sandwiched between two giants: India and China. Every Bhutanese I spoke to was aware of his or her distinct identity as Bhutanese and wanted to do everything to preserve the traditions and religion of the country. Since this topic is so broad, additional research is necessary.

I was shocked by the nuns' poor image of themselves. Those I talked with regarded themselves as inferior to the monks, as more dirty because of menstruation, and as less religious because of a folk belief that women cannot reach enlightenment. This made me sad, because to me the ultimate compassion – and compassion is a core value in Buddhism – is the compassion of a mother toward her child. I talked to the nuns about this and they had never thought about this. I also found this negative self-image with regard to religion among "uneducated" village women. However, this does not mean that women have an inferior position in society. But there is a contradiction with being a nun in Bhutan. I asked my female conversation partners if they were interested in becoming a nun one day in their lives; interestingly, most of them, even the highly educated women, had thought of it or would like to become a nun at a certain point in their lives, But, talking to the nuns, it seems that they are happy being a nun – but not happy to be a woman. They are happy to be able to live a "clean" life and get Buddhist education as a nun.

To me, Wikan's article shows that anthropologists can be biased. This reflection was for me the main reason for my inquiring conversations with Bhutanese.

Post Script: Impressions and reflection of my last visit in 2007

February 2007. I went back to Bhutan. This time, I could use my mobile phone. Many new hotels have been built, five-star hotels with luxury as in Bangkok and other big cities in the world. The number of tourists who can visit the country has grown from 5,000 per year to 20,000. Tourism is a very lucrative industry. Before one enters the Thimphu valley is a site where the biggest Buddha in the world will be built.

The beautiful small town of Wangdi, next to the *dzong,* will be destroyed and the town will be rebuilt on a paddy field a few kilometres from the *dzong.* Like Punakha, it will be a new concrete ugly town (satellite town) and the villagers who have to walk for hours from their villages to visit the *dzong* will have to walk much further to do their shopping.

In 2005, a nationwide ban on smoking was imposed. Even more shocking is that during religious festivals (lasting from three to nine days) in the *dzong*, there were carnivals next to the *dzong* where people could eat, drink, and play games. They were having a good time. One has to keep in mind that many visitors to the festivals are farmers from remote villages; for them, this festival is a welcome break in their life. They can meet other people from villages in the area. Now the government has banned the carnival next to the *dzong*. It has moved to a space more than five kilometres away from the *dzong*; and alcohol and gambling have been banned. At the same time, in Thimphu on Friday and Saturday nights, there are discos and bars for the city youth.

Bhutan is joining the rest of the world: consumerism is increasing; more cars are coming, more shops and malls; everybody has a mobile phone. It makes me sad, but do I have the right to be sad? I have a mobile phone; I like to drive; I like to shop; and I like the easy life. Why shouldn't the Bhutanese do the same?

During my conversations with Bhutanese people, especially in the city, they expressed the same feelings. Consumerism is increasing and people are realising that they like to have cars, computers, and mobile phones. One person said to me: "I have a car, but it would be handy to have a second car." She added, "it is strange that although I am very privileged and I do have a lot of things, I want to have more."

Glossary

Arra	Rice wine.
Bardo Thödol	Tibetan death-books. The Bon religion of Tibet and Tibetan Buddhism both maintain that crucial moments of transition are charged with great spiritual potential, especially the intervening moments between death and rebirth.
Bodhisattva	(Sanskrit) enlightened being, in Dzongkha: *changchub sempa.*
Chapdaula	Form of tax that the people have to pay.
Chiepen	Messenger.
Chokus	Rituals.
Chuko	A ritual which lasts for three days conditional upon the financial situation of a household.
Cimmi	Elected member of the National Assemble.
Dasho	Non-hereditary senior official; honorific title given by the king in recognition for services; also honorific title used for men of the royal family.
Desi	Title of Bhutan's temporal ruler.
Dhip	Negative energy, force.
Driglam namzha	Basic rules of disciplined behaviour, official Bhutanese etiquette.
Druk Yul	'Land of the Dragon' Land of the *Drukpa's* ; Bhutanese name for Bhutan.
Druk	'Thunder' dragon.
Drukpa	School of Buddhism, offshoot of the Kagyu tradition; also refers to the people of Bhutan.
Dung	'Bone', clan honorific title used for nobility of Bumtang and Keng.
Dzong	Fortress-monastery housing the civil administration and the *Drukpa* religious body.
Dzongdag	District head officer
Dzongkha	'Language of the fortress', national language of Bhutan.
Dzou	Puffed rice and a kind of popcorn.
Gandaula	Form of tax that the people have to pay is.
Getre	A retired monk.
Gewog	'Block'; administrative division of several villages within a district.

Gelong	A fully ordained monk.
Go	Man's dress.
Gomchen	Ascetic or hermit devoted to long periods of meditation.
Gompa	A hermitage. It should be situated at least thousand yards distant from a village or town.
Gup	Village headman.
Je kempo	Head abbot of Bhutan.
Katrim	Code of laws.
Kira	Women's wrap around dress, fastened at the shoulders with two brooches.
Konchog sum	Is used for Buddha, *dharma* and *sangha* – three collectively or separately. A precious gem of the rarest kind is useful only for worldly purposes, but Buddha, his teachings and the followers are of use to all living beings, both here, hereafter, for increasing and ensuring happiness.
Kundun	An embalmed body. A *tupa* containing relics or remains of a holy being.
La	Mountain pass.
Lama	Religious master, can be married.
Langdo	Is a measurement it means the amount of land that one person can work in one day.
Lha	Broad term used to refer to a variety of deities, gods or spirits.
Lhakang	Buddhist temple.
Lu	Serpent deity.
Lyonpo	Minister.
Marchoed	The tradition of animal sacrifice.
Ngejum	Shaman, oracle.
Ngalong	Generic name for the people of the five valleys of western Bhutan.
Pawo/pamo	Male and female oracles.
Puja	Ritual.
Rinpoche	'Precious one', term to address a reincarnated *lama*.
Shabdrung	"At whose feet one prostrates", title of the unifier of Bhutan.
Shidag	"Owner of the earth", category of local deities.
Stupa	Buddhist commemorative monument.
Terma	Concealed religious treasures, especially texts, awaiting rediscovery at a later time; many *terma* are said to have been hidden by Guru Rinpoche.

Tertön	Religious treasure revealer; person predestined to discover religious texts or objects.
Tormas	Small sculptures made of rice or wheat.
Trulku	Reincarnated lama, can have been married.
Tsawa sum	The "three foundations" of country, people and king.
Yulha	God of locality.

List of illustrations

Color illustrations following page 184

Literature

Acrewood, T. – tom.acrewoods.net/research/philosophy/ideology/marxism-capitalism

Allan, Ch., (1999) *The search for Shangri-La, a journey into Tibetan History.* Great Britain: Abacus.

Allison, E., (2004) "Spiritally Motivated Natural Resources Protection in Eastern Bhutan", in *The Spider and the Piglet.* Thimphu: Center for Bhutan Studies. P. 529.

Aris, M., (1979) *Bhutan.* Warminster, Wiltshire, England: Aris&Phillips.

Armington, S., (2002) *Bhutan.* Melbourne/Oakland/London: Lonely Planet Publications.

Arts, Hebinck, van Naerssen, (2002) *Voorheen de Derde Wereld, Ontwikkeling anders gedacht.* Alphen aan den Rijn, Haasbeek.

Arts, Dankelman & Rijniers, (2002) "Duurzame ontwikkeling. Dimensies, strategieën, valkuilen en perspectieven". In: *Voorheen de Derde Wereld, Ontwikkeling anders gedacht.* Alphen aan den Rijn, Haasbeek. Pp. 37-60.

Berghs, Harry (red.), (1991) *Denkwijzen* 6. Acco, Leuven/Amersfoort.

Bhattacharyya, N.N., (1977) *The Indian Mother Goddess.* New Delhi, Manohar publishers.

Boey, Koen, "De uitbuitingsleer van Karl Marx." In: *Denkwijzen*, Berghs, Harry (ed.). Leuven, Acco, 1991, p. 73-114.

Brauen, M., (1994) *"Irgendwo in Bhutan wo die Frauen fast immer das sagen haben",* Zurich, Waldut Verlag Zurich.

Boudon, R., (2001) *The origin of values.* New Brunswick, USA & London, UK, Transaction Publishers.

Bruntlandt, G., (ed.) (1987) *"Our Common Future"*: The World Commission on Environment and Development, Oxford: Oxford University Press.

Butler, J., (1990) *Gender trouble, feminism and the subversion of identity.* New York, Routledge.

Campbell, J., (2002) *Traveller in Space .* London: Continuum.

Carley M., Christie I., (2000) *Managing Sustainable Development.* London: Earthscan Publication Ltd.

Crapanzano, V.(2004) *Imaginative Horizons.* The University of Chicago Press, Chicago/London.

Cauquelin, J, Lim, P., Mayaer-Koenig, B., (2000) *Asian Values encounter with diversity.* Richmond:Curzon Press.

Centre For Bhutan Studies, (1999) *Development and it Challenges.* Thimphu.

Chah,A., (2003) in Palmer, M., Finlay, V., *Faith in Conservation New Approaches to Religion and Environment*. Washington D.C.: World Bank. P.79.

Chakravarti, B., (1979) *A cultural history of Bhutan*. Volume One, Calcutta: The Self Employment Bureau Publication.

Chakravarti, S.I. (1996) "The languages of Bhutan", in: *Bhutan society and polity*. New Delhi: Indus Publishing Company. P. 62.

Chhewang Rinzin, (2003) *Sustainability in Bhutan*, Thimphu: Royal Institute of Management, Thimphu (unpublished paper).

Clifford, J., (1988) *The Predicament of Culture Twentieth-century Ethnography, Literature and Art*. Harvard University press, Cambridge, MA.

Collingwood, R.G., (1945) *The Idea of Nature*. Oxford: Clarendon Press.

Commoner, B., (1972) T., *The Closing Circle, Confronting the Environmental Crisis*. London: Random House.

Cox, N., (1998) "An Introduction to Marx's Theory of Alienation", at http://pubs.socialistreviewindex.org.uk/isj79/cox.htm

Crins, H., (2004) "Gender values in a changing world" in *The Spider and the Piglet Thimphu: Centre for Bhutan studies*. P. 581.

Crins, H. , (1997) *"Bhutan"*. Landenreeks, Amsterdam: KIT press.

Crins, H., de Graaff, M., (1990) *F.M.I.S.* Tsachaphu research site, Thimphu: Department of Agriculture Irrigation Division. Royal Government of Bhutan.

Crins,H. ,Wangdi,K.P., (2000) *Women in Bhutan*. Amsterdam (Unpublished paper).

Crins, H. (1994) *Tsachaphu, een dorp in Bhutan*. Amsterdam Vrije Universiteit, Master's thesis.

Delphy, Ch., (1992) *Familiar exploitations a new analysis of marriage in contemporary Western society*. Cambridge: Polity Press.

Den Uyl, M. (1995) *Invisible Barriers*. Utrecht International books.

Department of Planning, Royal Government of Bhutan, Ministery of Finance (2003) *Convention on the Elimination of all Forms of Discrimination Against Women*. Thimphu:Kuensel Corporation.

Diamond, Orenstein, (1990) *Reweaving the World, The Emergence of Ecofeminism*, San Francisco, Sierra Club Books.

Dieren van, W., (editor) (1995), *Taking Nature Into Account*. New York: Springer Verlag Inc.

Dorji Thinley, (2004) *The Bone Tongue*. Kuensel Corporation Thimphu, Bhutan.

Dilgo Khyentse Rinpoche, (1996) *Excellent Path to Enlightenment*. Ithaca New York: Snow Lion Publications.

Dzongkha Development Commission, (1990) *Dzongkha Rabsel Lamzang,* Thimphu: Dzongkha Development Commission, Royal Government of Bhutan.

Eliade, M., (1972) *Shamanism. Archaic Techniques of Ecstasy.* Princeton: Princeton University Press.

Elstar, J., (1987) *An Introduction to Karl Marx.* Cambridge University Press.

Foster, K *et al.,* (2005) "Coming to Autoethnography: A Mental Health Nurse's Experience". In: *International Journal of Qualititative Methods* 4 (4) December 2005.

Fox Keller, E., Longino, E. (1996) *Feminism and Science.* New York/Oxford: Oxford University Press.

Gardner, K & Lewis, D., (1996) *Anthropology, Development and the Post–Modern Challenge.* Pluto Press, London/Sterling, Virginia.

Geertz, C., (1968) "Religion as a Cultural System" in *The Religious Situation,* edited by D. Cutler. Beacon Press.

Geertz, Clifford, (1973) *The interpretations of Culture.* Basic Books, Inc., Publishers. New York.

Goslin, D.L., (2001) *Religion and Ecology.* London: Routledge.

Giddens, A., (1991) *Modernity and Self-Identity.* Cambridge: University Press.

Griffin, S., (1990) "Curves along the road", in *Reweaving The World, The Emergence of Ecofeminism.* San Francisco: Sierra Club Books.

Gyatso, J., (1987) "Down With the Demoness: Reflections on a Feminine Ground in Tibet", in *Feminine Ground, Essays on women and Tibet,* J. Willis (ed.). New York: Snow Lion Publications. P. 33-52.

Han Sung Joo (1999) *Changing Values in Asia: Their impact on governance and development.* Tokyo: Japan Center for International Exchange 2003. Pp. vii-9.

Harding, S., (1991) *"Whose Science? Whose Knowledge? Thinking from women's lives".* Ithaca New York: Cornell University Press.

Hofstede, G., (1998) *Masculinity and Femininity.* London, Sage Publications, London.

Holmstrom, N., (1986) "Do women have a distinct nature?" in *Women and Values: Readings in Recent Feminist Philosophy.* Edited by Marilyn Pearsall. California: Wadsworth Publishing Company. P 50.

Horner, I.B., (1999) *Women under primitive Buddhism,* Delhi: Motilal Banarsidass Publishers Private Limited.

Imaeda, Y., (1994) *Bhutan: A changing Himalaya Buddhist Kingdom.* Tokyo: Daitou. (Translated from Japanese)

Ingram, P.O., (1988) *"Buddhist-Christian dialogue, two universal religions in transformation"* N.Y.: The Edwin Meller Press.

Jigmi Thinley, (1999) "Gross National Happiness and Human Development –searching for common ground", in *Gross National Happiness* Thimphu: Center for Bhutan Studies.

Jones, A., (1987) "From fragmentation to wholeness: a green approach to science and society", *The Ecolist*, vol.17, pp. 236-40 .

Karma Phuntsho, (2004) "Echos of Ancient Ethos: Reflections on Some Popular Bhutanese Social Themes", in *The Spider and The Piglet*. Bhutan: The Centre for Bhutan Studies. Pp. 564-581.

Karma Ura, (2002) "Faith on a Suburban Apple Farm", in *Festival and Faith at Nyimalung*. Japan: Hirakawa Shuppan Inc.. Pp. 215-218.

Karma Ura, (2001) "Deities and Environment", in *Kuensel: Bhutan's National Newspaper*, Nov.26.

Kinzang Dorji (Lyonpo), (1998) in National Environment Commission, Royal Government of Bhutan (1998)

The Middle Path, National environment strategy for Bhutan. Thailand: Keen Publishing.

Kunzang Choden, (1997) "Women in the city", in *Mountain Fortress of the Gods*, London: Serindia. P. 253.

Lham Dorji, (2003) *Sergamathang Kothkin and other Bhutanese Marriage Customs*. Centre for Bhutan Studies, Thimphu Bhutan.

Linton, R., (1961) *The cultural background of personality*. London: Routledge & Kegan.

Love, Nancy Sue, (1986) *Marx and Nietzsche: critics of the Rational Society*. Cornell University New York. University Microfilm International, Ann Arbor, Michigan.

Malinowski, B., (1960) *Argonauts of the Western Pacific: an account of native enterprise and adventure in the Archipelagoes of Melanesian New Guinea*. New York: Dutton.

Mancall, M (2004) "Gross National Happiness and Development: An Essay", in: *Gross National Happiness and Development*, Proceedings of the first international conference on operationalization of Gross National Happiness. Centre for Bhutan Studies, Thimphu. Pp. 191-203.

Marcus, E.G. & Michael M.J. Fischer, (1986) *Anthropology as cultural critique: an experimental moment in the human sciences* . The University of Chicago Press.

Makley, Charlene E., (2002) "On the Edge of Respectability: Sexual Politics in China's Tibet", in *Positions: East Asia Cultures Critique* – Volume 10, Number 3, Winter 2002, pp. 575-630.

Martine, G., (2001) "FAO women and population decision", at www.fao.org/WAICENT/FAOINFO/SUSTDEV/Wpdirect/WPan0020.htm

Marx, K., (1961) *Economic and philosophic manuscripts of 1844.* Foreign Languages Publishing House, Moscow.

Marx, K. (Jessup&Wheatley ed.), (1999) *Social and Political Thought, critical assessments of leading political philosophies, second series.* Routledge.

Marx, K., (1977) *Selected Writings.* Oxford University Press.

Marx, K., (1976) Capital. Vol 1. Penguin publishers. London.

http://www.marxfaq.org/archive/marx/works/1861/economic/ch13.htm   Karl Marx and the concept of time

McGee, R. Jon & Richard L. Warms, (2004) *Anthropological Theory: An Introductory History.* New York: McGraw Hill.

Mead, M., (1965) *Male and Female. A study of the sexes in a changing world.* Pelican Books.

Mellor, M., (1997) *Feminism and Ecology.* Cambridge, UK: Polity press.

Merchant, C., (1980) *The death of nature. Women, Ecology and the Scientific Revolution.* Harper, San Franscisco.

Ministry of Agriculture, (2002) *Biodiversity Action Plan for Bhutan*, Thimphu: Royal Government of Bhutan.

Ministry of Planning, (1996-2002) *Eight five year plan.* Vol.1 Thimphu: Royal Government of Bhutan.

Myers, D.K., (1994) "Textiles in Bhutan II: Cloth, Gender and Society", in : *Bhutan: Aspects of Culture and Development*, M. Aris & M Hutt (ed.). Kiscadale Sia Research Series, No. 5, pp. 191-201.

National Environment Commission, Royal Government of Bhutan, (1998)*The Middle Path, national environment strategy for Bhutan.* Thailand: Keen Publishing.

Newton, L. H,. (2003) *Ethics and Sustainability, Sustainable Development and the Moral Life.* New Jersey: Prentice Hall.

Norbu Wangchuk (2003) "GNH: Practicing the Philosophy". Royal Institute for Management, http://www.rim.edu.bt/rigphel

Oakley, A., (1972) *Sex, gender and society.* London, Maurice Temple Smith.

Oliver, K., (1997) *Family Values.* New York: Routledge.

Ortner, S., (1974) *Is Female to Male as Nature Is to Culture.* Berkeley: University of California Press. Pp 68-87.

Ortner, Sherry B., (1996) *Making Gender. The Politics and Erotics of Culture.* Beacon Press: Boston.

Palmer & Finlay, (2003) *Faith in Conservation. New Approaches to Religions and the Environment.* The Worldbank: Washington DC.

Pankaj, P., (2004) "Linking trade with the Environment in the context of WTO: Why is this option Good for Bhutan?" in *The Spider and the Piglet*. Thimphu: The Centre for Bhutan Studies. Pp. 466-529.

Pain,A. & Deki Pema, (2000) "Continuing Customs of Negotiation and Contestation in Bhutan", in *Journal of Bhutan Studies.* Thimphu : Centre for Bhutan Studies, Vol 2, nr 2., pp. 219.

Penjor Rimpoche, (2002) *How to follow a Spiritual Master,* Bangalore India: Gurudutt Printers.

Pommaret, F., (1998) "Traditional Values, New Trends", in *Bhutan, a Fortress on the Edge of Time. Selected Papers of the Seminar on Political, Social and Economic Developments in Bhutan.* AIC, Vienna. Pp. 13-28.

Pommaret, F., (1997) "The Birth of a Nation" in *Bhutan: Mountain Fortress of the Gods.* London: Serindia Publications.

Priesner, S., (1999) *Gross National Happiness-Bhutan's Vision of development and its challenges.* Thimphu: Centre for Bhutan Studies. Pp. 24-53.

Priesner, S., (1998) "Gross National Happiness – Bhutan's Unique Approach to Development", in *Bhutan: A Fortress at the Edge of Time.* VIDC Vienna: Austrian Development Cooperation, Pp. 37-60.

Radford Ruether, R., (1995) *Women Healing Eearth.* New York : Maryknoll.

Ramakant, M.R.C., (1996) *Bhutan society and polity.* New Delhi: Indus Publishing Company.

Ramos, A.R., (1992) "Reflecting on the Yanomami: Ethnographic images and the pursuit of the exotic," in: Marcus E.G. (ed.), (1992) *Rereading cultural anthropology.* Duke University Press. Durham. Pp. 48-69.

Random House, (1984) *College Dictionary.*

Redfield, R., (1959) *The primitive world and its transformations.* Ithaca: Cornell University Press.

Rinzin Wangchuk dz_editor@kuensel.com.bt

Rokeach, M., (1973) *The nature of human values,* New York: The Free Press.

Royal Planning Commission, (1999) *Bhutan 2020: A vision for peace, prosperity and happiness.* Thailand: Keen Publishing.

Rubin, G., (1975) "De handel in vrouwen. Opmerkingen over de "politieke economie" van de sekse", in: *Socialisties-Feministiese Teksten,* 4, pp. 196-253.

Samuel, G., (1993) *The Civilised Shaman.* Washington D.C.: Smithsonian Inst.

Schwartz, S. H. & Bilsky, W., (1987) "Towards a Universal in the Content and Structure of Human Values", in: *Journal of Personality and Social Psychology.* 53: 550-562.

Schwartz, H. & Bilsky, W., (1990) "Toward a Theory of the Universal Content and Structure of Values: Extensions and Cross-Cultural Replications", in *Journal of Personality and Social Psychology,* Vol.58, No 5, 878-891.

Schricklgruber, Ch., (1999) "Gods and Sacred Mountains", in *Mountain Fortress of the Gods,* London: Serindia. P.159

Schrijvers, J., (1986) *Mothers for Life,* Delft.

Simmer Brown, J. (2001) *Dakini's Warm Breath The Feminine Principle in Tibetan Buddhism,* London, Boston: Shambala

Sinha D., (ed.) (1988) *Social Values and Development: Asian Perspective.* New Delhi: Sage Publications.

Sonam Chuki, (1994) "Religion in Bhutan, 1: The Sacred and the Obscene", in Aris, M. & Hutt, M, *Bhutan, Aspects of culture and development* . Scotland: Paul Strachan-Kiscadale Ltd.

Sonam Gyaltsen (1996) *The clear mirror: a traditional account of Tibet's Golden Age.* Ithaca New York: Snow Lion publications.

Sonam Kinga (2003) *Impact of Reforms on Bhutanese Social Organization.* Thimphu: The Centre for Bhutan Studies.

Soules, M. (2007) "Notes Toward a Definition of Culture". http://www.mala. bc.ca/-soules/media112/culture.htm.

Stein, R.A., (1972) *Tibetan Civilization.* Stanford, California: Stanford University Press.

Sutton, P., (2001) "Sustainability: Getting Oriented". http://www.greeninnovations.asn.au/sustainability-getting-orientated.htm

Tashi Wangyal, (2001) "Ensuring social sustainability? Transmission of values", in *Journal for Bhutan studies*, Thimphu, Vol 3. No 1.

Thanh-Dam Truong, (2000) "'Asian' Values and the Heart of Understanding: A Buddhist View," in *Asian Values encounter with Diversity.* J.Cauquelin, P.Lim & B. Mayer-König (Eds.). Richmond, Surrey: Curzon Press. Pp. 43-70.

Triolo & Palmer (ARC), (2000) *A Capital Solution.* Northamptonshire: Pilkinton Press

Ueda, A., (2003) *Culture and Modernisation, from the perspective of young people in Bhutan.* The Centre for Bhutan Studies, Thimphu, Bhutan.

Westphal, Merold, (1993) *Suspicion and Faith. The Religious Uses of Modern Atheism.* William B. Eerdmans Publishing Company, Grand Rapids, Michigan.

Whitbeck, C., (1986) "Theories of Sex Difference", in *Women and Values:Readings in Recent Feminist Philosophy.* Edited by Marilyn Pearsall. Wadsworth Publishing Company: California. Pp. 34-51.

Whitecross, R. (2002) "Tha Damtshi, the foundations of Bhutanese moral values". *The Bhutan Society Newsletter.* London. No. 25, p. 4.

Wikan, U., (1996) "The Nun's Story: Reflections on an Age-Old, Postmodern Dilemma", in: *American Anthropologist*, New Series, Vol. 98, No. 2 (Jun., 1996), pp. 279-289.

Yonten Dargye (2001), *History of the Drukpa Kagyud School in Bhutan.* India: Omega Traders.

Samenvatting

In dit proefschrift, getiteld *Meeting The 'Other': Living in the Present: Gender and Sustainability in Bhutan*, onderzoek ik de categorieën gender en duurzaamheid en reflecteer ik op mijn ervaringen van 17 jaar Bhutan.

In 1990 heb ik voor het eerst kennis gemaakt met dit koninkrijk in de Himalaya. Ik maakte deel uit van een team studenten uit Nederland, dat door de Bhutanese regering werd uitgenodigd om onderzoek te doen. Samen met een studente irrigatietechniek werd ik naar een afgelegen dorp in Noord-West Bhutan gestuurd. Gedurende deze tijd maakte ik intensief kennis met de Bhutanese cultuur, hetgeen tot deze studie leidde. In het dorp, waar ik onderzoek deed naar de sociale organisatie rondom het traditionele irrigatiesysteem, werd ik in een premoderne gemeenschap ondergedompeld, waarin de mensen in harmonie met de natuur leefden. Ik leerde veel gedurende mijn verblijf. Met name dat bijvoorbeeld het begrip tijd in het dorp iets totaal anders was, dan zoals ik het kende. De mensen in het dorp leefden geheel in het heden. Verleden en toekomst speelden geen rol. In deze gemeenschap had het concept tijd een geheel andere betekenis dan in het Westen. Naast tijd speelde ook geld nauwelijks een rol. Wél belangrijk waren wederkerigheid en ruilhandel. Verder waren de man-vrouw relaties heel bijzonder voor een Zuid-Aziatisch land. Vrouwen hadden een sterke positie, zij stonden aan het hoofd van het huishouden, bezaten het land en het huis en het erfrecht ging van moeder op dochter. Vrouwen konden vrij hun partner kiezen, trouwen was niet nodig en scheiding al helemaal geen probleem. In de meeste gevallen ging de man bij de vrouw wonen, waar hij een waardevolle arbeidskracht was voor het huishouden en boerderij. De mensen in het dorp waren afhankelijk van de natuur waarin ze woonden en de natuur voorzag hen grotendeels van hetgeen ze in het dagelijkse leven nodig hadden.

Ik begin mijn boek met een *proloog* waarin ik een beschrijving geef van de ervaringen die ik opgedaan heb gedurende deze tijd in dit dorp. Ik was met name geïnteresseerd in de – in mijn ogen – zeer gelijke man-vrouw verhoudingen en de manier waarop men in harmonie leefde met de natuur. Ook wilde ik meer weten over de religie die voor mij zeer gecompliceerd leek gedurende mijn verblijf in het dorp. Ik had al kennis gemaakt met andere Aziatische landen, Maar Bhutan leek mij een verhaal apart. Na negen jaar ben ik terug gegaan naar Bhutan voor een bezoek en daarna ieder jaar, in 2004 voor onderzoek om antwoord te krijgen op de vele vragen die ik in de loop der tijd had gekregen op het gebied van religie, gender en duurzaamheid in Bhutan. In 2004 heb ik een onderzoek visum gekregen. Dat stelde in staat mensen te interviewen over deze onderwerpen.

In *hoofdstuk Een* ga ik in op de manier hoe dit proefschrift ontstaan is. Door de ervaringen in het dorp ben ik tot de conclusie gekomen dat in Bhutan misschien wel het animisme en Boeddhisme bepalen dat het leven zich afspeelt in het heden en dat gender (relaties tussen man en vrouw) wordt ervaren als deel van de kosmos waarin spiritualiteit allesomvattend is. Deze ervaring wordt in Bhutan (expliciet) geïdentificeerd met 'duurzaamheid'. Die observatie heeft mij ervan bewust gemaakt dat duurzaamheid geen deelkwaliteit is, zoals bijvoorbeeld politiek, economie of de manier van samenleving in het Westen ervaren wordt. Duurzaamheid in Bhutan kan gezien worden als een allesomvattende ontologie. In dit eerste hoofdstuk maak ik duidelijk dat deze dissertatie de vorm heeft van een essay, waarin ik Westerse thema's als gender, duurzaamheid en religie in Bhutan onderzoek en de invloed van de modernisering op het waardesysteem, waarop genderrelaties en het duurzaamheidbewustzijn zijn gebaseerd. Ik bestudeer de thema's vanuit een postmoderne, Humanistieke traditie. Dit betekent dat ik mijn onderzoek doe 'in relatie met Bhutanezen' waarin ik me bewust ben van mijn morele verantwoording te schrijven over 'de ander'. In dit proefschrift beschrijf ik mijn ontmoeting met 'de ander'. Ik heb naar de Bhutanese samenleving gekeken vanuit zelfreflectie: mijn interculturele verkenningen zijn gevormd door mijn ontwikkelingen in mijn schrijven van Westers antropologe, sociologe tot Humanistiek onderzoeker. Ik ben me ervan bewust dat mijn visie op de Bhutanese samenleving bevooroordeeld is door mijn Westerse blik. Vandaar dat zelfreflectie een belangrijke rol speelt in dit boek, naast de genoemde thema's gender en duurzaamheid. Mijn zelfreflectie heb ik in een kader gezet aan de hand van de kritiek op de gangbare antropologie van Crapanzano, Gardner & Lewis en Marcus & Fisher. Ik gebruik een artikel van de Noorse antropologe Wikan als voorbeeld over hoe subjectief antropologen kunnen zijn in het beschrijven van de 'ander'. In 1990 heeft Wikan, evenals ik, onderzoek gedaan in Bhutan. In een artikel gepubliceerd in een Amerikaans antropologisch tijdschrift, beschrijft zij het leven van een oude non in Bhutan. Daarbij beschrijft ze alleen de moeilijke tijden van de non, hetgeen een vertekend beeld geeft van met name de Bhutanese samenleving. Om die reden heeft het artikel stof doen opwaaien in Bhutan. In *hoofdstuk Twee* komen tien conversaties aan bod. Deze conversaties zijn geheel uitgewerkt. De rest van de 46 conversaties zijn samengevat in de hoofdstukken religie, gender en duurzaamheid. Dit hoofdstuk begint met een 'waarden' theorie, voornamelijk ontwikkeld als analytisch instrument in de Westerse wereld door Bilsky & Schwartz. Ik heb deze theorie gebruikt om een begin te maken van het in kaart brengen van waarden in een Boeddhistische Bhutanese context. Een gedeelte van mijn vragen tijdens de conversaties zijn gebaseerd op deze theorie.

Hoofdstuk Drie behandelt de theoretische debatten die de achtergrond van dit onderzoek vormen en die tevens de invalshoek bepaalden. Verder behandel ik het begrip gender en relateer ik het aan waarden, gebruikt in de feministische filosofie. De kruisverbinding gender, duurzaamheid en religie keert vooral terug in het eco-feminisme en debatten daaromtrent, die ik als theoretisch kader gebruik. Ook de relatie met gender en de discussie natuur-cultuur vindt men daarin terug.

Ik heb geprobeerd de combinatie gender, duurzaamheid en spiritualiteit in een eco-feministisch theoretisch raamwerk te plaatsen. Maar ik realiseerde me dat deze theorieën niet tot weinig aansluiten bij een Bhutanese context. De waardering van vrouwen en genderrelaties zowel socio-economisch als cultureel-symbolisch verschillen ingrijpend van de Westerse context. Ook de visie op de natuur en de dierenwereld verschillen fundamenteel van de Westerse categorieën gender en duurzaamheid die als zodanig uiteindelijk tekort schieten in de Bhutanese context. Het was voor mij een vreemde gewaarwording dat ik met mijn Westerse begrippen uiteindelijk niet veel kon aanvangen. Als laatste perspectief in dit hoofdstuk gebruik ik Marx' filosofisch materialisme als model om de verandering van een premoderne samenleving naar een moderne samenleving te begrijpen. Het dorp waar ik in 1990 woonde bevond zich nog in de premoderne tijd. Deze samenleving zou door Karl Marx als een ideale gemeenschap gekenschetst zijn: volgens hem leeft zo'n ideale gemeenschap in het heden.

Om toch meer van Bhutan te kunnen begrijpen ben ik eerst in de geschiedenis en religie gaan duiken om zo een inzicht te krijgen in de cultuur van het land. Religie en geschiedenis is alom aanwezig, onder andere in de vorm van grote burchten (*dzongs*) *stupa's* en gebedsvlaggen en de vele tempels. In *hoofdstuk Vier* ga ik daarom in op de religie en de geschiedenis van Bhutan. Om de genderrelaties en duurzaamheid in de Bhutanese context te kunnen begrijpen, is het belangrijk inzicht te krijgen in het ontstaan van de Bhutanese identiteit en cultuur, die weer onlosmakelijk verbonden zijn met de religie van het land. Naast het Boeddhisme speelt het preboeddhisme een grote rol. In het preboeddhisme is het landschap heilig. Bergen, meren, rivieren en lucht zijn de habitat van goden, zowel mannelijke als vrouwelijke. Het is van belang hun habitat niet te verstoren, omdat zij zich anders zullen wreken in de vorm van ziekten en natuurrampen voor mens en dier. Aan het begin van mijn onderzoek ging ik ervan uit dat in Bhutan religie het belangrijkste was maar gedurende mijn onderzoek ben ik tot de conclusie gekomen dat de Bhutanese wereld eigenlijk bestaat uit een holistische kosmologie waarin alles ondergeschikt is gemaakt aan de natuur.

In *hoofdstuk Vijf* ga ik in op de genderrelaties in Bhutan. Aan de hand van de Boeddhistische geschiedenis probeer ik de hoge status van vrouwen in de samenleving te verklaren. Boeddhisme was ten tijde van de Boeddha (ongeveer vijfhonderd jaar vóór onze jaartelling) de eerste religie, die vrouwen de mogelijkheid gaf non te worden en een religieus leven te leiden. Maar circa tweehonderd jaar na de Boeddha's dood kregen vrouwen een inferieure status toebedeeld in de geschriften die conservatieve mannelijke *lama's* opstelden.

De vrouw heeft weliswaar een hoge maatschappelijke status, maar ze heeft die niet in het Boeddhisme. Met name ongeschoolde vrouwen en nonnen blijken een negatief zelfbeeld te hebben. Ze stellen zelfs, dat je als vrouw negen keer moet incarneren om als man wedergeboren te worden. Deze respondenten menen dat alleen mannen de verlichting kunnen bereiken. Voor de geschoolden Bhutanezen is dit volksgeloof zonder enige waarde. In de interviews komt duidelijk naar voren, dat zij vrouwen en mannen als gelijkwaardig zien en dat het enige verschil is biologisch bepaalt. Uiteindelijk realiseerde ik me dat gender als Westers begrip, als *mijn* begrip tekort schiet in deze context. Gender in Bhutan maakt ook deel uit van de holistische kosmologie en kan dus gezien worden als natuur: er wordt dan ook geen waardeoordeel uitgesproken over levende wezens: mens (vrouw of man) en dier zijn even waardevol.

In *hoofdstuk Zes* komt duurzaamheid aan bod. Ook duurzaamheid heeft in Bhutan een ander betekenis dan in het Westen. In het Westen is het een concept, maar in Bhutan is het de natuurlijke levenswijze een vanzelfsprekendheid. Duurzaamheid doordrenkt dan ook het waardensysteem, de cultuur, spiritualiteit en tradities. Het respect voor alles wat leeft in het Boeddhisme en preboeddhisme is daarvan een uiting. De antwoorden in dit onderzoek op vragen over duurzaamheid gingen over de zorg voor de natuurlijke omgeving, het brengen van offers aan de vele goden die overal in de natuur aanwezig zijn, en het niet verstoren van hun habitat. Landschap en natuur zien Bhutanezen als een verlengstuk van henzelf; zij staan niet los van de mens. Deze waarden zijn diep geworteld. Verder betekent duurzaamheid in Bhutan ook, dat men streeft naar behoud van de Bhutanese manier van leven. Duurzaamheid is in Bhutan een holistische benadering van het dagelijks leven, gericht op behoud van spirituele waarden en tradities. In het overheidsbeleid staan deze waarden centraal: toename van het Bruto Nationaal Geluk krijgt voorrang boven groei van het Bruto Nationaal Produkt.

De mens in Bhutan voelt zich niet boven ander levende wezens verheven. Alles is met alles verbonden en daardoor is menselijke dominantie ten opzichte van ander leven afwezig. Deze afwezigheid van dominantie geeft een belangrijke basiswaarde aan ten opzichte van de natuurlijke omgeving, maar ook ten opzichte van de genderrelaties. Mannen staan niet boven vrouwen en de mens staat niet boven andere levende wezens. Mannen en vrouwen delen hetzelfde holistische, samenhangende wereldbeeld en dezelfde waarden op het gebied van duurzaamheid.

In *hoofdstuk Zeven* vat ik de punten samen, die in eerdere hoofdstukken aan de orde komen en interpreteer ze. Hierbij reflecteer ik kritisch op mijn eigen werk.

In deze studie ben ik tot de conclusie gekomen dat de concepten religie, gender en duurzaamheid, zoals ik deze ken van mijn Westerse achtergrond, slechts gedeeltelijk de situatie in Bhutan doen begrijpen. Als we in het Westen spreken over Boeddhisme, dan vind ik in Bhutan in mijn onderzoek: Boeddhisme is als het ware animisme, met als consequentie dat er sprake is van een *allesomvattend levenswijze*. We kunnen spreken van een holistische kosmologie. Als we in het Westen spreken over gender dan vind ik in Bhutan: gender is meer een compassie voor leven. Er wordt geen waardeoordeel toegekend aan de verschillen tussen de seksen en andere vormen van leven. Al het leven is even waardevol en het is niet aan de mens daaraan een waardeoordeel toe te kennen. Deze zienswijze past ook in het holistische kosmologische wereldbeeld. Als we in het Westen spreken over duurzaamheid, dan vind ik in Bhutan de nadruk op natuur. Het gaat bovendien zover dat natuur het belangrijkste is en dat zelfs religie en gender hieronder vallen. Dit is ook weer het gevolg van een holistisch kosmologisch wereldbeeld.

Als we in het Westen Bhutan als Premodern samenleving zouden duiden en willen nagaan hoe zo'n samenleving op modernisering reageert, dan blijken onze indicatoren voor economische ontwikkeling niet toereikend en zoekt men naar andere indicatoren namelijk Bruto Nationaal Geluk. De consequentie is dat we ook hier concluderen dat er een relatie wordt gelegd met de holistische kosmologie.

Veel Bhutanezen zijn zich er zeer bewust van, dat met ontwikkeling en modernisering ook veranderingen zullen plaatsvinden. Tot slot van deze dissertatie sta ik stil bij mijn eigen veranderingen als onderzoeker in de Bhutanese context. Door in te gaan op de vraag, waaróm ik dit essay over Bhutan schreef en bijvoorbeeld niet over een land in Europa. Mijn eerste verblijf in Bhutan had zo'n invloed op mij, dat het land me altijd is blijven fascineren. Ik leerde in Bhutan niet te snel te oordelen over wat je ziet; dingen zijn niet altijd wat je dénkt dat ze zijn. Ik heb er geleerd respect te hebben voor een andere samenleving en dat hetgeen ik zie eerder mijn visie en mijn waarheid zijn.